MW00389461

THE DIVISION OF CONSCIOUSNESS

THE DIVISION OF CONSCIOUSNESS

THE SECRET AFTERLIFE OF THE HUMAN PSYCHE

PETER NOVAK

HAMPTON ROADS
PUBLISHING COMPANY, INC.

for the evolving human spirit

THE DIVISION OF CONSCIOUSNESS
THE SECRET AFTERLIFE OF THE HUMAN PSYCHE

PETER NOVAK

for the evolving human spirit

HAMPTON ROADS
PUBLISHING COMPANY, INC.

Copyright © 1997
by Peter Novak

All rights reserved, including the right to reproduce this work in any form
whatsoever, without permission in writing from the publisher, except for
brief passages in connection with a review.

Cover art by Bob Holland
Cover design by Marjoram Productions
Graphics by Grace Pedalino

For information write:

Hampton Roads Publishing Company, Inc.
134 Burgess Lane
Charlottesville, VA 22902

Or call: (804)296-2772
FAX: (804)296-5096
e-mail: hrpc@hrpub.com
Website: www.hrpub.com

If you are unable to order this book from your local bookseller, you may
order directly from the publisher.
Quantity discounts for organizations are available.
Call 1-800-766-8009, toll-free.

ISBN 1-57174-053-8

10 9 8 7 6 5 4 3 2 1

Printed on acid-free paper in the United States of America

for

Ayriel Gold

CONTENTS

PREFACE

Suffering from a crippling psychological disorder, my beautiful young wife took her life in the summer of 1985, just months after having given birth to our daughter, Ayriel Gold. The devastating grief I felt over this tragedy, rather than subsiding over time, grew ever greater as I agonized over what I would tell Ayriel when she was old enough to start asking questions.

Following her suicide, I had three extraordinary dreams which affected me deeply. In the first, I saw my wife laid out on a high, rocky ledge, and was told that she was well, sleeping comfortably, and was in the process of "healing." Coming shortly after her death, this dream brought an irrational but nonetheless deeply felt sense of relief. In the second dream a few months later, I again saw this high place, but my wife was no longer there. While looking for her, I was told that, having awakened healed, she had flown away. While renewing my relief, this dream also brought an entirely new sense of loss, as if only then had our ties been truly broken.

The third and most powerful dream came years later, when our daughter had grown to childhood. In this dream, I had taken Ayriel to a school conducted in a sunny, spacious field. While at this field, I was summoned by a high authority to attend a special meeting, with whom I could not even imagine. Crossing a small stream, I was led far away from the field, eventually descending into a clean and well-built subterranean structure, and was left to wait alone in a neutral, empty room. Although no windows were in evidence, I somehow understood that the meeting about to take place was going to be monitored and carefully controlled. Shortly after entering the room, I was shocked and delighted to see my wife hesitantly enter, also alone, from the other side of the room. I will never forget the feeling of that moment—it was glorious, delicious, indescribable. Embracing her, I was overwhelmed with gratitude, sensing that this meeting was a supremely rare privilege granted us by an unseen authority. Without a word spoken, volumes passed between us; I simultaneously felt, saw, and understood that she was well, happy, in good hands, and had begun a new and interesting future, and that no ill feelings existed between us. We were both surprised and delighted we had been given such a precious chance to say our goodbyes, and we parted satisfied and at peace.

Immediately awakening, I marveled at the vivid sense of reality this dream had possessed; entirely unlike any other dream I'd ever known, it had felt bright, clear, fairly pulsating with life. Had the meeting really taken place, I wondered? While realizing I could not intellectually know for sure, I also knew it had felt as real (perhaps, if such a thing is conceivable, even more real) than waking reality itself.

Although I did not make the connection until years later, it was at this point in time that I began to earnestly seek answers to my own questions and uncertainties about death. Through past browsings, I'd learned of some variety of ideas and beliefs about death, but until that moment it had not concerned me that these different beliefs contradicted one another. After the third dream, I became consumed by the need to settle the matter in my own mind once and for all. As I reread the holy books of humanity's religions, the question of death seemed to grow ever larger and more inscrutable. The East believed one thing, the West another, and it seemed the twain indeed would never meet since each side had what appeared to be equally legitimate reasons for following its own ancient traditions.

I persisted in asking, seeking, and knocking, studying the classics of religious and psychological thought in hopes of comprehending how humanity's many different perceptions about death could possibly fit together. I consumed everything that seemed even remotely relevant. One week found me more or less simultaneously reviewing Jungian psychology, Swedenborgian theology, both the Tibetan and Egyptian Books of the Dead, a collection of Hindu Upanishads, a handful of previously unknown Christian Gospels unearthed in Egypt in 1945, and the Biblical prophecies of a Universal Resurrection and Judgment Day. Slowly, over the course of that week, in the chaos of all this, the question which unlocks the entire mystery took form in my mind: How might such a Universal Resurrection transpire if reincarnation indeed is a fact?

With the simple asking of that question, something profound changed. A door opened; a new perspective dawned; an alternate possibility presented itself. Maybe I just had an idea, or maybe it was something more. Whatever else it may have been, it seemed (and continues to seem now, after nine years of inspection) to be the genuine article—one of life's ultimate answers, for which I, like untold billions before me, had searched.

For a long time I hesitated; such a discovery would be so monumental that I could scarcely suspend my own disbelief. For nine years I studied this thing, examining it from every angle I could think of, always expecting its premise to fall apart at the next turn. Scared that I had lost touch with reality altogether, I wondered how I could have possibly discovered what so many others had not. How? Simply by being in the right place, asking the right question at the right time? Wouldn't it be the height of egotistic arrogance and ignorance to even suggest one might have discovered such a thing?

As much as these questions scared me, a final thought kept drawing me on—if one assumes that the psyche survives death in a whole state, that assumption doesn't lead anywhere. It most particularly doesn't lead in any logical way to reincarnation, heaven or hell, or the sort of automatic repetitive ghosthood so typical of ghost reports. Nor does it lead in any rational way to the existence of a Devil, a Fall from Grace, a Judgment Day, or a Universal Resurrection. That road, one finds, simply leads nowhere. But if you suppose instead that the psyche survives death in a divided state, you find to your amazement that this premise leads *everywhere.* That single, deviously simple twist leads logically and directly to the entire tradition of death we find in existence today. From that single assumption, all else—all our tradition, all our religion, even all the findings of our most modern scientific afterlife research—can be deduced.

> Whenever a true theory appears, it will be its own evidence. Its test is that it will explain all phenomena.
> — Ralph Waldo Emerson[1]

---

1   Ralph Waldo Emerson, "Nature," as quoted by George Seldes in *The Great Thoughts* (New York: Ballantine Books, 1985), 127.

Whether this "Division Theory" is correct may, of course, long remain ultimately unconfirmable, at least on this side of death's door. Even so, the evidence insists at the very least that the majority of the founders and authors of our ancient religions were under the impression that it is.

The implications of that alone are staggering. The full implications of Division Theory being true seem beyond any ability to anticipate.

INTRODUCTION

Religion and the Division of Consciousness

True Science and true religion are twin-sisters, and the separation of either from the other is sure to prove the death of both. Science prospers exactly in proportion as it is religious; and religion flourishes in exact proportion to the scientific depth and firmness of its bases.
—T.H. Huxley[1]

What is death?

Imagine if we knew. Living under the shadowy pall of the mystery of death may be the defining characteristic of the human experience; of all living things, only people suffer an awareness of their own mortality. Indeed, this apprehension has been one of only a very few real constants for the human race down through the millennia, one of only a handful of things that have never changed throughout all the ages of Man. If such a fundamental and primary constant as this ever did change, every other facet of human culture and experience might be expected to be transformed, perhaps beyond recognition.

Death is the ultimate uncertainty, both religious and scientific: to define death is to define human life. Compared to the Secret of Death, all other issues, political agendas, scientific achievements, and historical developments become completely insignificant. The answer to this one question is, in the long run, the answer to all questions; it could make all the difference in the world. What awaits us on the other side of death might bring complete fulfillment of

---

1   Leonard Huxley, ed., *Life and Letters of Thomas Henry Huxley*, as quoted by Seldes in *The Great Thoughts*, 198.

all our cravings for love and justice, or it might simply bring a bitter and futile ending to everything. All wrongs could be righted, or everything we cherish could be lost. Either way, one thing is certain—the discovery of the true nature of death would be the greatest development in human affairs since man first started walking upright.

But we don't know. We aren't able to define Death. Humanity finds itself today in exactly the same position as it was thousands of years ago, deadlocked in an ancient stalemate, frozen in place by a seemingly insurmountable conflict of opinion over the true Secret of Death. An endless parade of different religions have attempted such definitions, yet each doctrine seems hopelessly different. The ancient Egyptians, the Australian aborigines, the Hindus of India, the native tribes of the Americas, and every other culture have had perfectly sincere and honorable "holy men" who earnestly strived to understand and pass on the Secret of Death. From among all the different ideas and theories that people have entertained about death through the ages, two great traditions have come to reign supreme. Half the world believes in the Judeo-Christian-Muslim heaven-or-hell scenario, an afterlife containing a judgment followed by an eternal reward or punishment, while the other half believes in the Hindu-Buddhist-Taoist reincarnation scenario, in which people are continually reborn into new bodies, forever forgetting their past lives and identities. Instead of one of these traditions ultimately proving more valid than the other, they have remained stubbornly locked in a stagnant debate for at least the last several thousand years; like wrestlers immobilized by a balanced struggle, each has been unable to topple the other. Meanwhile, finding no clear winner, we as a species have consented to honor both traditions equally, bestowing upon each the place of supreme importance in its own culture. Each is recognized as the Ultimate Truth and utterly accepted by millions.

These two, the "reincarnation" tradition of the East and the "heaven-or-hell" tradition of the West, constitute practically the entire legacy of mankind's search for the Secret of Death. Unfortunately, according to these traditions, they are utterly irreconcilable.

In addition to formal religions, more "scientific" sources have also claimed possession of legitimate information about death. The standard scientific position, for example, has long maintained that death completely extinguishes the human personality. In the modern era, however, there have been studies that question this long-held scientific position. Once hypnosis began to be used as a tool for exploring the unconscious, it became almost commonplace to hear of people uncovering vivid memories of previous lives. And, too, numerous studies in recent years have shown that those who live through near-death experiences tend to report remarkably similar accounts of traveling down "a long dark tunnel" to heavenly or hellish afterlife locations, typically meeting a variety of deceased friends, relatives, angels, and gods.

When the findings from such afterlife research were first made public, it seemed to the world for a hopeful instant that the ancient deadlock between our two great traditions might be broken, that the real truth about the Secret of Death might finally be ascertained. Unfortunately, while some fairly compelling evidence has been obtained, in the end it has not helped. On the one hand, the findings of the regression research suggest the validity of the theory of reincarnation. On the other hand, the findings of the near-death research offer contradictory testimony; most near-death experiences include encounters with long-dead friends and relatives who, since they still possess their familiar pre-death forms, identities, and memories, apparently never reincarnated into new bodies after their own deaths.

Thus, after many millennia without any headway in the great afterlife debate, science seems to have chosen this moment in history to reinforce each side of the argument simultaneously, just pressing the ancient deadlock that much tighter.

So here we are. Our human family has been on this planet for a minimum of 40,000 years, our scientists now agree, and every moment of that time has seen more and more of us fall through those doors of death. Yet, after all this time we still don't understand death or agree about it at all. Our sciences don't agree, our religions don't agree, our ideas don't even agree. After hundreds of centuries and an endless parade of theories, we don't understand death at all. Curiously, few of us anticipate its secret ever being revealed. Perhaps carrying the numbing weight of this unsolved mystery has left the world collectively convinced that there just isn't any hard answer, that this mystery will never really be solved. Such a position could be correct; it is at least conceivable that mankind will never understand death. But somewhere a real answer to this mystery *must* exist—an answer that addresses and explains each of the legends, reports, and traditions about death that have been passed down to us over the ages.

Any truly satisfactory answer would need to resolve the ancient debate between our two primary traditions, the heaven-hell scenario of the West and the reincarnation scenario of the East. It might also be expected to account for the contradictory findings coming in from today's near-death and hypnotic regression research. It would need to explain the worldwide reports of ghost phenomena, the bizarre death-religion of ancient Egypt, and, in fact, the majority of human-ity's beliefs about death around the world and throughout time. Perhaps it would even shed light on that unique event deemed responsible for launching the Christian era, history's only reported occurrence of a man rising from the dead.

Introducing what may prove to be that answer, this work submits an unfamiliar, uncharted—and therefore unorthodox—vision to the world. While this extraordinary approach to the nature of death may seem completely alien to us today, it is doubtful that it could constitute a truly original proposition, since the highly improbable conclusions at which this theory arrives are virtually identical to certain prophecies repeated over and over down through history by some of the world's most legendary religious figures. This simple yet cogent hypothesis, evidence suggests, may actually have been advanced before, perhaps even widely pro-pounded, in our very distant past.

Whether or not this model of human mortality is in fact a fully accurate representation of the processes involved can, perhaps, never be confirmed on this side of death's door, but the findings presented herein do at least establish that this hypothesis pos-sesses all the prerequisites for being that answer. For this answer makes our religions agree. It makes our sciences agree. It even makes our ideas agree. Most of all, it makes sense.

The Secret of Death has to do with the way that people are put together, and, therefore, with the way we come apart. Human beings are composed of three parts. Every culture in every time and place has recognized this three-part composition, but none has ever known any of these parts perfectly and completely. (Nei-ther, of course, do we.) Different cultures focus on different characteristics of these three parts, providing each people with its unique but inevitably limited perspective.

In a certain culture, these three were called "body, soul, and spirit." In other places they were known by other names, and while many today refer to them as "body, mind, and soul," perhaps a more appropriate terminology for this scientific age would be "the body, the conscious mind, and the unconscious." The Secret of Death has to do with this three-part design and how it relates to humanity's most ancient legends, beliefs, and prophecies.

The nature of death has generally been thought, by those who presume any afterlife at all, to be the separation of the person's entire mental self from the body and the subsequent experiences of that entire mental self. This assumption, however, leads to a pivotal question: "What happens when death tries to make three parts divide into two?"

It's certain that the body doesn't survive, of course, but both the soul and spirit, the unconscious and conscious components of the human psyche, might. And compelling evidence for such a binary afterlife is found in the uncanny coincidence that the natures and qualities of religion's two traditional afterlives—familiar legends that have been around for thousands of years—are fully consistent with the natures and qualities of science's conscious and unconscious minds, which were discovered and defined only in this century.

The unconscious, if it survived the death of the physical body only to then be divided from its conscious half as well, would find itself alone and still, with no external stimuli to experience or elicit responce. Left with nowhere else to direct its attention, it would fall inward, becoming totally preoccupied with redigesting its own memories, doomed to eternally experience its own reactions and responses to those memories. If those responses were approval and appreciation, it would know absolute, unending joy and fulfillment; but if those responses were disapproval and self-condemnation, it would experience absolute, unending misery.

It would, in effect, go through a judgment and then experience either heaven or hell.

Meanwhile, the conscious mind, cut off from both the body and the unconscious, would find itself floating free, but suffering from total amnesia. It would have lost all its memories, including even its memory of its own identity, since, in the human psyche, memory is always stored in the unconscious. Finding itself cut loose in this way, without any identity, knowledge, or bearings of any kind, it could only wander aimlessly, eventually entering into new experiences and building up an entirely new sense of identity.

It would experience, in effect, the essence of reincarnation: repeatedly beginning new cycles of experience while severing all memories of the past.

Surprisingly, the mere introduction of the humblest, most elementary principle in psychology into the hallowed realm of religion is all it takes to reawaken the suspicion, suppressed for 1,500 years, that reincarnation may be neither inconsistent with nor alien to Western theology. Simply by introducing the foundation belief of psychology (that the human psyche is divided into two parts) to the foundation belief of theology (that the human psyche survives physical death), one is forced to acknowledge the underlying implication that there may be two different parts of a human being which survive physical death. If so, this would make it possible for both the East's doctrine of reincarnation and the West's doctrine of heaven and hell to be fully legitimate, though incomplete, descriptions of the very same event.

While humanity seems to take a certain bittersweet pride in its awareness that everything which lives must die, this belief is not, in fact, absolutely true—science has long known of curious exceptions to this rule—single-celled creatures which, instead of dying in our fashion, just divide and multiply. Their example, although modest, is precious beyond estimation, for it shows that nature already contains instances in which death takes the form of division. The question is—could the form that death takes for these most elemental of all earthly creatures secretly reflect a truth about all death—that it is always, at its most fundamental level, a division? Humanity has always instinctively followed the Biblical command to "multiply" in life; in death, do people find that this command then changes to "divide"?

Hinting of further correlations to the world's other, lesser-known afterlife traditions in addition to the primary Eastern and Western models, this Division Theory suggests ways in which many of the world's religious traditions could all fit together into the same simple truth. Instead of just one or another of the world's faiths holding a monopoly on religious truth, as almost all of them claim, this theory suggests that a number of different religions may have been originally founded on accurate glimpses into the ultimate nature of life and death; it argues, in fact, that most early religion originally focused on the exact same issue: the Primordial Division of the human psyche.

From the vantage point of a theology based on the division of the human psyche, many of humanity's afterlife beliefs fit together, almost as if each separate tradition were but another piece to a cosmic jigsaw puzzle. And, compelling by its very simplicity, the picture that comes into focus by fitting all these different pieces of the theological puzzle together, instead of resulting in some awkward, incongruous, and artificial construction as might be expected, strikes one as a simple and natural, even elegant and perfect, whole.

This is the reassembled story of the Secret of Death: all three components of a human being—the body, the unconscious soul, and the conscious spirit—can be and usually are divided from one another by death. This alien yet somehow strangely familiar message has resurfaced again and again down through the ages and has left evidence of its passing in nearly every culture on Earth. The re-discoverers of this ancient Secret, some of humanity's most revered teachers, have attempted to show people how to live so as to avoid being split apart in this way at death; such teachings have always focused on wholeness and integrity of the self. If you are different on the inside than on the outside, such teachers warn, you are in danger of losing your very soul at death. Great religions have grown up around such teachings and around the names of such teachers.

Each time this message resurfaced, it gradually became changed and refocused and compromised, until it was quietly lost all over again. During the brief, rare periods of the message's renewal, when its original simple truth was once again fresh and whole and uncorrupted, a precious few people could be taught how to successfully maintain their psyches' integrity at death, instead of dividing into their separate conscious and unconscious components. And when such seekers occasionally succeeded, fabulous tales of radiant, immortal beings arose to note their passage, tales which even today can be found in cultural traditions all around the world.

These rare exceptions notwithstanding, countless generations of souls continued, millennium after millennium, to plunge headlong into the ravenous, ballooning, dark unconscious pit. Prophets continued to come and go throughout these endless bleak ages, as did every other manner of teacher, saint, and holy man, always bringing the same message of salvation; yet the hordes flooding into the pit continued unabated.

Every culture has known its own prophets and holy men, thought to have somehow acquired special understanding of the secrets of life and death, often setting their cherished insights down in writing. An extraordinary phenomenon arises when the material written by such sages is examined from the perspective of Division Theory; a surprising transformation takes place, lifting an entirely new level of latent meaning from millennia-old pages. When placed within the context of Division Theory, such books bloom, almost exploding with newly relevant connotations and fresh nuances of meaning. Vast reservoirs of unexplored textual undercurrents are brought to light, suggesting that humanity now enjoys an unprecedented opportunity to examine those ancient teachers' fuller message and meaning.

As if penetrating to the very heart of religious doctrine, Division Theory's illumination of humanity's sacred writings seems both genuine and fruitful—time and time again, the simple path of its logic uncovers intelligent, credible solutions to many of the most daunting doctrinal paradoxes. As if distilling sense from nonsense, it draws out rational, intellectually honest solutions to some of the most deeply inscrutable riddles of the world's faiths. It seems, in short, to do exactly what one might expect the Secret of Death to be able to do—solve the mysteries of the ages themselves.

After untold ages, a dramatic chapter came to be written into the saga of the Secret of Death. A teacher came, teaching much the same message as his predecessors, that of how to avoid dividing at death and having one's soul trapped in an inescapable unconscious prison. The teacher's message was simple—he taught love and integrity.

When this teacher died, his soul and spirit did not remain united, as at least some of the earlier teachers had succeeded in doing; despite his own perfect integrity, he split apart. The legends report that this teacher chose to voluntarily suffer death's division, somehow taking upon himself the corrupted integrity of all the rest of us, willfully suffering being split apart on account of the failures and shortcomings of the whole of humanity.

But somehow, perhaps because of his own perfect integrity, this teacher's soul and spirit, after having been split fully apart, returned and became reunited once more, like separated lovers finding each other again. A miracle and a mystery, this reunion was something entirely new; it had never happened before in all the history of humanity. When the reunion took place, it involved, or perhaps produced, such power that it actually revived the physical body of the teacher who had died. And he rose from the dead.

Even that great wonder, however, pales compared to what happened to the teacher's soul—it grew. His soul exploded to huge—perhaps infinite—proportions, expanding throughout the entire universe of the unconscious. His soul enlarged so forcefully that it permeated all soul-stuff everywhere. A new religion dawned, teaching that its dead founder, the teacher, could yet be found and contacted, as he still lived, deep inside the souls of all people everywhere.

The final chapter to this saga of the Secret of Death remains unwritten in human history. According to that Secret, however, the day must come for every living spirit, including that of the teacher, to incarnate again. And with this idea, the prophecies agree fully; the teacher will surely return, they insist.

The prophecies have much to add; the teacher will return in the "Last Days," a mysterious time when all the world's dead are to return, somehow, to physical life, a time when the world is to see a final, decisive confrontation between good and evil.

If this teacher, or any such being, were to incarnate again, such an event, in and of itself, would be capable of bringing about just such a scenario, just such a threat for the human race. For, as that newly reborn infant teacher grew older and his young mind began once again to take shape, his perfect integrity would eventually prompt him to reawaken and raise up his inner soul, to try to become completely one with it once more. Such an instinct might otherwise be harmless enough, but if all of humanity's souls past and present were still linked to his own, then all of those other souls would also be restored to full living consciousness right along with his own, lifted back up in us as well as in him.

On such a day, everyone on Earth would find their own minds becoming battlegrounds, watching helplessly as legions of old abandoned souls and forgotten past selves surfaced to consciousness right inside of them, "rising from the dead" into living bodies just as the ancient prophecies had always predicted. Like an invasion of an "ancient and enduring nation," each of those newly reawakened dead (who, as the prophecies point out, would be "the most ruthless of all nations") would begin a desperate struggle to gain control over the individual's bodily self.

Such chaos could lead to, and indeed could itself be, that "great and terrible" event obliquely described in those ancient prophecies, a time widely feared but never truly understood: Judgment Day.

If this theory connecting the long inscrutable Secret of Death with humanity's ancient Division of Consciousness indeed is correct, then this represents humanity's first real look at our self-imposed "covenant with death" since the very inception of that fateful pact. If so, then religion, after remaining divided and buried under the guise of myth for ages, has finally come of age merely by broaching this ancient secret.

This book traces the origin, legacy, and ultimate destiny of humanity's Division of Consciousness, identifying and distinguishing the soul and spirit and exploring how each might be affected differently by the trauma of physical death. Thanks to the focus of Division Theory, a new, panoramic chronicle of mankind's spiritual history has been reassembled from the original visions of humanity's legendary teachers and wise men, tracing our collective destiny right down to what would seem to be its inevitable conclusion: the full reintegration of our fragmented selves. The voices of some of humanity's most honored leaders and intellects, voices which once seemed widely divergent, are now shown to have all been singing together in a chorus, all of them unknowingly harmonizing with the universal song of humanity's Primordial Division.

Over the last century, a new chorus of voices has been heard, heralding the imminent arrival of some momentous religio-cultural development: some have written, for example, of an upcoming marriage between psychology and religion; others, of the impending birth of some new, world-embracing form of Christianity; and following this century's twin discoveries of the Biblical-era Dead Sea Scrolls and the Nag Hammadi scriptures, many more wonder if new, possibly profound revelations about the earliest forms of Christian theology may be close at hand.

It remains to history to determine if any such predictions ever come to pass. A far more important question is whether or not this new Division Theory might work like the proverbial pinch of yeast, "leavening the entire loaf." If Division Theory is correct, it would be a marriage not only of science and religion, but also of East and West and past and present, and as such, it would span many of the chasms dividing our world today; thus, it must be asked—could such a marriage of religion and psychology be truly seminal enough to do what is so desperately needed in our world today—to not only transform, but actually integrate the great network of humanity's belief structures?

Of course, the only truly compelling argument for any hypothesis is not to be found in any cultural changes it might seem poised to produce, but in the soundness of its reason; and Division Theory strikes its defense, its only defense, with the one virtue so pure that no power or ideology has ever successfully stood against it: it makes sense. Division Theory behaves exactly the way correct answers usually behave: it explains all the phenomena, it puts all the pieces together, and it makes sense. It fits the facts.

And isn't that, after all, what we've been waiting for?

> Creeds must become intellectually honest. At present there is not a single credible established religion in the world. That is perhaps the most stupendous fact in the whole world situation.
> — George Bernard Shaw revised [1]

---

1 George Bernard Shaw, the preface to *Major Barbara*, as quoted by Seldes in *The Great Thoughts*, 381.

CHAPTER 1

YOU WILL BE BROKEN
INTO PIECES

The Body, Soul, and Spirit
and Three Traditions About Death

*The word of God is living and active and sharper than any two-edged
swordد, and cuts so deeply it divides the soul from the spirit.*
        —Hebrews 4:12
. . . I cut you in pieces with . . . the words of my mouth.
        —Hosea 6:5
Consider this, or I will tear you to pieces . . .
        —Psalm 50:22
*[Those who] have altogether broken the yoke, and burst the bonds . . .
shall be torn in pieces . . .*
        —Jeremiah 5:5-6
. . . ye shall be broken in pieces . . . ye shall be broken in pieces.
        —Isaiah 8:9

Death had always been both inevitable and inscrutable. No one
knew what was on the other side, but all knew they'd end up there
eventually.

In a world saturated with chaos and injustice, humanity came
to view death as the only certainty. Nothing else could be counted
on. Subject to everything from thirty-second tornadoes to 1,000-
year ice ages, and earthquakes that seemed to be constantly
decimating cities, shifting rivers, or altering landscapes, the world
never seemed very stable. For tens of thousands of years, humanity
watched slack-jawed and uncomprehending as oceans became
deserts and mountains became islands, as sea levels rose and fell,

as the Earth's magnetic poles wandered drunkenly across the globe, as the very constellations in the sky slowly rearranged themselves. It registered upon humanity's developing psyche, albeit dimly, that the sky could change; comets, supernovas, and eclipses reminded humanity again and again that even the very heavens were subject to inconsistency and upheaval. Every generation learned the hard way that nothing—neither land nor sky nor even country or culture—could be counted on; political powers came and went as regularly as the breath of a sleeping child, and cultures were forever evolving, degenerating, or being conquered. Generation after generation, age after age, mankind observed everything under the sun, but ultimately saw nothing but change.

The point was impossible to overlook, having been hammered into humanity's psyche every day for tens of thousands of years: everything changed. Everything, that is, except death. Death was the only constant the human race ever encountered, the only equalizer, the only certainty. Death owned everything. Death was forever, eternal, like a god. Death was everything.

Once Man determined that death was the only thing that could be counted on, he did count on it, heavily. The leaders of the world were so thoroughly convinced of the reliability of death, in fact, that they based all their power and position on it, founding the empires of the world on the simple hypothesis that when a man was killed, he would stay dead.

For tens of thousands of years, the heavy shadow of death hung unchallenged over all the world, silently denying the reality and value of life, and this fact, as much as anything, shaped the development of the human psyche. For tens of thousands of years, every family, nation, and race came up with its own ideas about death; religions, cultures, even great civilizations were founded on such beliefs. In the inner recesses of the human psyche, the great and mysterious Secret of Death took on proportions so enormous they were barely even hinted at by humanity's ultimate tribute to death, the Great Pyramid of Egypt. Death felt like the oppressive shadow of just such a mountain; looming monstrously over everything, it was simultaneously unknowable yet unforgettable, undeniable yet unalterable.

It's doubtful whether anyone living today could fully appreciate how profound an impression it must have made upon humanity when, 2,000 years ago, an entirely new wrinkle appeared in this mystery, a wrinkle which forever altered the image of death in the human psyche. An unprecedented report began circulating at that time, insisting, despite all reason, that someone came back. From the most wretched slave to the most exalted prince, people everywhere found their grasp on reality challenged by the idea that somebody had risen from the dead.

The story changed the human psyche, and the world it ruled, forever. The idea that life could triumph over death had entered the human psyche for the first time, and nothing would ever be the same again. Death remained inscrutable, but it no longer seemed to be quite so inevitable. In response to this change, the whole world changed.

However, while death may have seemed somewhat less inevitable than before, people still didn't know what death was, except now a man was supposed to have risen from the grave, and no one understood how that could be possible, either. The legends surrounding this man claimed that his death represented a great boon to humanity, that through it, somehow, many others would be saved from death; but no one pretended to understand the actual logical mechanics of how this was supposed to work. Conquering death, it seemed, only deepened its mystery. With Jesus' entry into the picture, the nature of death became—and remains today—the central mystery of the Judeo-Christian tradition, around which all else ultimately revolves.

These all-important questions remain unanswered 2,000 years later. In fact, in all these years not a single theory has surfaced offering intellectually honest explanations of the nature of death, the Christian Resurrection, or the promise of eternal life. These three mysteries are all really just different facets of the same question—what is death?

Those few traditions we do have about death offer three mutually exclusive answers to its mystery, and the origins of each stretch back into the unrecorded depths of time. One school of thought simply holds that there is no afterlife at all, that physical death completely terminates the individual; another promises an afterlife of perpetual reincarnation; and the third warns of an eternal afterlife in either heaven or hell. These three conflicting traditions have remained deadlocked since the dawn of history; today, as in every age, each enjoys massive support from equally enthusiastic devotees.

Science and Death

People today tend to take for granted that modern science will provide solutions for all the dreary problems that plagued previous generations. However, even though it has proven itself marvelously capable of untying many of the other thorny knots of reality, science doesn't seem to provide much help in solving this particular dilemma.

The primary scientific opinion is that once the body dies, the individual is entirely dead and nothing remains. However, two new branches of scientific investigation have arisen in the latter half of the twentieth century, both offering formidable rebuttals to that opinion. Unfortunately, these new studies also seem to contend with each other. The data coming in from past-life regression research strongly suggests that the reincarnation tradition is correct; subjects who delve hypnotically into their unconscious memories consistently come up with convincing recollections of past lives.[1] The data coming in from near-death experience research, however, indicates just the opposite—that after death people permanently enter heaven-or-hell type experiences, generally found to be populated with long-deceased friends and relatives. Finding those friends and relatives there directly conflicts with the data from the past-life regression research: those long-lost friends and relatives have obviously not reincarnated, since they still remain in that "heaven" or "hell" the near-death experiencers briefly visit.[2] So, according to science, after death we either die entirely, or we reincarnate, or we permanently enter a heaven or hell.

Science doesn't seem to be much help.

On the other hand, traditional religions are known to have preserved some of humanity's oldest and most valued teachings. Possessing mysterious origins, many such traditions seem to be older even than any specific culture or civilization. Religions have always claimed to safeguard invaluable information from primordial times, including, they say, the secrets of life and death. Since science, that celebrated panacea of the twentieth century, has failed thus far to solve this mystery, such traditions deserve, if for no other reason than their very longevity, to be examined as well.

---

1 R.A. Moody, Jr., *Coming Back: A Psychiatrist Explores Past-Life Journeys* (New York: Bantam, 1992), 179.
2 R.A. Moody, Jr., *Life After Life* (Boston: G.L. Hall, 1975), 23-24.

The Binary Mind

In his chronicle of humanity's origins, the author of Genesis betrays a pronounced interest in binary systems. Apparently perceiving nature itself as fundamentally binary, Genesis suggests that everything was originally created in complementary units of twos: chaos and light, heaven and earth, sun and moon, day and night, water and firmament, plants and animals, man and woman, and soul and spirit (Genesis 1:3-27). Today, science would add a few more items to such a list: the brain, perfectly divided into left side and right side, and the human psyche itself, with its conscious and unconscious halves.

But it wasn't always realized that the human psyche possesses a binary structure; it was only in the last century that science even conceded the existence of the unconscious. Before Freud, fully half of all human consciousness went essentially unrecognized by science;[1] today, the scientific world universally acknowledges that the human psyche is indeed formed of two separate and distinct components.

Study of the mind has revealed that the conscious and unconscious are, despite what their names suggest, not merely two different forms of the same substance; the unconscious is not just a lesser or lower form of consciousness. They are fundamentally different types of mind, with completely different modes of operation.

> Consciousness proceeds in terms of analysis and differentiation, in terms of special attention to "the most minute details." The unconscious, on the other hand, has an opposite way of thinking. Non-analytical, undifferentiated, it takes its symbols as they are, and does not break them down as consciousness does. . . . [T]he basic categories and ways of procedure are different in consciousness from those that prevail in the unconscious. . . . Its mode of thinking is altogether different from what we understand by "thinking."[2]

Each side of the psyche possesses characteristics and capacities unique to itself. However, neither part is sufficient alone;

---

1 C.G. Jung, *Aion: Researches into the Phenomenology of the Self*, in *The Collected Works of C.G. Jung*, Vol. 9.ii, trans. by R.F.C. Hull (Princeton: Princeton University Press, 1969), para. 11, p. 6.

2 Ira Progoff, *Jung's Psychology and Its Social Meaning* (New York: Grove Press, 1953), 75.

each needs the input of the other. The two sides of the mind thus complement one another, together forming a whole—the self—far greater than the sum of their parts.[1]

The conscious mind's objectivity allows it to distinguish and differentiate between forms,[2] providing humanity with its logic and analytic reasoning, the foundation of all science, technology, and civilization. And, more importantly still, the conscious mind has free will, the power to make choices and decisions. The basic design of the human mind grants all the free will to the conscious and none to the unconscious, which risks letting the mind become one-sided. The conscious is able, under this design, to repress and inhibit its other half, the unconscious;[3] and since it is essentially masculine, or self-assertive, in nature, it tends to use this ability regularly.

The unconscious has equally essential qualities. Although much of its activity occurs outside our awareness, the unconscious is constantly releasing material into the conscious mind; this secret participation of the unconscious is vital, providing the balance necessary for a healthy psyche.[4]

Whereas the conscious is logical, the unconscious is emotional; and since it lies below the threshold of awareness, we tend to experience the emotion it releases into the conscious not as something we have chosen, but as something which happens to us.[5] And whereas the conscious is active and enterprising and takes the initiative, the unconscious is almost purely reactive in nature; much of what it does is in response to outside stimuli. It is also receptive and therefore functions as the mind's memory center, receiving and storing all information, experiences, and other memory data.[6] The unconscious contains a complete,

---

1 Jung, *Two Essays on Analytical Psychology*, in *Collected Works*, Vol. 7, para. 274, p. 177.

2 Jung, *Psychology and Religion: East and West*, in *Collected Works*, Vol. 11, para. 785, pp. 492-93.

3 Jung, *The Structure and Dynamics of the Psyche*, in *Collected Works*, Vol. 8, paras. 132-140, pp. 69-71.

4 Jung, *The Structure and Dynamics of the Psyche*, paras. 158-59, pp. 78-79, and para. 702, p. 364; *The Archetypes and the Collective Unconscious*, in *Collected Works*, Vol. 9i, para. 505, p. 282.

5 Jung, *Aion*, para. 15, p. 9.

6 Jung, *The Structure and Dynamics of the Psyche*, para. 270, p. 133.

perfectly preserved, unedited record of all the thoughts, feelings, and experiences of a person's past. However, since the memory-bearing unconscious is also emotionally-based, memory recall tends to be an emotional experience; memories are generally found to be imbued with an aura of emotion.[1] Memories which lack an emotional charge, having little personal meaning or importance, tend to be more difficult to recall than memories which contain strong emotional ingredients. Storing all memory, the unconscious is necessarily both vast and deep and has often been likened to a limitless dark ocean within the psyche.

Essentially female in character, the unconscious is the source of value-awareness in the human psyche.[2] While the conscious will coolly note an object's outer characteristics, it takes the unconscious' more intuitive perspective to recognize if those characteristics hold any personal value or meaning; the conscious quantifies, the unconscious qualifies.

Although the unconscious is subjective, allowing feeling, rather than law, to form the ultimate basis of its value system, it also possesses an innate understanding of good and evil,[3] making it the source of humanity's moral consciousness.[4] And, as the inner creator of images and patterns, the "matrix-mind" that gives birth to thought-forms in the psyche,[5] it is also the source of all instinct, intuition, and dreams.[6]

While the conscious mind tends to recognize specific details and differences between things, the unconscious focuses on issues of connectedness and unity; thus, the unconscious often reflects a certain timeless quality, a feeling of oneness and universality.[7]

These two halves of the mind are fully dependent upon one another; each lacks and needs what the other possesses. While the conscious is the seat of free will, able to make new and creative

---

1 Frances G. Wickes, *The Inner World of Choice* (Englewood Cliffs: Prentice-Hall, 1963), 165.
2 Ibid., 220, 204.
3 Jung, *Two Essays*, para. 30, p. 27; para. 224, p. 140; *The Structure and Dynamics of the Psyche*, para. 275, p. 135; para. 281, p. 137; *The Practice of Psychotherapy*, in *Collected Works*, Vol. 16, para. 391, p. 193.
4 Jung, *Two Essays*, para. 218, p. 136.
5 Jung, *Psychology and Religion*, para. 782, pp. 490-91.
6 Jung, *The Structure and Dynamics of the Psyche*, para. 265, p. 130; para. 266, p. 130-31; para. 269, pp. 132-33; para. 338, pp. 156-57; para. 341, p. 158.
7 Jung, *Psychology and Religion*, para. 784, pp. 491-92.

decisions, by itself it has no ability for recall, and must rely on the unconscious to provide it with memory data when it needs it. The unconscious, the equal but opposite partner of the conscious, lacks free will; like an automatic computer, it is incapable of making any independent decisions whatsoever. But the unconscious instinctively recognizes all subjective value content, automatically processes all command messages, and, as the seat of all memory, precisely records all input from the conscious.

Although psychology first discovered this binary mind in the days of Freud and Jung in the early 1900s, it took biology nearly a full century longer to make the same discovery for itself. In recent years, however, medical research on the hemispheres of the human brain has reached essentially the same conclusions as those arrived at by Freud and Jung—that a fundamental division exists within the psyche. Each hemisphere seems to have a mind of its own; or, rather, each hemisphere seems to be related to a different half of the whole mind. The two hemispheres, again, seem to have completely different styles of processing information: the left hemisphere seems language- and analysis-oriented, while the right seems to process information holistically.[1] The left brain, like the conscious, is critical and detail-oriented, while the right brain, like the unconscious, seems emotional, creative, comprehensive, pattern-matching, and analogy-forming, and is even suspected of being the source of dreams.[2]

Two Minds, Two Scenarios

Since, in apparent support of modern psychological theory, medical research also seems to have found evidence of two distinct realms of consciousness in the human psyche,[3] the question now becomes, "What happens to such a binary mind at death?"

The fate of this binary system is the key to the Secret of Death: whatever happens to one's mind after death would indicate the nature, if any, of the afterlife. If personal consciousness continues on in any fashion after physical death, then there is such a thing as an afterlife; but if no threads of one's psyche survive at all, there is not. It has always seemed, quite reasonably, that these were the only two

1   Sally P. Springer and Georg Deutsch, *Left Brain, Right Brain* (New York: W.H. Freeman and Company, 1985), 55.
2   Ibid., 301, 367, 328.
3   Ibid., 62, 333.

alternatives, that death could only go one way or the other. Yet not one of Earth's present philosophies or religions has taken into account the binary structure of the human psyche in connection with the question of post-death survival of consciousness. Instead, only two dominant theories postulate an afterlife—either a never-ending flow of reincarnations or a never-changing eternity in either heaven or hell.

Hinduism, Buddhism, and Taoism subscribe to the theory of reincarnation, in which an individual's consciousness and life force are believed to re-enter a new body after each death, being born again. Individuals are thought to go through an endless number of incarnations, but, as they go from life to life, they continually get cut off from all memory of their previous identities and experiences. The people of the East believe their destiny is just to live a life and forget it, live another and forget that one too, on and on forever.

On the other hand, among Christians, Jews, and Muslims, the afterlife is thought to include a moral judgment followed by an eternity of either heavenly reward or hellish punishment. Only one lifetime is to be had, and the subsequent afterlife is permanent, unchanging, and either absolutely pleasing or absolutely unpleasing. Curiously, there is thought to be no variance in the quality of happiness in many of these scenarios; the experience is always at the furthest extreme. The pleasure of the heaven experience, tradition maintains, is always at maximum and never wavers; the displeasure of the hell experience is likewise always at maximum, also never wavering.

According to Christian theologian Emmanuel Swedenborg, the human unconscious would itself produce the entire afterlife experience of the individual. As early as the eighteenth century, Swedenborg dimly recognized the existence of the unconscious and directly equated it with that ancient, mysterious religious unit known as the "soul." According to Swedenborg, after death the whole experience of the individual would be that of the unconscious; following death this side of the mind eventually "contracts and condenses" into its own "most essential nature."[1] If a person had lived a life which brought peace and joy to his inner soul, according to Swedenborg, at death the unconscious would, upon condensing, find these attributes to be its essential nature and

---

1   Emmanuel Swedenborg, *Heaven and Hell* (New York: Swedenborg Foundation, Inc., 1979), 423.

would enjoy a "heaven" type experience. If, however, the individual had lived a life which brought only pain, discontent, and self-condemnation to his inner self, then upon condensation his unconscious would experience those feelings on a more absolute level of intensity, suffering a "hell" type experience.[1]

Division of the Self

There exists today no philosophy or organized religion which supposes that each side of this argument has held but half the answer. Perhaps this is because religions are in the business of encouraging and comforting people; it would be hard to try to comfort people while at the same time suggesting to them that after death their very identities would rupture down the middle. This would be considerably less optimistic an outlook than the pearly heaven of Christianity or the blissful nirvana of Buddhism; yet, if the two sides of the mind do correlate somehow with humanity's two predominant concepts of the afterlife, then such a "splitting" might be exactly what does take place.

Perhaps it has been a mistake for humanity to assume that the "self" is indivisible. Consider the world of physics—each time science finds a new subatomic particle that might be the final, smallest indivisible building block of nature, it inevitably discovers later that this particle can also be split into even smaller pieces. At death, might we not also divide into smaller pieces? Do we, in fact, break apart into our three fundamental components—a body, a conscious, and an unconscious—when we die? And if so, does this not call to mind the ancient maxim that each living person is composed of a body, a soul, and a spirit?

If dying splits us apart in this way, then in a sense dying truly means extinction; the individual as he had been during life would be rendered completely nonexistent. But then, in just as real a sense, the individual would also be multiplying, becoming two new selves, like an amoeba. Following the separation from a dead body, the two sides of the mind would also separate from each other, and each half, one conscious and one unconscious, would have an equally valid claim to the identity of the individual.

---

1 *"The mind is its own place, and in itself can make a Heav'n of Hell, a Hell of Heav'n."* — John Milton, *Paradise Lost*, as quoted by Seldes in *The Great Thoughts*, 292.

Would both of these parts be the real individual, or would neither? Where does identity lie?

Curiously, although Swedenborg maintained that just such a splitting of the conscious mind away from the unconscious occurs shortly following death,[1] he never pursued this curiosity further by inquiring what happens to that conscious mind following the separation.

The Soul and the Spirit

Although the two terms tend to be equated today, "soul" is not properly the same as "spirit." The blurring of distinctions between these two is, historically speaking, something of a recent development; it used to be understood that they referred to two completely separate substances. In the ancient Hebrew of the Old Testament, just as in modern English, there was one term for "soul" and a different one for "spirit." The Old Testament consistently distinguished the two; they were referred to as having completely different attributes. Souls were regularly referred to as "feeling" this or that; a spirit, however, was always "doing" or "thinking," but never "feeling" anything. The soul was thought to be capable of dying or experiencing death, but the spirit was never referred to as having died. After death, the spirit was said to "return to God," while the soul generally wound up in She'ol, the Jewish version of hell.

In the New Testament, the Greek scriptures continued this practice; again, there was one word for soul and a different one for spirit. Each was spoken of in different ways and as having different attributes, and occasionally both were even mentioned separately in the same sentence.

We see, then, that although it was only relatively recently that modern science distinguished the existence of two different parts to a person's inner self, labeling them the "conscious" and the "unconscious," religion had long before distinguished two different parts to a person's inner self, calling them the "spirit" and the "soul."[2] Are these the same?

It may be that Jesus Christ believed they were, identifying the unconscious with that same soul thought to survive death—in a number of passages, he referred to a dead person as "not dead,

---

1 Swedenborg, 237, 420-423.
2 Isaiah 26:9.

only sleeping."[1] It seems, from his terminology, that Jesus perceived some very real, existential similarity between the state of death and the state of unconsciousness.

And if the soul might be identified with that same psycho-spiritual unit modern science knows as the unconscious mind, as both Jesus and Swedenborg (and Freud) seem to suggest, then might not that other mysterious unit, the spirit, actually be what is known today as the conscious mind?

Considerable evidence suggests that the soul and spirit of ancient Jewish culture have reappeared in today's language as these unconscious and conscious elements. The Hebrew prophets consistently used terminology appropriate to the right-brain unconscious when referring to the soul. More than 110 times in the Old Testament, the soul is reported as possessing attributes which today we know belong exclusively to the subjectively-oriented, emotionally-based unconscious, such as loving, hating, abhorring, loathing, lusting, grieving, longing, and mourning, and as feeling bitterness, joy, humility, thirst, desire, anguish, weariness, enjoyment, satisfaction, comfort, contempt, and delight.

The distinction is both clear and striking—nowhere in either the Old or New Testament is it stated that the spirit experienced such feelings.

Thirty-two times in the Old Testament, the soul is referred to as being able to die, twenty times as being in danger of being "cut off," seven times as being in "the pit," three times as being in "hell," three times as being rent "in pieces," four times as being destroyed, twice as being "taken away," and once each as being thrust into "total darkness" and "total silence," being "dried up," being "in prison," and being "gathered with sinners."

Not even once is the spirit referred to in any of these contexts. While the soul is thought able to die, to be "cut off," thrown into a pit, taken away, destroyed, and all the rest by the ancient Hebrews, the spirit is spoken of in only one way in reference to death:

> The spirit returns to God who gave it.
> —Ecclesiastes 12:7

Just as Israel's prophets spoke of the soul using terminology modern science reserves exclusively for the unconscious, so too they credited

---

1   Matthew 9:24; John 11:11-14. See also Psalm 13:3; Acts 7:60, 13:36; I Corinthians 15:6.

the spirit with the very traits science recognizes as belonging to the conscious, such as intelligence and comprehension:

> There is a spirit in man, and the inspiration of the almighty giveth them understanding.
> — Job 32:8

Over and again in both the Old and New Testaments, the spirit is held up as the exclusive source and repository of knowledge, understanding, wisdom, and logic, the same characteristics modern science attributes to the conscious half of the human psyche:

> . . . the spirit of wisdom and understanding, the spirit of council and might, the spirit of knowledge . . .
> — Isaiah 11:2

And just as with the conscious mind of today, the spirit of old was also associated with the characteristics of perception and awareness, being thought of as the "lamp of consciousness":

> The spirit searches everything . . . who knows a man's thoughts except the spirit of the man which is in him?
> —I Corinthians 2:10-11

> The spirit of man is the lamp of the Lord, searching all his innermost parts.
> — Proverbs 20:27

And, further mirroring the human conscious, the spirit was also thought to possess the key characteristics of free will and conscious intent.[1]

People's inner spirits, the ancient Hebrews believed, came directly from the deity at their births, and, although residing within them throughout their lives, continued to belong to Him, being parts of the deity's own spirit. They believed that this inner spirit was what animated them and gave them life, associating it with that most fundamental symbol of life, breath itself:

> . . . God . . . breathed into his nostrils the spirit of life, and man became a living soul.
> — Genesis 2:7

---

1   Psalm 32:2; Exodus 35:21; Matthew 26:41.

When thou sendeth forth thy spirit, they are created . . .
—Psalms 104:30

Don't you know that you are the temple of God, and the spirit of God dwells within you?
—I Corinthians 3:16

Spirit, however, was only a temporary gift; it was given at people's births only to be taken away again at their deaths:

. . . the Lord said, "My spirit shall not abide in man forever, for he is flesh, but his days will be 120 years."
—Genesis 6:3

No man has power to retain the spirit, or authority over the day of death . . .
—Ecclesiastes 8:8

The ancient prophets believed that the same spirit which animated human beings also resided in and animated all other living creatures:

If he gather onto Himself his spirit and his breath, all flesh would perish together.
— Job 34:14-15

While they fully expected the spirit to separate from the body at physical death, returning to God, there was thought to be yet another separation which also threatened one's passage from physical life, a second death far worse than the first:

He who has an ear, let him hear what the Spirit says to the churches. He who overcomes will not be harmed by the second death.
—Revelation 2:11

The soul, they thought, could also be separated, "cut off" from its spirit as well as its body; this separation would prevent the soul from accompanying its spirit on that return journey:

The word of God is quick, and powerful, and sharper than any two-edged sword, piercing even to the dividing asunder of soul and spirit . . .
—Hebrews 4:12

To suffer such a division, it was thought, was to have God Himself turn away from a person, taking away His living spirit; thereafter, one's experience would be limited to the crippled perspective of the dying soul:

> ... he makes me dwell in darkness like those long dead ... my spirit grows faint within me ... my spirit faints. ... Do not hide your face from me or I will be like those who go down into the pit.
> —Psalm 143:3-7

This dreaded separation, however, was not thought to be fully inevitable, and early Christians prayed fervently that it would not happen to them:

> May the God of peace himself sanctify you absolutely whole, and may your spirit and soul and body be kept sound ...
> —I Thessalonians 5:23

There seems to have been a conflict within the Judaism of Christ's day over the concept of resurrection from the dead, as the following passage illustrates, but what is particularly telling in this passage is the underlying suggestion that Jewish culture of the time recognized the possibility that there might be two different parts of a person's self that survived physical death:

> ... the Sadducees say there is no resurrection, neither of angel nor spirit, but the Pharisees confess both.
> — Acts 23:8

There seems little room for doubt—within the ancient culture of the Hebrew, there existed a widely-held belief that the soul and spirit were separate and distinct internal elements which could and at least sometimes did part from one another at physical death. Although rare today, such a doctrine is known to have been present in many of the native belief systems surrounding Israel, and from the evidence preserved within the Old Testament, it seems that it was within the ancient Hebrew culture as well.

The Two-Edged Sword of Death

If death divides the individual mind into its two separate components, it would be possible for both of the traditional afterlife scenarios to be correct, each being a different, partial view of the same event. Modern psychological theory predicts that such a division would produce conditions consistent with the two traditional afterlife scenarios. The correlation is so perfect, in fact, that even if the "reincarnation" and "heaven and hell" afterlife scenarios had never been heard of before, both would be summoned into existence the instant modern psychology pondered the fateful question "What if both parts of the psyche were to survive physical death, but separately?"

If, in leaving its dying body, the conscious also separated from its unconscious, it would be struck with total amnesia, losing every last thread of its memory and sense of identity, because the unconscious is where all memory is stored. Without the unconscious' memory, instinct, and intuition, nothing it observed around it would seem to make any sense. And without the unconscious' subjective perspective, it would not feel related or connected in any way to the world around it. In fact, without the unconscious, it would not experience any feeling or emotion whatsoever. Objective to the end, the conscious would then just be a bodiless, identityless, emotionless point of pure, living awareness.[1] In time, such an amnesic conscious spirit could be expected to drift innocently into new experiences, from which it would slowly build up a new sense of identity. Free as a lark, it would be likely to repeat this pattern indefinitely, perpetually creating new identities and leaving behind a steady stream of discarded past selves, like a plant endlessly growing shoots that are pruned as soon as they are grown.[2]

---

1   Perhaps not so coincidentally, just such a state *has* been found, in past-life regression research. When hypnotically regressed to a time between lives, subjects consistently describe themselves as bodiless, floating in nothingness, possessing no memory of any identity or past life, and seemingly free of any emotion whatsoever.

2   It seems no matter how much soul is discarded into unconsciousness, it never seems to run out; as a spirit entered a new body, more memory-recording soul-material would be needed to join with it. *"Man is . . . a complex being: the substance which gives a power of motion to the body . . . men call the . . . spirit. Another internal spirit called . . . the . . . soul attends the birth of all creatures embodied . . . convey[ing] a perception either pleasing or painful. These two, the . . . spirit and . . . soul, are closed united . . ."* — From The Hindu Laws of Manu, quoted in W.Y. Evans-Wentz, trans., *The Tibetan Book of the Dead* (London: Oxford University Press, 1981), n. 47.

Meanwhile, any afterlife for a separated unconscious would necessarily be both permanent and unchanging; such an unconscious would be unable to change after having parted from the conscious mind, since that conscious holds the free will, the power to make choices and decisions when alive. Once parted from its conscious half, it would lose all capacity for objective, rational thought; unable to think clearly, it would be doomed to remain in whatever automatic, subjective, emotionally-based patterns it had forged during life. As Swedenborg suspected, if an individual died still holding onto desires which, on an unconscious level, brought only grief and pain, then his unconscious would continue to experience that grief and pain, yet would also continue to desire the object which brought it that pain. Having lost the capacity for intelligent decisions, the unconscious would find itself frozen in form, permanently holding whatever opinions, psychological habits, and unresolved emotional complexes it possessed at the moment of death.

And, also as Swedenborg anticipated, it seems that the unconscious would more or less "fall in upon itself" after death, but only if, in that dying, it also became separated from the conscious. By separating, it would lose the source of all its energy, vitality, and drive and could do nothing except sit, utterly unable to move. Being cut off from the input of both the physical body and the conscious mind—cut off, in effect, from all mental and sensory stimuli—it would find itself in ultimate darkness and ultimate silence, imprisoned by the bars of absolute isolation. Sitting alone and abandoned, cut off from all it had known outside itself, cut off from all objective reality, the unconscious would turn its attention inward. Since it is naturally subjective anyway, full self-absorption under such isolation would be inevitable, perhaps even instantaneous.

Turning within, it would find all the memories it had stored up over the lifetime and would quickly focus all its attention on them. Collapsing into itself, such a separated unconscious would become completely preoccupied with redigesting its own memories.[1] Since, as the source of humanity's moral consciousness the unconscious is also naturally sensitive to issues of "good and evil" and "right and wrong," during this digestion process

---

1 One is reminded of the archetypical ghost sighting, in which a disembodied specter is seen unconsciously acting out scenes from its past, apparently replaying the same scene over and over, like a skipping record.

it would become acutely aware of all the moral shortcomings illustrated within those life memories; in effect, it would judge itself. And because the unconscious is also naturally reactive and responsive, it would then automatically react to those memories as well, experiencing internal emotional responses which reflected those judgments. In other words, not only would a separated unconscious judge itself, but it would also reward or punish itself accordingly, through its automatic emotional responses to those judgments.

Due to its absolute isolation from all outside stimuli, these emotional responses would come to fill its entire field of awareness, and so would be felt on an absolute level of intensity. And since the unconscious is emotionally-oriented, it would focus intently on those responses, feeding blindly on their emotional content; like a winepress, it would press the same material over and over for the ever-increasingly intense emotional responses this would elicit.[1] Thus, if its judgments of its memories were self-approving, the corresponding emotional experience would be absolute, unending, ever-increasing joy; but if those judgments were self-condemning, the emotional response would be absolute, unending, ever-increasing misery.

Established psychological theory, then, would seem to predict that if an unconscious separated from both its physical body and its conscious mind, yet continued to function, it could be expected to automatically make, and then feel, its own value judgment of itself;[2] the unconscious' own fundamental nature would, in effect, force it to judge and carry out sentence upon itself.

It can be readily seen that in each case, both the conscious and the unconscious would experience more or less just what the Eastern and Western religious traditions have always claimed they

---

1   This perhaps is the origin of the "winepress" metaphor used so curiously in many Biblical passages, such as Job 24:11; Isaiah 5:2 and 63:2-3; Jeremiah 25:30; Lamentations 1:15; Joel 3:13; Matthew 21:33-41; and Revelations 14:19-20 and 19:15.

2   According to Ecclesiastes 9:5, the dead know nothing. Yet, elsewhere in the Bible, the dead do register some sort of experience, if not actual objective awareness: Isaiah 14:9-16; Job 3:18, 22, 10:21-22, and 12:24-25; and, especially, Job 26:5—"The dead are in deep anguish." The dead *would* "know" nothing, of course, if they were subconscious psyches, which *never* think, but only feel. They would "know" nothing of the real world, yet they would "feel"; they would continue to record experience in their own fashion.

would, but only if they separate from each other. The conscious would lose its memory and go on to new cycles of experience, while the unconscious would find itself forsaken and abandoned in an eternally unchanging "heavenly" or "hellish" experience.

The East's tradition of reincarnation and the West's tradition of heaven and hell are each thousands of years old; science's discovery of the natures and qualities of the conscious and unconscious are less than a single century old. Nonetheless, they are somehow the same; somehow, the latter has reconstructed the former. Science, it seems, has arrived at conclusions religion embraced ages ago.

CHAPTER 2

EVIDENCE OF TWO SELVES
THAT SURVIVE DEATH

Findings of Modern Afterlife Research

We shall some day catch an abstract truth by the tail, and then we shall have our religion and our immortality.
—Henry Adams[1]

The most amazing—indeed, awesome—scientific development of the twentieth century occurred in the past few years yet was all but ignored by the scientific community. After 200 years of having the scientific world maintain that the concept of an afterlife was nothing more than a fairy tale, bold independent researchers have started collecting the first hard evidence to the contrary. Long a concern of only the religious, the question of life after death has now become a rallying call for those on the frontiers of science. Extensive research is now being done, primarily in two areas: hypnotic past-life regression and near-death experience.

Past-life regression research began with the almost incredible discovery that the human unconscious functions as a perfect memory machine. Once hypnotized and thus able to more fully interface with their unconscious minds, ordinary people have demonstrated a phenomenal ability to recall, in exact detail, virtually anything and everything they ever encountered or experienced while awake, at virtually any moment in their pasts. It is easy, for instance, for a hypnotized subject to recall all the sights,

---

1   Henry Adams, as quoted by Ernest Samuels in *Henry Adams: The Middle Years*, 1958, as quoted by Seldes in *The Great Thoughts*, 5.

sounds, and smells of a particular day in school that occurred more than thirty years in the past, just as easy as recalling what occurred only one day in the past. It has been demonstrated time and again that the unconscious records and is able to recall virtually every detail of an individual's life experience.

In past-life regression, a subject is hypnotized and then, thanks to this total recall, is regressed all the way back into what are supposedly earlier lives. Near-death experience research, on the other hand, investigates the reports of those who go through what is believed to be the actual death experience and are lucky enough (or unlucky enough, according to many of these subjects) to be revived.

Each of these fascinating areas promises to add much to humanity's understanding of life after death and the processes involved. Although they seem so full of promise, however, there is a glaring dilemma involving these two areas of research, a problem which has thus far allowed the greater scientific community to completely disregard them: the data from the near-death experience research seems to contradict the data from the past-life regression research.

Regression Research

In a typical past-life regression, individuals supposedly return in their memories to a period prior to their actual birth, to a time when, typically, they report finding themselves in a state of bodiless limbo, "floating," as they tend to describe it, with no sense of identity, past, or location. Subjects calmly report a most peculiar existence at this stage in their regressions: being utterly alone, experiencing no emotions or subjective feelings of any kind, completely unaware of having ever had any name or identity, completely unaware, in fact, of having ever been anywhere else or experienced anything besides the limbo they are in at that moment. It is almost as if they exist merely as a spark of consciousness, aware of nothing except being conscious. Continuing further back in such regressions, detailed and convincing memories of previous lives are reached;[1] reports of such past-life journeys have found their way into a number of popular "life after death" books over the past few years.

---

1   Moody, *Life After Life*, 6-20.

Near-Death Experience Research

In typical near-death experiences (NDEs), on the other hand, subjects report traveling at high speeds through some sort of tunnel immediately after leaving their bodies. After coming out on the other side, which is often described as a beautiful, love-permeated, heaven-like place,[1] these subjects typically report meeting up with deceased friends, relatives, and various divine God-like figures. Once encountering a God-like figure, subjects often report undergoing a memory review, which covers their life histories in extreme depth; such reviews tend to be described as profoundly emotional experiences. Typically the subjects are then told that it isn't their time to die yet, and they suddenly find themselves back in their bodies.

Interestingly, Swedenborg's reports are, in certain respects at least, strikingly similar to these near-death scenarios; however, Swedenborg seems to have gone one step further, claiming that following the memory scan, the person's conscious separates from the unconscious, and thereafter the unconscious soul enters heaven or hell.

These new fields of study are wonderfully intriguing, but what weight can these rigorously researched reports actually be given if the data coming from the past-life regression research continues to conflict with the data from the near-death experience research? Regression research suggests that after death (between lives), a person just floats around in an empty limbo, an experience devoid not only of body, but also of emotion, memory, and even sense of identity; near-death experiencers, on the other hand, claim to still possess a body of sorts in the afterlife, and, speaking vividly and emotionally of actually visiting traditional heaven- and hell-like environs, return convinced they genuinely met their long-lost, previously deceased relatives and friends.

Acknowledging the Obvious

Division Theory offers a rational explanation for this dilemma; its hypothesis of the separation of body, soul, and spirit at death successfully accounts for all the phenomena being reported in these investigations. Division Theory offers a humble yet

---

1   Some reports, however, speak of emerging into a far different, horrible, hell-type place.

irresistible suggestion—that these two areas of research are reporting two different kinds of afterlife scenarios precisely because there *are* two different kinds of afterlife scenarios.

The data coming in from the regression research is in perfect agreement with Division Theory's scenario of a disembodied spirit separated from its soul. The spirit indeed would be expected to be left alone, bodiless, seemingly floating in nothingness, just as these past-life regressions consistently report. And such a spirit would possess no feeling, memory, or sense of identity, as these would all have departed along with the soul.

Likewise, most of the data coming in from the near-death research also seems consistent with a disembodied soul that was separated from its spirit. Subjects report the very heavenly and hellish experiences the separated soul would be expected to have.

An Emotional Void

Yet, a question remains concerning a curious emotional void which is often reported early on in near-death cases, a state which does not seem, at first glance, to correspond with the anticipated experience. As subjects first discover themselves to be separating from their bodies in near-death experiences, they often report experiencing a delightful sense of freedom from all bodily sensations, and, strangely enough, freedom from all emotional experience and reaction as well:

> It was just like I floated up there . . . very detached. I think the thing that impressed me the most was that I was devoid of emotion. It was as though I was pure intellect. I wasn't frightened. You know, it was very pleasant and obviously emotionally detached from the whole situation . . .[1]

> I was detached from it, it was as if I was there watching and I was the third party. I felt no emotion, just nothing, like looking at a picture.[2]

Encountering this sort of emotional detachment, it seems, is typical in the earliest moments of an NDE; later, however, the

---

1   Dr. Michael Sabom, *Recollections of Death: A Medical Investigation* (New York: Harper & Row, 1982), 116.
2   Margot Grey, *Return From Death: An Exploration of the Near-Death Experience* (London: Arkana, 1985), 126.

experience moves to the other end of the spectrum with the emotionally intense memory scan.

Encountering emotional detachment at this stage in an NDE seems to suggest that the initial separation of the psyche from the physical body might cause the connection between soul and spirit to first be wrenched, but not immediately severed; if so, this would account for the near-death experiencers' reports of momentarily feeling, immediately after quitting their bodies, as if they were pure intellects devoid of emotion. And other evidence even suggests that such a partial, wrenched separation of the soul and spirit occasionally occurs prior to the actual physical death; it is a widely recognized phenomenon in the medical field that people often report a pleasant calmness washing over them minutes before they quit the body.

If the memory scan following separation from the body produces the fuller separation of soul and spirit (as Swedenborg believed), this would explain why subjects' reports generally indicate stronger levels of emotional content starting at that point in their experiences.

It seems that if the evidence is approached from the presumption that there is no division of the individual's psyche following death, the actual data coming from this modern afterlife research offers, at best, inconclusive evidence or, at worst, proof that the whole concept of an afterlife is invalid. But if the evidence is examined impartially, purely on its own merits and without any preconceptions, it quite plainly indicates the existence of two completely distinct forms of the afterlife.

CHAPTER 3

TWO VISIONS OF DEATH

The Netherworld and Reincarnation

*On the day you were one you became two. But when you become two,
what will you do?*
— The Gospel of Thomas 11

The Netherworld

If, as Division Theory postulates, the conscious and unconscious both survive physical death but in vain, being separated
from each other as well as from the body they had shared, the
unconscious could be expected to experience certain very specific
conditions. It would find itself enveloped in unbroken silence and
impenetrable darkness, having been cut off from both the conscious mind and the body's senses. It would feel naked, having no
body to wear. It would also feel cold, hungry, and empty, lacking
the vibrant and fulfilling presence of its living spirit. Losing the
intellectual capacities of its conscious half would make it dull-wit-
ted, and losing the animating vigor of that conscious spirit—the
source of all its vitality while alive—would severely enfeeble it.
Such an intellectually incapacitated soul, having actually descended into the deep, dark recesses of the unconscious, might well
assume instead that it had fallen into some murky underworld
realm far beneath the abode of the living. And, as the unconscious
is essentially without limit, this would seem like falling into a
bottomless pit. In fact, submerging deeper and deeper into the foul
dregs of that unconscious wasteland would probably seem like
sinking into the miry waters of the great deep itself. And due to the
"collective" nature of that watery unconscious, such disembodied

souls would, over time, coalesce together into a single undifferentiated mass, a united semi-conscious collective sitting like a stone at the bottom of the unconscious.[1]

This is not a new picture.

The idea of the land of the dead being an "underworld" is perhaps the most common of all concepts of the afterlife, being found in diverse cultures all around the globe.[2] From the ancient civilizations of the East to the Maori of New Zealand, from the tribes of the Algonquin and the Ojibwa in North America to those of the Zulu, Ashanti, and Dogon in Africa,[3] the peoples of the earth seem everywhere to have come to the same conclusion—that the souls of the dead descend to some dark realm located far below the land of the living.

The legends of the earliest Vedic Indians describe the souls of their dead entering a gloomy netherworld, a gigantic abyss far below the earth. This bottomless pit was thought to be shrouded in total darkness[4] and perfect silence,[5] and, completely lacking any food or water, was populated by "pale, emaciated specters."[6]

In Mesopotamia, disembodied souls were believed to descend to a subterranean realm, thought to be the absolute lowest level of the earth, a dreary netherworld of total darkness, silence, immobility, and hunger.[7] The abode of the dead was also believed by the people of ancient Sumer to be underground; once there, the souls of the dead were thought to become severely weakened, both physically and mentally. The later Babylonians held similar beliefs, but they seem to have also held the peculiar notion, shared by their Western neighbors in Israel and Egypt, that the dead would be obligated to consume their own waste in the netherworld:[8]

---

1 For more on this phenomenon, see Appendix A: Fruit of the Division.
2 T.P. Van Baaren, "Afterlife: Geography of Death," in *The Encyclopedia of Religion* (New York: MacMillan, 1987), 1:119.
3 J. Bruce Long, "Underworld," in *The Encyclopedia of Religion*, 15:127.
4 *Rig Veda*, ed. by Barend A. Van Nooten and Gary B. Hilland (Cambridge, MA: Harvard University Press, 1994), 2.29.6; *Atharvaveda: Sanskrit Text with English Translations*, trans. by Devi Chand (Colombia, MO: South Asia Books, 1982), 8.4.
5 *Rig Veda* 7.104.5.
6 Long, "Underworld," 127.
7 Steven Davies, "Soul," in *The Encyclopedia of Religion*, 13:431.
8 For more on this, see Chapters 5 and 6.

The house of darkness, the house the inhabitants of which lack light, the place where dust is their food, and excrements their nourishments, where they see no light and live in darkness.[1]

The Greeks believed that the dead descended to Hades, an enormous cavern deep below the ocean,[2] a morose netherworld utterly lacking both in sunlight and self-consciousness. The souls of the dead, they believed, were condemned to a wretched subterranean world forever shrouded in mist and shadow. These souls were consistently described in ancient Greek texts as weak, cold, joyless, unconscious, and incommunicative.[3]

Ancient Egypt's underworld of Nun was thought to be the primordial chaos of the universe, conceived of as a boundless ocean, a deep, watery, black abyss,[4] and the souls of the dead who were there were described as naked, starving, deaf, and blind.[5]

Even in faraway China, the dead were believed to descend to a murky subterranean land, known there as Huang Ch'uan, in which the Chinese expected to suffer through eternity in a semiconscious state.[6]

The ancient Hebrews, of course, also believed that the dead descended deep below ground,[7] to a netherworld known as She'ol. Like the netherworlds of the Greeks and Egyptians, She'ol was thought to be located far below the murky waters of the sea,[8] and, again, was thought to be a place pervaded by deep silence,[9] thick darkness, and endless chaos:

... I go to the place of no return, to the land of gloom and deep shadow, to the land of deepest night, of deep shadow and disorder...
— Job 10:21-22

---

1 Babylonian myth of Ishtar's descent into hell, from James B. Pritchard, ed., *Ancient Near Eastern Texts Relating to the Old Testament*, 3rd ed. (Princeton: Princeton University Press, 1969), 107.

2 Long, 126.

3 S.G.F. Brandon, *The Judgment of the Dead* (New York: Charles Scribner's Sons, 1967), 81, 126-7.

4 Norman Cohn, *Cosmos, Chaos, and the World to Come* (New Haven: Yale University Press, 1993), 6, 30.

5 Jan Zandee, *Death as an Enemy According to Ancient Egyptian Conceptions* (New York: Arno Press, 1977), 14-41.

6 Anna Seidel, "Afterlife: Chinese Concepts," in *The Encyclopedia of Religion*, 1:124-27.

7 Job 11:8.

8 Job 26:5; Psalms 69:1-2, 15 and 88:4, 6-7.

9 Psalm 94:17.

And Jewish traditions described the dead as weak,[1] naked, cold, hungry, and thirsty, just as did the traditions of their neighbors:

> Lacking clothes, they spend the night naked; they have nothing to cover themselves in the cold. . . . they carry the sheaves, but still go hungry. . . . they tread the winepress, yet suffer thirst.
> — Job 24:7-12

Hebrew tradition held that people's souls continued to register very intimate experiences after death, suffering "deep anguish" and "unrelenting pain" in the land of the dead:

> Oh, that I might have my request, that God would grant me what I hope for, that God would be willing to crush me, to let loose his hand and cut me off! Then I would still have this consolation—my joy in unrelenting pain—that I had not denied the words of the Holy One.
> — Job 6:8-10

> The dead are in deep anguish.
> — Job 26:5

The ancient Israelites believed that the dead were stripped of both their physical strength and their conscious reason in the netherworld, and then were left to stagger blindly through the barren and chaotic wasteland of She'ol:

> He deprives the leaders of the earth of their reason; he sends them wandering through a trackless waste. They grope in darkness with no light; he makes them stagger like drunkards.
> — Job 12:24-25

The Sleep of Death

It seems curious that the Jews commonly referred to the state of death as "sleeping." This choice of terminology has always stood in marked contrast to the perspective of the cultures surrounding Israel, which as a whole tended to focus on the continued activity of the dead in an underground realm. But Division Theory provides a very satisfactory explanation for such a discrepancy. According to Division Theory, the abode of the dead indeed would

---

1   Isaiah 14:10.

be "below" and "beneath" that of the living, but "below" in consciousness rather than in geography. And the souls of the dead, being deeply unconscious, indeed would in a sense be "sleeping," just as Biblical tradition has long maintained:

> But man dies and is laid low . . . til the heavens are no more, men will not awake or be roused from their sleep.
> — Job 14:10-12

Assimilation into the Collective

Division Theory predicts a post-death amalgamation of souls trapped in the unconscious,[1] which is interesting, for this curious detail seems also to have been a belief shared by early Jewish tradition:

> Prior to the Babylonian exile of 597 BCE, the dead were not thought of [by the Jews] as having an existence in which individual identity was preserved beyond life on earth, but rather were conceived as a faceless collective . . .[2]

And in a remarkably similar conception, the Greeks suspected that the souls of the dead did not maintain their separate identities, but instead merged into a collective state:

> In time, the individual soul becomes just a member of the countless number of "all souls." The souls move in "swarms" in the Homeric underground.[3]

Part of the Universal Human Experience?

Ancient legends frequently contain some precious nucleus of truth, and, indeed, humanity's ancient concept of the post-death abode of the soul is in remarkable agreement with the scenario anticipated by Division Theory. Perhaps even more interesting, however, is the fact that these ancient peoples all possessed similar ideas about the afterlife many thousands of years ago, in

---

1   Again, see Appendix A: Fruit of the Division.
2   Linda M. Tober and F. Stanley Lusby, "Jewish Afterlife," in *The Encyclopedia of Religion*, 6:238.
3   Jan Bremman, "Soul: Greek and Hellenistic Concepts," in *The Encyclopedia of Religion*, 13:436.

cultures even as widely separated as those of the Chinese and the Egyptian. How could such a remarkable uniformity of afterlife beliefs have existed at the dawn of recorded history, within cultures separated by thousands of miles? And how is it that those beliefs, thousands of years old, are now found to agree not only with each other, but also with the very scenario modern science itself would predict for a disembodied human unconscious?

Although ancient, this classic vision of the underworld is apparently not ancient history. A genuinely universal human experience, of course, would cut across not only all cultural boundaries, but also the boundaries of time itself; and this same vision is, as it turns out, being reported even today, by near-death experiencers. Within a span of only two days, according to one near-death researcher, the same horrifying vision was separately witnessed by four complete strangers; while suffering his own brush with death, each subsequently reported seeing:

> A landscape of barren, rolling hills filled to overflowing with nude, zombie-like people standing elbow-to-elbow doing nothing but staring straight at [the experiencers].[1]

Far more similar to the classic "cold and barren" underworld known to the ancients than to the younger Roman church's "fiery" version, the hell being described by most modern experiencers is in complete accord with what would be anticipated by Division Theory. Today, just as thousands of years ago, the most common characteristics of the "hell" vision are "lifeless apparitions" suffering "surges of anxiety" in "suffocating darkness" or "barren expanses." The majority of experiencers still describe the hells they visit as "cold and clammy" and "hard and empty," with "dull," "gray," "dim," "darkened," or "heavy" light,[2] just as their counterparts were reporting thousands of years ago.

Reincarnation: From Universal Creed to Christian Heresy

> Jesus said to them, "Can the wedding guests mourn as long as the bridegroom is with them? But the days will come when the bridegroom shall be taken away from them, and then they will fast.

---

1   P.M.H. Atwater, *Beyond The Light* (New York: Birch Lane Press, 1994), 36-37.
2   Ibid., 41, 92, 242.

And no one puts a patch of raw cloth on an old garment, for the patch tears away from the garment, and a worse rent is made. Nor do people pour new wine into old wine-skins, else the skins burst, the wine is spilt, and the skins are ruined. But they put new wine into fresh skins, and both are saved."
— Mark 2:19-22

If any religious belief could be said to be even more universal than that of the netherworld, it is doctrine of reincarnation. Repeatedly appearing among the most ancient beliefs of every continent, the belief in rebirth seems also to be a naturally-occurring element of native religions. From the Indians of North America to the tribesmen of Africa, from the Aborigines of Australia to the teeming masses of India, China, and Japan, people everywhere seem to have independently reached the same conclusion: that after death, a person is reborn again, given a new chance, a new life, and a new identity.

The belief in reincarnation has covered the entire world at one point or another. In the East, the Zoroastrians of Persia, the Egyptians of Africa, and the Pythagoreans and Platonists of Greece all held this belief. In ancient Europe, this doctrine was native to the Finns, Danes, Norse, Saxons, Celts, and Prussians, among others. In the Americas, similar views were held by the Incas and the Aztecs and later by the Mayans, Hopi, Iroquois, Algonquins, Dakotas, Tlingits, and many, many other tribes.[1] Since this doctrine has been found in native cultures all across the world, from Africa to South America to Alaska to Australia to a myriad of completely isolated oceanic islands, rebirth cannot be a tradition handed down from any one source, but instead must be considered a truly universal indigenous belief.

Today as well, this doctrine is taught far and wide; besides the larger reincarnational nations (Hinduism's India and Buddhism's China, Tibet, and Japan), the doctrine of rebirth is still alive in the native religions of more than a hundred African tribes and, among ocean peoples, in the religions of the Australian Aborigines, the New Zealand Maoris, the Tasmanians, the Tahitians, the Solomon Islanders, and the Okinawans, to name just a few.[2]

---

1 Joseph Head and L. Cranston, *Reincarnation: The Phoenix Fire Mystery* (New York: Crown, 1977), 112-114, 119-121, 195-216.
2 Ibid., 190, 192-193.

Hidden Western Roots

Although it is often assumed to be completely foreign to the West, reincarnation theology is also found thriving within the religions of Abraham, most notably in Islam's Sufism and Judaism's Cabalism. The place of reincarnation within Judaism[1] has long been debated; according to the famed Jewish historian Flavius Josephus, in fact, only one of the three schools of Jewish philosophy at the time of Christ was known to clearly reject the doctrine of reincarnation: the Sadducees. The Pharisees' pro-reincarnation views were well known, "that . . . the souls of good men . . . are removed into other bodies." The Essenes' views were less well known; but they acknowledged the pre-existence of the soul, a necessary prerequisite for the belief in reincarnation.[2]

Reincarnation and the Church

The Christian tradition does not overtly join the rest of the world in accepting this doctrine; upon inspection, however, it has more in common with reincarnation theology than is officially acknowledged. One of the most fundamental tenets of Christianity, of course, is that Jesus Christ will return to earth again one day. This return is not, however, usually anticipated to occur by reincarnation into the body of a newborn baby; he is expected, rather, to spontaneously return already full-grown, floating in the sky, still wearing the same skin he was wearing 2,000 years ago. Traditional Western theology expects him, in other words, to put the "new wine" of his new life into the "old skin" of his A.D. 33 body. Even though Christian theological tradition lacks any established or even reasonable mechanism which might allow a person to make such a return appearance, and even though much of the rest of the world's theological traditions are based on just such a mechanism, reincarnation is simply not considered to be an option.

---

1   *"[Even today] in mystical Judaism, we believe in reincarnation. It's called gilgul. We believe each time we incarnate, we move a step forward."* — Rabbi Zalman Schacter-Shalomi, as quoted by William Elliot in *Tying Rocks to Clouds* (Wheaton, IL: Quest Books, 1995), 180.
2   Head and Cranston, 124-126.

Belief in reincarnation was condemned by church authorities in the Dark Ages, in the year A.D. 553.[1] Prior to that condemnation, the first 500 years of Christianity apparently held a much less intolerant position on reincarnation; in fact, many of the earliest Church fathers are known to have openly and enthusiastically endorsed this doctrine.[2] For example, the Gnostic branch of the Church, which flourished during the first three centuries, taught a form of Christian doctrine which included a belief in reincarnation. And since Gnostic Christianity arose in the very years the New Testament was itself being written,[3] this tenet of the new religion received wide respect back then, at least until the politically organized Roman church resolved to terminate it. However, just as Gnosticism started to come under attack by the Roman church, reincarnation found a second path into Christian theology, through the third-century movement known as Manichaeism.[4] This new sect thrived throughout the fourth and fifth centuries and managed to hold out, in one form or another, all the way until the thirteenth century. But well before Manichaeism had disappeared, reincarnation was being reintroduced into Christian theology yet a third time, nestled this time within the doctrine known as Cartharism. This latest pro-reincarnation Christian sect flourished in Europe between the tenth and thirteenth centuries, and its unexpected success so alarmed Church authorities in Rome that the bloody Albigensian Crusade was finally launched to destroy it.[5]

No longer seen as a threat to Christian doctrine, reincarnation is held to be fully alien to the Judeo-Christian scriptures; however, even a cursory examination suggests that this is not truly the case. While the Bible never overtly addresses the doctrine of rebirth, either to support or condemn it, certain passages appear to carry clear reincarnational implications—either that reincarnation has occurred, in some passages, or promises of future incarnations, in others. Biblical scriptures, in fact,

---

1 Ibid., 144-48, 156-60.
2 Quincy Howe, *Reincarnation for the Christian* (Philadelphia: Westminster Press, 1974), 62-97. See also Origen, *On First Principles*, 1.4.1, 1.8.4, 2.8.3, 2.9.7 (Peter Smith Press).
3 Willem A. Bijlefeld, "Gnosticism as a Christian Heresy," in *The Encyclopedia of Religion*, 6:578-80.
4 L. Bruce Long, "Reincarnation," in *The Encyclopedia of Religion*, 8:265.
5 Gorden Leff, "Cathari," in *The Encyclopedia of Religion*, 2:115-117.

actually seem to explain why reincarnation keeps knocking on Christianity's door more than they explain why it keeps getting turned away.

The Elijah-John Connection

In the most famous instance of reincarnational thought in the Bible, it is predicted in no uncertain terms in the Book of Malachi that the prophet Elijah would return to life on earth:

> See, I will send you the prophet Elijah before that great and dreadful day of the Lord comes.
> — Malachi 4:5

And later, in the Gospel of Matthew, Jesus himself maintains, in plain and unmistakable language, that the one known then as John the Baptist was in fact the same man who had lived centuries earlier as the prophet Elijah:

> "This is the one . . . there has not risen anyone greater than John the Baptist. . . . And if you are willing to accept it, he is the Elijah who was to come. He who has ears, let him hear."
> — Matthew 11:11-15

> "To be sure, Elijah comes and will restore all things. But I tell you, Elijah has already come, and they did not recognize him, but have done to him everything they wished. In the same way the Son of Man is going to suffer at their hands." Then the disciples understood that he was talking to them about John the Baptist.
> — Matthew 17:11

Traditional Christian doctrine steadfastly denies that these John-Elijah passages constitute a true reference to reincarnation. Although these passages seem to be quite clear in their meaning, certain other passages are invariably used in rebuttal:

> The angel said to [John the Baptist's father] ". . . he [John] will go . . . in the spirit and power of Elijah . . . to make ready a people prepared for the Lord."
> — Luke 1:17

[John] confessed freely. . . . They asked him, "Who are you? Are you Elijah?" He said, "I am not." "Are you the prophet?" He answered "No."

— John 1:21

Although these passages may have once seemed capable of refuting reincarnation, Division Theory argues instead that they fully support it. In using Luke 1:17 to rule out reincarnation, in fact, Christian theologians resort to the use of a questionable interpretative procedure—in order to defend the Church's official position on reincarnation, they have been forced into the unenviable position of insisting that in this passage and this passage alone, the Greek word *pneuma*, which is translated everywhere as "spirit," does not in fact refer to a living spirit, but rather to an impersonal enthusiastic feeling or energy, oft likened to a "school spirit" or a "national spirit." This usage of the word "spirit," while common in our modern era, is completely alien to the scriptures' use of the term, which consistently uses the term *pneuma* in referencing a living autonomous being. This same Greek word was used a total of sixty-two times in the Gospels alone and always referenced a living autonomous being, as in the following examples:

He saw the spirit of God descending like a dove and lighting on him.
— Matthew 3:16

He sighed deeply in his spirit and said, "Why does this generation ask for a miraculous sign?"
— Mark 8:12

So, instead of refuting reincarnation, the passage of Luke 1:17, which suggests that John the Baptist possessed Elijah's spirit, is fully consistent with Division Theory; if reincarnation had taken place, it would have been exactly as the scriptures state—Elijah's living spirit would have returned again as John the Baptist. Furthermore, John 1:21 is also consistent with Division Theory. Since it would have been Elijah's living spirit, and not his memory-bearing soul which did the reincarnating, John would not have had access to any of his memories as Elijah, and thus would have been fully unaware that he had lived before, as Elijah or anyone else; naturally he would have denied it. Thus, rather than conflicting with Division Theory, both of these passages instead actually offer support for it.

Ancient Public Opinion

Due to the condemnation of reincarnation by church authorities some 500 years after Jesus left the scene, this doctrine has become an alien, even enemy concept to the Judeo-Christian West. However, it is reasonably certain that reincarnation was not an alien concept to the people to whom Jesus preached or, probably, to Jesus himself. To the chagrin of traditional Christian doctrine, in fact, it was apparently rather common for Christ's contemporaries to innocently wonder aloud if Jesus himself were the reincarnation of some earlier prophet:

> When Jesus came to the region of Caesarea Philippi, he asked his disciples, "Who do people say the Son of Man is?" They replied, "Some say John the Baptist; others say Elijah; and still others, Jeremiah or one of the prophets."
> — Matthew 16:14

Considering such widespread conjecture about the doctrine of reincarnation in first-century Israel, the people of his own time undoubtedly assumed Jesus had been openly promoting this doctrine when he claimed that the man now known as John the Baptist was the same man who centuries earlier had been the famous prophet Elijah.

There is at least one other reference to reincarnation in the Gospels—an indirect reference, yet an unmistakable one. In all three of the synoptic Gospels, Jesus promised that anyone leaving their homes, wives, mothers, fathers, children, or farms to follow him would personally receive hundreds more such homes, families, and so on in the future:

> Jesus [said] "No one who has left home or brothers or sisters or mother or father or wife or children or land for me and the Gospel will fail to receive a hundred times as much in this present age—homes, brothers, sisters, mothers, children and fields . . . and in the age to come, eternal life."
> — Mark 10:29-30

Outside of the doctrine of reincarnation it's difficult to imagine how such a promise could be fulfilled. In one lifetime, one can have only a single set of real parents, and no one seriously proposes that each of the seventy original disciples, who actually left their homes and families, ever received as compensation a hundred wives, a hundred fields, and so on. Either this statement of Jesus' occurred when he was waxing so poetic as to allow a falsehood to pass his lips, or he was making a promise that only many reincarnations could fulfill.

To read such passages yet insist that the Judeo-Christian scriptures denounce reincarnation is to be like a man who looks at a white card and decides that it should be black. After making this decision, the man may be able, through clever reasoning, to convince himself that the card is black, and then, either by a persistent search or through coercion, he may even be able to get someone else to agree with him that the card is black. The card, of course, will remain white nonetheless.

This is the way of these passages. They say what they say. It may be argued that they do not mean what they say, and a clever case might be used to support this claim.[1] But a person of integrity must admit to an inner unconvinced uneasiness, for these passages do say what they do say.

The argument invariably used against reincarnation is found in Hebrews 9:27: "Man is destined to die once, and then to face judgment." This passage has served as Western theology's ace in the hole whenever reincarnation has been brought up, and, until now, it's been a very effective rebuttal. However, Division Theory allows both this passage and reincarnation to be accurate at the same time. The natural division of humanity's binary psyche allows the possibility that one side of our being could go on to reincarnate, while the other side, the one with the memory and sense of identity, could still die "but once and then go on to judgment," just as Western religion has insisted for millennia. Division Theory would fully expect each individual soul to live but once on our planet, but even so, our spirits would be free to reincarnate. Thus, the question has now become: What is "a man"? Division Theory suggests that the standard definition, and indeed, general human understanding of this most basic term may be fundamentally inaccurate, misleading, and not fully understood.

---

1 This sort of twisted oppression of rational thought is precisely what the Christian Church eventually found itself forced to resort to: "We should always be disposed to believe that what appears to us to be white is really black, if the hierarchy of the Church so decides." —St. Ignatius of Loyola, *Exercitia Spiritualia*, 1541, as quoted by Seldes in *The Great Thoughts*, 251.

CHAPTER 4

THE PRIMORDIAL DIVISION

The Fall of the Soul and the Origin of the Unconscious

Now the earth was formless void, and darkness was upon the surface of the deep, and the Spirit of God was moving upon the surface of the waters. . . . God divided the light from the darkness. . . . God divided the waters. . .

God took one side of the human and . . . made a female from the side he had taken . . .
—Genesis 1:2,4,7; 2:21-22

Herewith a great crisis, a rift, splits the created world into two apparently contradictory planes of being . . .
The lines of communication between the conscious and the unconscious zones of the human psyche have all been cut, and we have been split in two.
—Joseph Campbell[1]

Division Theory does something absolutely unprecedented and profoundly transformative: it finds, in the natural binary structure of the human psyche, a cogent basis, a real-world foundation, for the whole of holy writ. Nowhere is this more evident than in the startling undercurrents of meaning Division Theory brings to light within humanity's sacred scriptures. Once one is acquainted with Division Theory, many passages never read in quite the same way again—a threshold is crossed; a barrier is broken; an ignorance is lost.

---

1   Joseph Campbell, *The Hero with a Thousand Faces* (Princeton: Princeton University Press, 1949), 281, 388.

Thanks to the fresh perspective Division Theory provides, a surprisingly foreign but now scientifically relevant chronicle is found peering out from the familiar pages of the Judeo-Christian scriptures. Uncovering a chilling yet all-too-human tale, Division Theory exposes a horror story hidden for many thousands of years, a legend dating from the very beginning of our racial memory, in which humanity unwittingly entered into a "covenant" with death itself. Just how we came to foolishly consent to such a devastating pact, how something we originally deemed an insignificant "divorce of convenience" ultimately resulted in the fall, alienation, and afterdeath exile of the human soul itself, is examined at length in these ancient holy books. Newly relevant passages abound in these scriptures, exploring in nightmarish detail the awesome ramifications and ultimate destiny of that covenant, that divorce, and that exile.

Genesis Rediscovered

> Then God said, "Let us make man in our own image, in our likeness." [Note the use of "us" and "our," plural tenses appropriate to a two-part God.] . . . So God created man in his own image, in the image of God he created him; male and female he created them.
> — Genesis 1:26-27

Division Theory suggests that the original basis of human religion might be able to be rediscovered by exploring the deeper implications of the binary structure of humanity's psyche. For example, the Western tradition that mankind possesses a two-part design, as illustrated in the above passage, now seems even more relevant; not only is the entire species differentiated into members of two different sexes, it is now also known that each individual member is mentally androgenous as well, each possessing two parts to his or her whole mental self. The masculine, conscious "spirit" forms our objective awareness, while the feminine, unconscious "soul" forms our subjective awareness. These two, modern science has taught us, interact in a dynamic partnership, together forming a whole far greater than the sum of their parts.

The spirit, we know, operates on a fully conscious level and makes its own decisions. The soul, on the other hand, functions almost exclusively on an unconscious level, from which it automatically generates feelings and stores memories. The conscious mind chooses for itself what it will think and do. The unconscious soul does not choose for itself how to feel or react; everything it does is triggered by automatic reflexes dictated by its own inner programming. To some degree, as modern science has discovered, the unconscious can be reprogrammed; to a large degree, however, it cannot.

This is the way the human psyche currently functions; it may not be the way it has always functioned.

Even that celebrated discoverer of the human unconscious, Freud himself, believed that the existence of a secondary, sub-level of consciousness must, somehow, be unnatural.[1] Division Theory is founded on the same premise, that the current partial separation between the conscious and unconscious sides of the human psyche, although common, is not natural. Division Theory, however, takes this premise one step further with its suggestion that this unnatural partial separation, if not repaired during life, inevitably becomes an even more unnatural, total, and permanent division at the onset of physical death.

> Every kingdom divided against itself will be ruined, and every city or household divided against itself will not stand.
> — Matthew 12:25

The Primordial Soul

If it is indeed not natural for the spirit and soul to be separated or alienated, then they must have once existed in a state substantially different from that found today; if so, some truly profound change must have occurred to produce the separation currently found between them. Before that change, while these two were still in their original primal state, the human soul might not have been unconscious at all, but may instead have formed just as immediate and direct a presence in the human psyche as the conscious spirit holds today. During such

---

1 *"As Freud puts it, 'We are all ill'—neurosis is of the very nature of the mind . . . we are all . . . malfunctioning."* — From Lionel Trilling, *Sincerity and Authenticity* (Harvard University Press, 1972), cited in *Modern Critical Views: Sigmund Freud*, ed. by Harold Bloom (New York: Chelsea House Publishers, 1985), 99.

a time, when no parts of the memory-bearing soul had yet separated away from the spirit, memory would not have been limited in any way; all humanity would have possessed a complete and unbroken mental record going all the way back to its very beginnings.

Humanity would still remember its Maker.

If the soul was once a more equally conscious element of the human psyche than it is today, it may have originally functioned as a teaching and guidance mechanism. Fully conscious souls could have easily been capable, for example, of making people feel bad whenever they behaved badly. Since people's souls would have still contained their original programming—designed and installed, presumably, by their Creator—whenever people made wrong choices, their souls might have automatically responded by flooding their entire psyches with painfully strong doses of negative input.[1] Just as governments have long found it necessary to install checks and balances into their nations' constitutions, perhaps the Creator also felt it necessary to install His own checks-and-balance system into the human constitution.

Making choices that conflicted with design specifications imprinted directly into humanity's souls would have brought immediate repercussions; while individuals would have been free to consciously choose how to think and behave, they would not have had any control over the vivid feelings that could follow—shame, pain, or any number of other unpleasant, non-negotiable feelings. Such "disobedience," then, would have carried a price; but it would not seem to have been capable, by itself, of bringing about humanity's exile from God.

And They Hid from the Presence of the Lord . . .

After making choices prohibited by their own inner makeup, and then immediately feeling the agony those choices automatically evoked within their souls, would people's first inclination have been to try to avoid this new input, this pain which instantly filled their inner beings?

---

1 "*Every disorder of the soul is its own punishment.*" — Saint Augustine, *Confessions*, as quoted by Seldes in *The Great Thoughts*, 25.

> He poured out on them his burning anger. . . . It enveloped them in flames, yet they did not understand; it consumed them, but they did not take it to heart.
> — Isaiah 42:25

Instead of taking it to heart, people may have opted instead to disassociate from those feelings, to disconnect from their own souls. In what would have been history's first violation of personal integrity, people may have arrogantly decided that since they didn't want those bad feelings, they simply weren't going to tolerate them, and they stubbornly blocked the input of their souls out of their conscious awareness altogether. If so, then this would have been the true "fall" of humanity.

> With one accord they . . . had broken off the yoke and torn off the bonds.
> — Jeremiah 5:5

In attempting to push their own souls away, the human race would have been denying its own design; in rejecting the inner feelings which the Creator had intended to be felt, feelings which had been expressly designed as appropriate and balanced counterpoints to their own conscious choices, humanity would have been attempting to hide from its own Maker. The Judeo-Christian scriptures agree; humanity was not ejected from paradise immediately after they disobeyed God, but only when they then tried to hide from Him as well.[1]

Consequences of Breaking the Covenant

The current existence of the human unconscious carries with it the unnerving implication that ancient humanity indeed was successful in just such an attempt to "break the eternal covenant"[2] between their souls and spirits. Apparently discovering that it was possible to at least partially suppress their souls, people seem to have pushed them just as far as they could out of their conscious awareness, creating in the process an entirely new sub-stratum of

---

1 Genesis 3:6-23.
2 Isaiah 24:5; Jeremiah 5:5, 11:4, 3:18; Malachi 2:14-15.

human consciousness,[1] that same unconscious which Freud discovered again millennia later.[2]

Making such a choice to suppress and disassociate from people's own souls would have had consequences no one could have foreseen. It would have, for example, cost people their memories, including the memory of their Maker, thus alienating them from God[3] and, ironically, even the memory of having made this choice in the first place, since it was in those souls that all their memories would have been located.[4] And because the memory of that choice to suppress unpleasant feelings would have fallen into the unmonitored, unconscious depths of the still very fertile soul, from there it would have been free to produce an unconscious behavioral chain reaction, making people always somewhat prone from that point on to suppress and disassociate from their more unpleasant "guilty" feelings. People would more and more frequently disassociate from all uncomfortable feelings rising from within their souls, eventually becoming so adept at this that they would permit themselves to suffer only the tiniest twinge of inner discomfort before initiating the disassociation process. Upon considering some immoral act, for instance, a person might briefly experience a moment of shame or sadness, but then instantly push this out of his mind, consciously rationalizing that he could not afford to have a "bleeding heart," thereby cutting himself off from the input coming from his own soul:[5]

> They are darkened in their understanding and separated from the life of God because of the ignorance that is in them due to the hardening of their hearts. Having lost all sensitivity [to their own

---

1   Jung saw the Genesis division as the source of all subsequent disorder and conflict: *"What happened on that day was the final separation of the upper from the lower waters by the interposed 'plate' of the firmament. . . . this unavoidable dualism . . . points to a meta-physical disunity"* — Jung, *Psychology and Religion*, para. 619, p. 392. See also Psalm 33:7; Proverbs 9:16; Isaiah 50:6.

2   *"[Freud] single-handedly changed the way we look at being alive. . . . he came up with the idea of the unconscious . . . which [was] like realizing that the earth moved around the sun. Once we understand that, we see everything else differently."* — Rabbi Harold Kushner, quoted by Elliot in *Tying Rocks to Clouds*, 109.

3   On humanity losing its memory of God, see Jer. 50:6; Hosea 4:6-10, 8:14.

4   *"You lose your immortality when you lose your memory."* —Vladimir Nabokov, *Ada, or Ardor: A Family Chronicle*, as quoted by Seldes in *The Great Thoughts*, 305.

5   I John 2:24; Revelation 2:25, 3:3,11.

souls], they have given themselves over to ... indulge in every kind of impurity, with a continual lust for more.

— Ephesians 4:18-19

It does seem, then, that humans may have once willfully chosen to ignore the input from their own souls, preferring instead to push these messages down below conscious awareness; people apparently hoped to completely rid themselves of their troublesome consciences in this manner, to "slaughter" them and eliminate the whole inconvenience altogether.[1] However, as Freud discovered, humanity's souls were in fact neither lost nor destroyed, but had merely been "put out to pasture" into an undetectable lower level of consciousness.

An Ignored Warning Leads to Partial Separation

Perhaps, upon observing that the human race had been purposely choosing to behave contrary to the guidelines He had written into their very souls, the Creator's first reaction was to "withdraw His favor," allowing people for the first time to experience unpleasant feelings within those souls. But when that warning failed to deter people and instead propelled them to draw back even further from their souls' input, did humanity's Designer then decide to give people what they seemed to be asking for, and completely "break the union" between the soul and spirit?[2]

This is what the Lord my God says: "Pasture the flock [souls] marked for slaughter. Their buyers [conscious spirits born into new bodies] slaughter them and go unpunished ..." So I pastured the flock [saved them in a sub-level of consciousness] ... I took two staffs and called one Favor and the other Union. ... The flock detested me, and I grew weary of them and said, "I will not be your shepherd. Let the dying die and the perishing perish. Let those who are left eat one another's flesh."[3] Then I took my staff called Favor and broke it, revoking the covenant I had made with the

---

1   *"The tragedy of man is what dies inside himself while he still lives."* — Albert Schweitzer, *The Philosophy of Civilization*, Pt. 1, as quoted by Seldes in *The Great Thoughts*), 376.

2   On the soul separating from the spirit, see also Hosea 6:4-5; Amos 3:3; Matthew 12:25.

3   See Chapter 9: Judgment Day.

nations . . . Then I broke my second staff called Union, breaking the brotherhood between Judah and Israel [between the soul and spirit].

— Zechariah 11:4-14

Partial Separation Leads to Full Division

Such a decision to suppress the soul may well have been capable of producing the very sort of full, static afterdeath rupture of soul and spirit envisioned by Division Theory. Even after having been hidden safely away in the unconscious, that original decision would not have ceased to function;[1] instead, its eternally operational presence in that lower level of the psyche would only have enhanced and perpetuated its insidious effects. Once in the unconscious, that decision would be free to operate completely unmonitored and unfettered, using its subtle influence to constantly induce people to retreat from all painful or frightening experiences, causing individuals to continually split off more and more pieces of their own souls, secreting those pieces away in an ever-enlarging unconscious. At physical death, surely the most painful and frightening experience of all, such an unconscious complex would inevitably produce its greatest effect, perhaps even going so far as to cut the entire personal-soul, containing the person's ego, memories, and habits, his entire sense of identity, away from the spirit. Then, at the onset of death, a person's entire sense of self would feel itself passing through the barrier between the conscious and the unconscious, losing in the process all ability to perceive the real world of the living:

> Therefore, Son of Man, pack your belongings [your memories] for exile. . . . Then in the evening [at death] . . . go out like those who go into exile. . . . dig through the wall [the barrier separating the

---

1   Note Jung's comments on the nature of the subconscious being such that it locks in belief and behavior patterns: ". . . *complexes in the subconscious do not change in the same way that they do in consciousness . . . they are not corrected, but are conserved in their original form . . . they take on the uninfluencable and compulsive characteristics of an automatism, of which they can be divested only if they are made conscious.*" — Jung, *The Structure and Dynamics of the Psyche*, para. 383, p. 186. See also Ecclesiastes 11:3.

conscious from the unconscious] and take your belongings out
through it. . . . carry them out at dusk [at death]. Cover your face
so you cannot see the land [of the living] . . .
— Ezekiel 12:1-6

And Division Leads to Ignorance, Guilt, and Exile

Just as Western tradition has always maintained, both the
alienation of the living from their Maker and the afterdeath exile
of the soul might indeed be humanity's own fault. If not for that
ancient choice to reject the input of the Primordial Soul, humanity's present lack of knowledge about life, death, and God might
have never had to be. Rather than having been designed or
intended by our Maker, the mysterious aspect of these matters
may be our own fault; perhaps if we hadn't once decided to
separate from our own souls, we'd never have forgotten what we
now crave to know.

And, also in accordance with Western tradition, such a wa-
tershed decision would have left a permanent flaw in all people,
writing the effects of that "Original Sin" upon every newborn,
causing it to be faulty, incomplete, "soiled." It would be missing
huge parts of its eternal soul, to which it would owe a massive
debt. Each newborn's unconscious would still contain its perfect
memory of each and every violation of the original design
specifications during all the millennia that followed the original
separation of soul and spirit. An inconceivably monstrous accumulation of soul debt, with all of the painful feelings that each
separate violation would have normally evoked if conscious,
would still be lurking down below in the unconscious of every
newborn child, still waiting for its chance for conscious expression.

Critics of Western religion have always found the doctrine of
Original Sin an easy target for ridicule, pointing out the obvious
miscarriage of justice in holding newborns guilty for sins committed by others millennia ago. But Division Theory echoes the
somber assertions of Judeo-Christianity's ancient sages, suggesting that the burden of that Original Sin indeed justly belongs on
each newborn, charging that each newborn did itself willfully
choose to separate soul from spirit all those long eons and lifetimes ago.

> To accuse others for one's own misfortunes is a sign of want of education; to accuse oneself shows that one's education has begun . . .
>
> —Epictetus[1]

Making such a decision to separate soul from spirit would have set a self-perpetuating series of events into motion, quickly resulting in an ever-growing accumulation of personal-souls being forcibly ejected into the afterdeath prison of the unconscious:[2]

> This is a people plundered and looted, all of them trapped in pits or hidden away in prisons. They have become plunder, with no one to rescue them.
>
> — Isaiah 42:22

Because of an ill-conceived act, then, humanity would have placed itself in an extremely dire situation without any apparent way to correct its mistake.

Echoes of the Primordial Division

> You, O God, divided the sea . . . you broke the heads of the monster in the waters. You broke the heads of Leviathan in pieces.
>
> — Psalm 74:13-14

> Was it not you who cut Rahab to pieces . . .?
>
> — Isaiah 51:9

In the beginning, working backwards from Division Theory, there would have been only "soul" and "spirit," joined together in an eternal embrace. The spirit would have had a purely objective perspective, the soul, a purely subjective one; the spirit would have been the decision-maker, but the soul would have always been placing conditions and restrictions on those decisions. The soul's water-like feeling and the spirit's wind-like thought would have thus been intertwined together like husband and wife, like male and female twins occupying a single egg. The two would have functioned as one, comprising a dynamic, self-sufficient whole, complete unto itself.

---

1 Epictetus, *The Manual of Epictetus,* as quoted by Seldes in *The Great Thoughts* 130.
2 See Psalm 9:15.

But this original idyllic condition changed, according to Division Theory; there was some great "falling-out" between these two primordial parts, some catastrophic fracture of their perfect unity. The spirit seems to have risen up against its partner, perceiving the soul's programming as dictatorial, unnecessarily limiting its freedom of behavior and self-expression. When the spirit overpowered the soul and forced it down into submission, down into unconsciousness, the era of the soul's overt control over the behavior and expression of the spirit would have effectively ended.

Following such a primordial conquest, the spirit, believing it had legitimately won the right to all power and authority, would have seen itself as a great conqueror, a champion of intelligence, rational order, and vitality. However, the soul, while defeated, would not have been out of the picture entirely; although condemned to a lower status, it would have nonetheless continued to exist and function in the unconscious depths of the psyche. There, it would make itself felt and known only as something dreadful and mysterious, a source of dreams and chaos, a murky, black abyss, an underworld haunt for the dead.

According to Division Theory, before such a change had taken place, before such a "fall from grace," there would have been no such thing as death in the human experience. With the fracture between these two primordial parts, death of the individual would have also entered the picture.

Such a Primordial Division would have been a questionable trade; not only would humanity have ended up paying for the "freedom from conscience" it wanted so badly with the price of death—it would also have had to given up both "destiny" and "justice" in the deal as well. Before the Fall, the as-yet uncompromised memory of the Primordial Soul would have made it easy to tell if justice really did operate naturally and automatically, whether or not a person really did "reap what he sowed" in life (as the reincarnationists' theory of karma maintains today). For, in such an era, both causes and their effects would have remained ever-present in each person's conscious memory. But with the Fall, the soul's memory would have been carved up and lost, and thus, not knowing the past, it would have become unable to anticipate what might happen in the future, what "destiny" would hold. And since the effects, the long-term consequences of people's actions and choices, would no longer always be able to be traced back to their forgotten causes, any natural workings of justice that actually were taking place would have been rendered unrecognizable and unprovable, and would seem, in fact, to be altogether nonexistent. While justice before the Fall might have seemed obvious and inevitable, justice after the Fall would have become a beautiful but seemingly impossible dream. A cause could come in one lifetime, its effect in quite another, and without the memory of the soul to connect the two, true and perfect justice would seem, instead of a certainty, merely a vain hope.

Is this story of humanity's origins true? Outside of the scientifically unconfirmable possibility of direct divine revelation, there is no way to know. However, the world does hold a full measure of evidence in support of this theory, in the form of creation myths that closely echo the very scenario described above.

In the writings of many of the ancient civilizations of the Near East, including Babylon, India, Egypt, Canaan, Sumer, and even Israel, the same archetypical creation myth appears, describing a primordial binary system, two parts existing as one at the very dawn of time: a negative, feminine, watery chaos-creature (a perfect symbol for the Primordial Soul), and a masculine god of wind and light (a perfect symbol for the Primordial Spirit). At first, these two coexist and interact peacefully, but at some point the wind god rises up against its partner, subduing the primordial watery chaos-creature and dividing it into pieces. In these legends, the feminine chaos-creature originally holds the power to restrain and control the masculine wind-god (just as the Primordial Soul would have held the power to restrain the spirit in Division Theory), but loses this control when the wind-god rises against it. After the wind-god conquers the chaos-creature, he seems to be in possession of absolute power and authority (just as the spirit would have felt after successfully subduing the soul and all its restrictive programming). And even after the chaos-creature has been vanquished, somehow it still continues to exist,[1] posing a constant threat to the order of the universe (just as the soul, although similarly overthrown and exiled in the unconscious, still makes its continued existence known through seemingly irrational urges and impulses which rise up from the depths of the human psyche). Further echoing Division Theory, elements of these myths declare that death did not enter human experience until after the defeat of the

---

1   *"The beast, which you saw, once was, now is not [and yet somehow still is]."* — Revelation 17:8.

feminine watery abyss, and that some all-important "record of destiny," which was originally a possession of the watery chaos, was lost during the conflict.

Babylon's Enuma Elish

This archetypical myth is perhaps best represented by the Enuma Elish, the Babylonian creation epic. In this version, nothing originally existed except a chaos in which male waters, *Apsu*, mingled with female waters, *Tiamat*. From these two first parents, male gods were born. Tiamat, the great mother who ruled the universe, was envisioned as a fearsome monster.[1] Feeling that Tiamat was a threat to their free self-expression, the male gods eventually rebelled against her, choosing the storm-god Marduk, the embodiment of youthful strength and creative intelligence, to be their leader. Tiamat appointed her second husband, the god Kingu, to defend her in this battle, giving him the all-important Record of Destinies to guarantee his success, but to no avail. Tiamat was slain, Kingu was deprived of the Record of Destinies, and, splitting Tiamat's body in half, Marduk formed heaven and earth from its parts. Thus crowned the supreme god of heaven and earth, Marduk was given a new function—maintaining order in the universe. Still, the world was never secure; although Tiamat had been killed, somehow she continued to exist, posing a constant threat to the world order.[2]

The Hindu Myth of Indra and Vritra

This story is also found in India's Rig Veda; in this version of the myth, the storm-god Indra overcomes the primordial chaos and brings the ordered world into existence. In the beginning there were again the cosmic waters, being held in restraint by Vritra, who represented primordial chaos. Although thought of as a "cosmic mother," Vritra's very name means "restrainer," and she was thought of as a giant dragon living in eternal darkness,[3] covering all the space between heaven and earth.[4] In an effort to free up the cosmic waters, Indra, a young storm-god of limitless vitality and creative energy, agrees to fight

---

1   Cristiano Grottanelli, "Dragons," in *The Encyclopedia of Religion*, 4:432.
2   Cohn, 45-49.
3   Ibid., 65.
4   *Satapatha Brahmana* 1.1.3.4-5.

Vritra, but only on the condition that, if he succeeds, he would be granted all power and authority, becoming the leader of the gods.

Indra promises not to kill Vritra either by day or by night, neither with anything wet nor anything dry; but then Indra does kill Vritra, with foam, at the juncture of day and night.[1] This curious detail fits Division Theory perfectly, suggesting that the actual primordial event represented by this legend must have taken place before opposites such as "day and night" and "wet and dry" had first been separated and distinguished from one another in human consciousness, i.e., before "God separated the light from the darkness," before the separation of the subjective perspective of the soul from the objective perspective of the spirit.

When Indra pierces Vritra, releasing the primordial waters from the chaos-monster's belly, Vritra asks him "now cut me in two."[2] (This image of the primordial chaos being cut into two parts appears in most of these Near Eastern myths.) After this, Indra uses the pieces of Vritra's body to create the world, while confining the primordial chaos beneath the earth, which becomes the netherworld abode of demons and the dead. And again, although Vritra has been defeated, she still somehow remains as well, in the form of other demons who also represent chaos; whatever their names, they are all really Vritra, who must be battled over and over again to keep chaos at bay.[3]

The Egyptian Myth of Seth and Apophis

A parallel legend is found in Egyptian mythology, in the story of Seth and Apophis. Apophis, the embodiment of chaos, a demon of falseness and injustice, is envisioned as a monstrous serpent living in an eternally dark abyss, the primordial chaos of the netherworld. Seeking to overturn the order and stability of the world, Apophis tries to restrain the sun-god by drinking up the water on which his boat sailed. But again a young and powerful storm-god—Seth—opposes him. The storm-god stabs the chaos-monster and cuts him into pieces, allowing the cosmic waters to flow so the sun-god could continue.[4]

---

1   Ibid., 12.7.3 1-2.
2   Ibid., 1.6.3.1-17.
3   Cohn, 64.
4   Ibid., 12, 21.

The Canaanite Myth of Baal and Yamm

This archetypical myth is found in what is believed to be its earliest fully intact version in Canaanite mythology. In the beginning, the people of Canaan taught, there was a rivalry between two great primordial deities, Yamm and Baal. Yamm, known also as Prince Sea, was "identified with or accompanied by two fearsome sea monsters, Litan (the Biblical Leviathan) and Tunnan (the Biblical Tannin)."[1] This sea-god Yamm was itself thought to be a sea-monster, being variously referred to as "the dragon," "the twisting serpent," and "the seven-headed monster." Since this Canaanite sea-god may be an ancient symbol for the Primordial Soul, which would have functioned as a controlling "judge" over its partner the spirit, it is worth noting that the other name commonly used for Yamm was Judge River. And Baal, in the role of the young storm-god, was variously called Lord of the Storm, Rider of the Clouds, and Conqueror.[2] Again, at first this sea-god Yamm was master over Baal, holding power and control over him. But Baal ultimately overthrew Yamm:

> The club danced in Baal's hands,
> like a vulture from his fingers;
> it struck Prince Sea on the skull,
> Judge River between the eyes;
> Sea stumbled;
> he fell to the ground;
> his joints shook;
> his frame collapsed.
> Baal captured and drank Sea
> he finished Judge River.[3]

Successfully defeating Sea, Baal gained absolute authority, securing an eternal kingdom for himself. But after this supreme victory, Baal was defeated by Mot, the god of death, and was forced to enter the underworld.[4]

---

1 Alan Cooper, "Canaanite Religion: An Overview," in *The Encyclopedia of Religion*, 3:39.
2 Ibid., 38.
3 Michael David Coogan, "Canaanite Religion: The Literature," in *The Encyclopedia of Religion*, 3:47.
4 Ibid., 45-57.

The Lost Sumerian Myth of Kur and Enlil

In the recently rediscovered mythology of ancient Sumer, one of the oldest civilizations to leave written literature[1] (and the supposed birthplace of Judaism's patriarch Abraham), yet another parallel to this archetypical creation myth has been found. Thought to predate the Egyptian, Hebrew, and Hindu versions by more than a full millennium, and even the Canaanite version by at least half that time,[2] the Sumerian version may be the original, from which all the others were adapted.

In the beginning, Sumer's mythology relates, there was only the goddess Nammu, the primeval Sea, eternal and uncreated. This Sea brought forth a cosmic mountain, known as Kur, which was a binary system, composed of heaven and earth united. Kur, although a mountain, was somehow also recognized as being both the Great Below and the Sumerian netherworld, and was even identified with a great dragon thought to live at the bottom of the Great Below where it came into contact with the primordial waters and restrained them. This same Kur, Kur the mountain, Kur the Great Below, Kur the dragon, Kur the union of heaven and earth, was split in two by a storm-god named Enlil (Lord Wind), thus forever separating the male heaven-god from the female earth-goddess. (In some versions of the myth, however, it is Enlil's son Ninurta, god of the Thunder-storm, who conquers Kur.)[3] This storm-god Enlil, curiously enough, also had a strong association or identification with a mountain, and is referred to, in certain myths, as "cohabiting" with a mountain, and even as himself being a mountain.[4] (This further strengthens the connection between this myth and Division Theory's concept of the spirit originally "cohabiting" with the soul.) After dividing the female earth from the male heaven, Enlil, like all the other storm-gods who followed him, then became supreme in the Sumerian universe;[5] being honored as Lord of Heaven and Prince of the Earth, he was given

---

1   5,000-2,000 B.C.
2   S.N. Kramer, *Sumerian Mythology* (Philadelphia: American Philosophical Society, 1944), 20.
3   Ibid., 38-41, 76-80.
4   Thorkild Jacobsen, *The Treasures of Darkness* (New Haven: Yale Press, 1976), 103, 101.
5   Kramer, 38-41, 73-74.

authority to plan and order the affairs of the entire world and even organize the universe itself.[1]

It is particularly interesting that, after Kur is vanquished, Ninurta builds up a great wall over the body of the dead Kur, to hold back the mighty waters which threaten to destroy the land[2]—just as Division Theory suggests that the spirit's suppression of the soul formed a wall that held back the soul's flow of input to the spirit.[3]

There is yet another mythical reference to Enlil which parallels Division Theory. Enlil, the myths report, once overpowered the female goddess Ninlil, forcing himself sexually upon her, and for this crime he was condemned to death and sent into the netherworld.[4] This story calls to mind Division Theory's image of the primordial male spirit forcing his dominance over the primordial female soul, after which death first entered human experience.

Israel's Myth of Yahweh and the Sea

Such an archetypical vision of a wind-god defeating a sea-monster also held an honored position in early Hebrew lore; some ancient legend of a storm-god defeating a watery primordial chaos, even though it is never addressed at any length, is hinted at repeatedly in the Jewish scriptures. Enough fragments of this tale remain scattered throughout the Old Testament to make it recognizable as the same myth that was obviously so well-known throughout the rest of the ancient Near East.

The Jewish Torah starts with the very same creation-myth scenario found throughout the rest of the Near East: a masculine storm-god interacting with a negative, feminine embodiment of chaos:

> Now the earth was formless and void, darkness was upon the face of the deep, and the Spirit of God moved upon the surface of the waters.
> — Genesis 1:2

The sea, or "deep," is here again a symbol for the primordial chaos; it is described as dark, empty, and without order. The feminine Hebrew word *teh-home'*, commonly translated in this

---

1 Jacobsen, 11, 99-100, 151.
2 Kramer, 80-81.
3 See Chapter 5.
4 Kramer, 103.

passage as "the deep," can also be given as "an abyss," or as "a surging mass of water,"[1] bringing it even closer into alignment with the universal image of the primordial chaos. And the word given here as "spirit," *roo'-akh* in Hebrew, is actually more accurately translated as "wind,"[2] and has traditionally been thought to refer to the breath of God. But, in fact, the most literal translation of this passage's original Hebrew would describe the wind of God hovering over a watery chaos-symbol, neatly recreating the same Near Eastern image of the beginning of time starting with a storm-god engaged with a primordial watery chaos.

While the full story line of the common myth is conspicuous by its absence from the Hebrew texts, an early tradition of Yahweh battling and overcoming a sea-chaos monster is discernable in various passages of the Old Testament, such as Psalm 74:13-14, Psalm 89:9, and Isaiah 51:9-10, as well as in the following:

> With his power he stilled the sea, with his skill he smote Rahab, with his wind he bagged Sea, his hand pierced the fleeing serpent.
> — Job 26:12-13

It is evident that much of the original version of this Near Eastern myth never found its way into the Hebrew scriptures in its earliest form; however, rather than just being dropped, the myth seems to have been revised and then inserted in the text in a different form. Still, just as in the Egyptian, Hindu, Babylonian, and Sumerian myths, the Hebrew God is shown overtly splitting various sea-chaos symbols into pieces:

> Was it not you who cut Rahab into pieces?
> —Isaiah 51:9

> God divided the waters.
> — Genesis 1:7

But instead of emphasizing this primordial battle between Yahweh and the Sea (which would imply that the Hebrew's deity was not all-powerful, since He would have had a formidable

---

1 James Strong, "Dictionary of the Hebrew Bible," in *The New Strong's Exhaustive Concordance of the Bible* (New York: Nelson Publishers, 1984), 123.

2 Ibid., 107.

opponent to overcome in that tradition), this ancient myth seems to have been edited in Hebrew literature into a different story of a primordial entity being cut into two parts: the legend of Eve being created out of Adam:

> God took one side of the human and . . . made a female from the side he had taken . . .
> — Genesis 2:21-22

In this passage, the Hebrew word *tsal-aw'*, usually translated as "rib," can also correctly be translated as the "side" of a *person;*[1] thus it seems that the Hebrew scripture might not have been originally stating that a single bone was removed from Adam, but instead that a complete side, a full half of his being was removed from him. Such an alternate translation would gain great relevance in light of Division Theory's hypothesis that humanity originally suffered just such a division, being broken into two separate but equal parts, a feminine, unconscious soul and a masculine, conscious spirit.

A Model of Our Division
> Humpty Dumpty sat on a wall,
> Humpty Dumpty had a great fall.
> And all the king's horses
> and all the king's men
> couldn't put Humpty together again.
> — Old English Nursery Rhyme

The Primordial Unity

In the beginning, the soul and spirit were as one, so perfectly intertwined it was not possible to tell where one ended and the other began; neither was any more conscious or unconscious than the other. Many cultures' creation myths describe the universe at this point as an egg, sometimes as a brother and sister intertwined together within an egg, or as two different kinds of waters swirling around each other within an egg.

---

1 ". . . tsal'ah, tsal-aw' . . . a side, lit. (of a person) or fig. (of an object or the sky, i.e. quarter) . . ." — Ibid., p. 100.

The Division

In an act of warlike aggression, the spirit asserted dominance, separating from and subjugating the soul into unconsciousness.[1] This act severed the intimate link between them, a connection that had existed from time immemorial (the eternal covenant). These efforts to push the soul down and reject its input created a wall-like barrier between them[2] which operated like a one-way door—data flowed freely from spirit to soul, but encountered resistance going from soul to spirit.[3] Although this Primordial Division seemed a rebellion at the time, and even now seems to have produced much trouble and disorder for the human race, since its ultimate results are not yet fully apparent, it may represent, or ultimately produce, an evolutionary step forward for human consciousness.[4]

---

1   "... *the conscious ... split off from the unconscious ...*" —Jung, *The Structure and Dynamics of the Psyche*, para. 339, p. 157. "*The only things we experience immediately [since that split] are the contents of consciousness.*" —Jung, *The Structure and Dynamics of the Psyche*, para. 284, p. 139. "*[The other side,] the absolute unconscious [possesses] a psychic activity which goes on independently of the conscious mind and is ... untouched—and perhaps untouchable—by personal experience ...*" —Jung, *The Structure and Dynamics of the Psyche*, para. 311, p. 148.

2   This wall was discovered by science nearly a century ago: "*The whole of psychoanalytic theory is in fact built on the perception of the resistance exerted by the patient when we try to make him conscious of the unconscious.*" — Sigmund Freud, *New Introductory Lectures in Psycholanalysis*, as quoted by Seldes in *The Great Thoughts*, 148. The existence of this Wall is easily demonstrable—who has not stirred from a vivid dream only to find that, upon awakening, his own mental wall came crashing down, blocking out all memory of that dream, leaving only the nagging suspicion that something which only a second ago had been extremely important could no longer even be guessed?

3   "To the mind, the heart and mind are two things, but to the heart, they are one." —Stephen Levine, as quoted by Elliott in *Tying Rocks to Clouds*, 156.

4   "*Repression of [the unconscious,] the collective psyche was absolutely necessary for the development of personality.*" — Jung, *Two Essays*, para. 459, p. 277. "*There is no birth of consciousness without pain.*" — Jung, *The Development of Personality*, para. 331, p. 193.

The Personal-Soul

Whenever the soul receives material from the spirit, it automatically responds by generating more material to be released back into the spirit.[1] This material, however, finding itself unable to pass through the wall, becomes stuck in the middle, forming a pocket of soul-material inside the wall. Usually distinguished from the much larger unconscious, this soul-pocket has been variously designated the subconscious, or the personal unconscious, by modern science.[2] This isolated pocket of soul-material represents an intermediate level of the psyche somewhat more available to conscious access than the rest of the unconscious Primordial Soul, and its contents are of a more personal nature.[3]

The Conscious Ego

Material flowing from spirit to soul then enters these pockets on its way through the wall and, finding soul material there, is tricked into thinking it has reached its destination and stops, thus also becoming trapped in these pockets. Within this pocket, then, material from both spirit and soul again commingle as they did in the primordial unity, but on a dramatically reduced scale. Since the conscious once again has, within the limited confines of this pocket, access to the unconscious, it therefore also has access to its own memories;[4] this allows it to turn its attention back upon itself, becoming aware of itself and its own consciousness. Thus,

---

1 Jung, *Two Essays*, paras. 289-92, pp. 182-85.
2 "*We have to distinguish in the unconscious a layer which we may call the personal unconscious.*" — Jung, *Two Essays*, para. 218, p. 135. "*. . . the rationally explicable unconscious . . . is only a top layer, and underneath is an absolute unconscious which has nothing to do with our personal experience.*" —Jung, *The Structure and Dynamics of the Psyche*, para. 311,, p. 148.
3 "*The materials contained in this [top] layer are of a personal nature . . . [the materials contained in this layer] are the integral components of the personality, they belong to its inventory.*" — Jung, *Two Essays*, para. 218, p. 36.
4 The soul-material within these pockets absorbs and records all spirit-input entering the pocket, thus creating memory-records of everything that occurs following the initial formation of the pocket. Thus these pockets are named the "personal" unconscious by modern science, because they contain all personal memory. In keeping with Division Theory, I rename them the "personal-soul."

this miniature remarriage of the soul and spirit creates its own "offspring," a dynamic, self-aware microcosmic reflection of the original primordial unity: the ego.[1] This ego, however, is aware of only a fraction of the whole true self, only that material which has found its way into the personal-soul.[2]

Death

At physical death, the pocket suffers convulsive spasms, being squeezed out from the wall. Once separated from the wall, but still encased inside a coating of wall material, the personal-soul finds itself completely immersed[3] within the deep blackness of the unconscious Primordial Soul. Having lost all contact with the energizing light of spirit consciousness, these personal-souls dry up, shriveling and shrinking into themselves, falling to the bitter depths of the unconscious Primordial Soul.

Rebirth

A new life would start the process all over again; with each new incarnation, the same dynamics of the wall would automatically conspire to reproduce an entirely new personal-soul, which unfortunately would be completely unaware of any other previous personal-souls trapped at the bottom of the unconscious soul.

Collectivization

Over many lifetimes, many such discarded personal-souls would have accumulated together on the lowest levels of the

---

1 ". . . [the ego is] acquired . . . during the individual's lifetime [and] . . . goes on developing from further collisions [between] the outer world and the inner." ". . . The ego rests on the total field of consciousness, and . . . on the sum total of unconscious contents." ". . . the ego is . . . the center of the field of consciousness." —Jung, *Aion*, paras. 6, 4, 1, pp. 5, 4, 3.

2 "[The self,] *the personality as a total phenomenon does not coincide with the ego, [or] conscious personality. . . . The total personality, which, although present, cannot be known, [is called] the self. The ego is . . . subordinate to the self and is related to it like a part is to the whole . . .*" — Jung, *Aion*, paras. 8-9, p. 5. "*The self . . . embraces not only the conscious but also the unconscious psyche, and is therefore . . . a personality which we also are. It is easy enough to think of ourselves as possessing part-souls.*" — Jung, *Two Essays*, para. 274, p. 177.

3 "Immersion" was the original term for baptism. A parallel?

Primordial Soul. At first, since these personal-souls would be confined within thin layers of the wall material, they would maintain their individual integrity. But since the soul material was able to partially penetrate the wall when it originally produced these soul-pockets, it is clear that some seepage can and does occur through the wall material. Thus it can be assumed that when all these personal-souls are sitting together on the bottom of the Primordial Soul, in time they would start to seep through their wall-material coatings, and would eventually congeal together into a partially unified mass. As it is the nature of the unconscious to recognize connections and similarities between things rather than their differences, it could be expected that these personal-souls would in time come to find their individual ego-identities coalescing together, forming a single mass of subjective self-awareness.[1]

Distortion

Since these pockets would have been formed out of soul-material meant to be released into the conscious spirit but which the spirit had never received, the conscious spirit would shrink a little with the formation of each new soul-pocket, while the unconscious Primordial Soul grew.

System Success

If the conscious ego within the soul-pocket were to fully incorporate and energize all of the soul-material within the pocket, so that no parts of the personal-soul remained unconscious and inert, this would effectively remove the buffer between the Primordial Soul and spirit; the amount of wall material that would be left between the soul-pocket and the Primordial Soul would be stretched too thin to any longer prevent the Primordial Soul from directly contacting the spirit. The pocket, filled through and through with spirit-saturated soul-material, would itself then be a source of spirit-input into the Primordial Soul. And receiving such spirit-input, the Primordial Soul would automatically release more material into the soul-pocket, and

---

1 *"Any large company has the morality and intelligence of an unwieldy, stupid, and violent animal. The bigger the organization, the more unavoidable is its immorality and blind stupidity."* — Jung, *Two Essays*, para. 240, p. 153. See also Appendix A: Fruit of the Division.

that material would then also be energized by the spirit within the pocket, stretching the pocket wall thinner still. A chain reaction would ensue, as the Primordial Soul flooded[1] the pocket with ever-greater amounts of soul-material which then became energized at an ever-increasing rate. Ultimately the pocket would grow at such a rate and to such a pressure that it would entirely burst through and break apart the wall; quickly, the entire Primordial Soul and spirit would be consumed by such a process, becoming a living, pulsing, fully self-aware singularity. It would be different than it was in the primordial unity; the isolating pressure of the wall would have been used as a tool, helping the primordial unity to achieve self-aware-ness—the ego. And once the pocket burst from the inside out, that ego would envelop and consume the entire system. The entire system would thus have achieved a single self-awareness.

System Failure

If, before such a singularity was achieved, the spirit's artificially-created wall ever broke down, the resulting chaos would allow consciousness to filter down, awakening the long-dormant dis-carded personal-souls. This would allow multiple numbers of these personal-souls, or soul-personalities, to simultaneously rise back up to join with the conscious spirit, playing havoc with the spirit's sense of identity.

---

1   *"The end will come like a flood."* — Daniel 9:26.

A PROPOSED MODEL OF
THE DYNAMICS BETWEEN SOUL & SPIRIT

The Original Unity

In the beginning, the Soul and Spirit were so perfectly intertwined it was not possible to tell where one ended and the other began; neither was any more conscious or unconscious than the other.

The Fall:
Creation of the Unconscious

Then the Spirit asserted dominance, becoming more fully Conscious, and separating from and subjugating the Soul into Unconsciousness

Creation and Dynamics
of the Wall

The Spirit's efforts to push down the Soul and reject its input created a wall-like barrier between them, completely preventing Soul input from reaching the Spirit. The more the Conscious Spirit rejected the Unconscious Soul, the heavier and thicker the wall became.

Movement Through the Wall

The wall was like a one-way door—data flowed freely from Spirit to Soul, but encountered severe resistance going from Soul to Spirit.

Formation of the Subconscious

When the Soul received data from the Spirit, it automatically responds by generating data to be released back into the Spirit. Finding itself unable to pass through the wall, however, this material became stuck in the middle. It formed a pocket of soul-material in the center of the wall which was not as conscious as the Conscious Spirit, but also not as unconscious as the Unconscious Soul. This was recognized in the 20th century, and labeled the personal Subconscious.

Personal Memory

Data flowing from Spirit to Soul also became trapped in these pockets of Soul-material, allowing these pockets to store memory records.

The System
Partially Self-Corrects

As the wall was stretched thinner around these pockets, some free movement of data could again flow from them into the Conscious Spirit, allowing the Spirit access to its memories stored in the Soul-pocket. Since these pockets were formed of Soul-material, in this way a limited degree of input from the Primordial Soul to the Conscious Spirit was restored.

Death

At physical death, the wall suffers convulsive spasms, squeezing out the pocket of Soul-material.

The Soul-Pockets
Fall Into the Pit

Separating from the wall, but still encased in a small coating of the wall material, the pocket of Soul-material finds itself surrounded by the Primordial Soul, having lost all contact with the Spirit.

Cut off from the energizing input of the Spirit, these Soul-pockets dry up, shriveling and shrinking into themselves, and fall to the bottom of the Unconscious Primordial Soul.

A new life starts the process all over again.

Formation of the Collective Unconscious

Over many lifetimes, many discarded Soul-pockets accumulate on the murky bottom of the Primordial Soul, congealing into a partially unified mass.

Gradual Distortion of the Soul-Spirit Balance

Since these Soul-pockets were formed out of Soul-material which had been meant to be released into the Conscious Spirit but which the Spirit did not receive, the Conscious Spirit shrinks a little with the formation of each new Soul-pocket, while the Unconscious Primordial Soul grows.

Judgment Day

When the Spirit's artifically-created wall finally breaks down, some of the discarded Soul-pockets will rise up immediately into the Conscious Spirit, playing havoc with the Spirit's sense of identity. Other Soul-pockets will remain below until finally exiting in a burst of light and power.

CHAPTER 5

MAKING THE TWO ONE

A Carpenter's Repairs

*When you make the two one, and when you make the inside like the outside
and the outside like the inside, and the above like the below . . . then you will
enter the kingdom. . . . If [one] is undivided, he will be filled with light, but if
he is divided, he will be filled with darkness.*
— The Gospel of Thomas 22 & 61

According to Division Theory, a person's conscious and unconscious split apart upon death, with no hope of ever being rejoined.

Or is there some hope after all? It does seem that there might be,
since that world-shaking report which first launched Christianity
suggests there may have been at least one exception to this scenario;
but if so, just what sort of spiritual, psychological, or physical contor-
tions would it take for a person to rise from the dead?

The Bible records Jesus' division. In Luke, Christ "com-
mended" his spirit into his Father's hands at his death, after just
promising a criminal beside him, "I tell you, today you will be with
me in paradise" (Luke 23:43).

All Biblical passages which refer to the afterdeath disposition
of the spirit consistently state that it returns to God. But the soul
is never specifically stated to "return to God"; instead, it is said to
"die" and then enter the Jewish underworld of She'ol.

In Jesus' case, this pattern is clearly discernable. While one part
of his full being, his spirit, was reported to have gone to paradise
to be with his Father, some other part is recorded to have gone
somewhere far different:

. . . he also descended to the lower, earthly regions.
— Ephesians 4:9

. . . he went and preached to [those] who disobeyed long ago . . . in the days of Noah.

— I Peter 3:19-20

. . . the gospel was preached even to . . . the dead . . .

— I Peter 4:6

At the same time that his spirit rose up, did Jesus' personal-soul then split away, contracting in upon itself, descending to the "lower regions," the deepest levels of the unconscious? If so, then something else must have happened as well, something that had never occurred before in all the history of humanity. For Jesus to have risen from the dead, his spirit must have reconnected with his personal-soul somehow. But how could such a thing happen?

Obviously, there would have to be something very exceptional about a person whose spirit couldn't bear to be parted from his personal-soul, but instead went searching for it again. Why might Jesus' spirit have been unwilling, perhaps even unable, to stay separated from his personal-soul after death, if this was the way the mechanics of death had always worked for everyone in the past? How might his spirit have been able to find and rejoin with its lost personal-soul?

Jesus' Resurrection carries the interesting implication that his spirit had somehow bonded with his personal-soul, that some sort of curious union, apparently powerful enough to withstand even death itself, had somehow been forged between the two halves of his psyche during his life. Could it have been, in fact, Jesus' intention while alive to unite his conscious and unconscious in a bond so strong that it could not be permanently undone even by physical death?[1]

The few traditions that have reached us about Jesus suggest he placed tremendous emphasis upon the issues of personal sincerity and inner integrity. Did he believe that the key to overcoming death ("Be of good cheer; I have overcome the world") was to be found in such integrity? This issue was clearly dear to his heart—after 2,000 years, the raw emotional charge behind his comments about hypocrisy can still be felt. The question begs to be asked: could devotion to such inner integrity during life

---

1 Perhaps this theory would explain what he was doing during those mysterious unrecorded first thirty years of his life.

conceivably result in an "integrity of being" following death? Perhaps, as the following passage suggests, Jesus' real purpose during his physical life was the achievement of such a union.

> For he himself is our peace, who has made the two one. . . . His purpose was to create in himself one new man out of the two [the soul and spirit?], thus making peace . . .
> — Ephesians 2:14-15

Perhaps during his life Jesus succeeded in achieving something most psychiatrists today consider a complete impossibility: an "intra-psyche marriage," a synergistic union between the conscious and unconscious in which the two parts are so perfectly integrated that they always work together in complete and unconditional harmony.[1] In order for such a "marriage" to be completely perfect, however, Jesus' conscious ego would have needed to fully incorporate all personal material within his Primordial Soul,[2] both in his personal unconscious and in his past-life personal-souls as well, making the two one—making, in effect, his unconscious conscious.

If he did, did he ever mention it?

The Son of Man: Past-Life Deficit and the Scroll of Remembrance

Curiously enough, Jesus seemed to actively avoid making any great definitive statements about who he was or what he believed his status or true nature to be. He never overtly stated that he was the Son of God (although he didn't deny it when others said it); the only way he would refer to himself was as "the Son of Man." This rather obscure phrase has generally been taken to mean either the son of a man, or the son of mankind, but neither definition is satisfactory. He was in fact not the son of a man, according to the virgin birth legend, and the phrase "the son of mankind" is meaningless except to say that he was a member of the human race. This too is unsatisfactory, since Jesus used the

---

1 Perhaps becoming, in the words of Wickes, "a being of superhuman, undivided and complete consciousness . . . this ultimate angel . . . won through loyalty to every choice of consciousness, through inner willingness to become aware of the nature of the one who speaks through the image." — Wickes, 22.
2 See Chapter 4: The Primordial Division, A Model Division.

phrase *the Son*, not *a son*, implying a uniqueness which other members of the human race did not share.

Significantly, this phrase stands in stark contrast to the phrase Jesus used when referring to all the rest of humanity: "all those born of women" (Matthew 11:11 and parallels). It seems almost as if Jesus defined the difference between himself and others as that between *man* and *woman*.

There was another who was also called Son of Man: Ezekiel. The scripture calls the prophet by that phrase repeatedly, a phrase which, prior to the book of Ezekiel, does not show up at all in the Hebrew Bible. If it had, the phrase *Son of Man* might be considered suitable for any prophet; but since it turns up only in references to Ezekiel or Jesus, one must ask if there is some quality which only Jesus and Ezekiel shared.

Ezekiel described an intense mystical experience in which he saw the Glory of God directly, face to face. After informing Ezekiel that he would become a prophet, God made him do something that no prophet before had been asked to do: God gave Ezekiel a scroll which had "words of lament and mourning and woe" written on both sides, and said, "Son of Man, eat what is before you, eat this scroll." Ezekiel did, commenting that the scroll tasted "sweet as honey" while in his mouth, but after he had swallowed it, he was filled with bitterness, and his "spirit" was angered. The whole mystical experience was so intense and moving, the scripture reports, that it left him dumbfounded and overwhelmed for seven days; only after recovering from this staggering experience was he able to begin his prophetic ministry for Israel.

What an extraordinarily odd episode this seems to be! Although this eating-of-the-scroll event is often assumed to be when God gave Ezekiel the words for His prophecies, this interpretation would appear to be mistaken, since it was much later in the book when God specifically issued Ezekiel the words of His prophecies. So what was that scroll with the "words of lament" on it?

A similar event is described in Revelation 10, when Saint John also "saw God," and he also was given a scroll to eat, being told as well that it would be as sweet as honey in his mouth but would turn his stomach sour, which, as John reported, proved again to be the case. And only after he ate his scroll, was John, like Ezekiel, allowed to prophesy.

Eating these scrolls, then, may represent nothing less than the full reunion of soul and spirit, reabsorbing and reintegrating all one's past lives, with all their history and soul-pain. When Ezekiel first ate his scroll, he reported that it tasted "as sweet as honey in his mouth"; yet after this experience, he went "in bitterness" and with "anger in [his] spirit." Such reactions make perfect sense; the first reunion with his past personal-souls, discovering the unimaginable richness of his long history and past lives, discovering he possessed eternal life, would seem a great delight, "sweet as honey in the mouth." However, as more and more of the forgotten soul-pain of all those lives was reabsorbed and consciously experienced, it would likely make one feel extremely bitter and angry inside.

Ominously, just as Ezekiel was forced into this reassimilation of his past, the Judeo-Christian scriptures suggest that the whole world will undergo a similar experience, having a similar scroll forced upon it:

> I looked again, and there before me was a flying scroll. . . . Then he said to me, "This is the curse that is going out over the whole land; for, according to what it says on one side, every thief will be banished, and according to what it says on the other side, everyone who swears falsely by the Lord will be banished."
> — Zechariah 5:1,3

When Ezekiel ate his scroll, his spirit was angered; like everybody else, he had been used to having the option of avoiding all that pain.

Ezekiel was made whole. His spirit and soul were reunited. And he was called "Son of Man."

In the long-lost early Christian scriptures recently rediscovered in Nag Hammadi, Egypt,[1] it is also suggested that unification of soul and spirit is the key to the mysterious designation "Son of Man":

> When you make the two one, you will become the sons of man, and when you say, "Mountain, move away," it will move away.
> — The Gospel of Thomas 106

In classic sexual symbolism, the male—man—represents a singularity, a whole, while the female—woman—has traditionally symbolized a lacking or division. Perhaps it is to such symbolism

---

1   See Chapter 6: Ever Hearing But Never Understanding.

that the Bible refers when it calls both Ezekiel and Jesus "Son of Man." Perhaps it was saying that they were each again complete, with their souls and spirits entirely reconciled. "All those born of woman," on the other hand, would refer to all of us whose souls and spirits still remain at least partially divided.

Resurrection Through Wholeness?

So, when Jesus referred to himself as the Son of Man, was he in fact making a veiled statement about his status and nature, declaring himself to be spiritually perfect, psychically whole and undivided? If Jesus indeed had possessed such a state of complete psychic unity at the moment of his death, it is conceivable that such a condition was able to prevent the normal separation of his personal-soul and his spirit from becoming permanent.

Perhaps, like a man searching for his lost lover,[1] Jesus' separated conscious groped about blindly for its lost unconscious half, searching three full days before a sliver of this living conscious spirit finally brushed up against his dead personal-soul again.

As that contact was first being re-established, his personal-soul would have been in a far different state than during life; by that time Jesus' personal-soul would have been severely contracted, having collapsed down upon itself into the wretched condition typical of the personal-soul's afterlife. What then would have been the effect when his living spirit suddenly touched his dead personal-soul again, flooding consciousness and life back into it while it was still in such an extremely compressed state?

A certain ancient wisdom-tradition has been preserved within the *Tao Te Ching*, the "bible" of Taoism, a simple lesson which might be relevant to such a situation:

What is to be shrunken is first stretched out;
What is to be weakened is first made strong;
What will be thrown over is first raised up;
What will be withdrawn is first bestowed.[2]

---

1 Reread The Song of Songs with this in mind.
2 Lao Tzu, *Tao Te Ching (The Way of Life)*, trans. by R.B. Blakney (New York: New American Library, 1983), Poem 36.

Might the opposite also be true? Is there a natural law also requiring a thing to first be condensed smaller before it will expanded larger? Science offers examples of such things: if a star is massive enough, when it starts to die it will first contract swiftly and deeply into itself and then suddenly explode to huge proportions, becoming a supernova. A nuclear bomb, as well, must first be intensely compressed into itself before the thermonuclear explosion can be initiated. Such a law may be universal; it certainly seems to apply in all physical circumstances—even a simple wire spring must be compressed before it will bounce upwards.

If there is some corresponding law covering matters of the psyche, might Jesus' personal-soul have become the human equivalent of a supernova? If his spirit had come back to rejoin his dead personal-soul, might that personal-soul, having contracted into a densely compressed state, have then exploded out of its own collapsed state, enlarging in all directions, perhaps even filling, as has been given, "the whole universe"?

> He who descended [into the world of the dead] is the very one who [later] ascended higher than all the heavens, in order to fill the whole universe.
> — Ephesians 4:10

Finding it impossible to incorporate the Primordial Soul in its entirety into his own conscious ego while physically alive, did Jesus purposely use the mechanics of death to forcefully slingshot his personal-soul throughout the entire length and breadth of the infinite Primordial Soul, incorporating it in that way into his ego after death?

If Jesus' personal-soul indeed had been strewn throughout the universe, the "universe" it filled would have been that of the unconscious, the universe of the Primordial Soul; and in order to fill that universe, Jesus' personal-soul would have had to have been forcibly injected into the unconscious psyche of every person past, present, and future by the forces released during his Resurrection. Of course, if such a marvelous and incredible event had once happened, it could reasonably be expected that now, throughout the entire realm of the human unconscious, in and behind and next to every mind in existence, Jesus' own personal-soul would still be sitting and waiting,[1] like an unconscious

---

1   John 14:16-20.

"ghost," ready to guide and teach that same path that Jesus himself originally followed.[1] And all anyone would need to do to find this out for himself would be to make the attempt to align his own conscious mind to become aware of this already-existing unconscious presence, to "knock on the door," to "step on the threshold," to contact it and allow its effects to occur automatically.[2]

Such a psychologically-based explanation of the Resurrection not only is consistent with Judeo-Christian scripture (if not with contemporary doctrine), but also offers intellectually honest explanations for some of Jesus' most baffling statements:

> Truly, truly, I say to you, before Abraham was, I am.
> — John 8:58

> Truly I say to you, as you did it to one of the least of these my brethren, you did it to me.
> — Matthew 25:40

Conventional Christian theory has never been able to explain or agree on just precisely what the new Holy Ghost actually was, where it came from, or even, for that matter, how Jesus went about "filling the whole universe." It can be no coincidental fact, however, that immediately following Jesus' death, an extraordinary historical event occurred—the birth of the Christian church. Utterly unprecedented phenomena began to be reported within that church—whole crowds collectively experiencing profoundly moving subjective episodes while gathered together in prayer. These phenomena were hailed as the arrival of the mysterious Holy Ghost which their leader had predicted would come following his death. Jesus freely admitted that this Holy Ghost was unavoidably connected to his death, explaining that there was simply no way it could come to them until after he had died:

---

1 And is this not exactly what the Christian church has been teaching for the last 2,000 years?

2 Wickes suggests that such indeed is the case: "*The god voice is always warning, suggesting, revealing. Thoughts come to you; feelings arise; emotions engulf . . . ". . . we may plead unconsciousness, yet, if we look back with honesty, we know that at a critical moment, an experience, or a dream, or a voice came to arouse a consciousness of new life . . .*" — Wickes, 11, 53.

> And now I am going to him who sent me. . . . It is expedient for
> you that I depart. For if I do not go, the Advocate [the Holy Ghost]
> will not come to you; but if I go, I will send him to you.
> — John 16:5,7

It seems possible, then, that Jesus may have used the mechanics
of death as a tool to expand his own personal-soul, using death,
the enemy of humanity, to save humanity. Although for 2,000 years
it has been assumed that his greatest sacrifice was dying on the
cross, perhaps he made an even greater sacrifice; maybe it was not
so much his body as his very own personal-soul that he sacrificed
for us!

> . . . make his soul an offering for sin . . .
> — Isaiah 53:10

Was this the great plan—to provide a helper, the Advocate,
the Holy Ghost, Jesus Christ's own infinitely expanded personal-
soul, which he promised to send to the world upon his departure?
If so, his love was so great that he literally gave us part of his very
self.

> World sovereignty can be committed to that man Who loves all
> people as he loves himself.
> — *Tao Te Ching* 13

Since the nature of the unconscious is always passive and
responsive, it could then indeed be assumed, just as Jesus promised, that he would (through the Holy Ghost) "be with us always."[1]
And since the nature of the conscious mind is active and expres-
sive, it would also have to be expected that Jesus' spirit would
eventually seek further ways to express itself. But how?

If this theory about death's divisive effects upon humanity's
binary psyche is correct, and the Holy Ghost of Christian tradition
is actually Jesus' own transfigured unconscious, then the other half
of this theory predicts that Jesus' conscious spirit would eventually
incarnate again. Such a reincarnation would unquestionably be an
event of the most monumental importance. Is it mere coincidence
that traditional Christian doctrine hinges on just such a promised
Second Coming for Jesus Christ?

---

1   Matthew 28:20.

Shared Experience

Neither Jesus' Resurrection nor the union of his personal-soul with those of the rest of humanity, marvelous as such wonders would be, could in and of themselves save the human race from the curse of death and the horrors of hell. However, Jesus specifically defined his mission as one of freeing captives and prisoners, and the measures the Bible has him taking to do so are fully consistent with the conditions proposed by Division Theory. What he did, in fact, would have been the only solution with any chance at all of repairing the separation of humanity's spirits and souls, reversing all the effects of the Primordial Division and freeing the lost personal-souls trapped in the unconscious.

> He has sent me to bind up the brokenhearted, to proclaim freedom to the captives, and release for the prisoners.
> —Isaiah 61:1

> The Son of Man came to seek and save what was lost.
> — Luke 19:10

God's teachings have always stressed the need to accept pain if necessary;[1] just as God once impressed upon Abraham, in threatening to sacrifice Isaac, the necessity of accepting any amount of pain when required, so Jesus also taught that nothing was more important than paying unflinching attention to all the input, whether pleasant or painful, that came from the soul.[2] Unlike the popular would-be prophets of every age, who echo the message to not worry, but just "be happy," Jesus took the perennially unpopular position of insisting that people not turn away from the troubles, and the troubled, of the world. In fact, not turning away from the painful and distressing truths which the soul recognized and bemoaned was the whole key;[3] and those who did not reject such impressions of the soul

---

1 See, for example, Ezekiel 21:13; Proverbs 3:11; Hebrews 12:7-11.
2 Soren Kierkegaard, severely criticized for his "negative" view of Christianity, understood this aspect of God's teaching: *"To be a Christian is the most terrible of all torments; it is—and must be—to have one's hell on earth."* — Soren Kierkegaard, *The Last Years: Journals, 1853-55*, as quoted by Seldes in *The Great Thoughts*, 229.
3 Isaiah 32:11-12; Jeremiah 6:26, 9:17-18.

were, according to Christ, guaranteed to find "the Kingdom of Heaven":

> Blessed are you who hunger now, for you will be satisfied.
> — Luke 6:21

> Blessed are you who weep now, for you will laugh. Blessed are the poor in spirit, for theirs is the kingdom of heaven. Blessed are those who mourn, for they shall be comforted. Blessed are those who hunger and thirst for righteousness, for they will be filled. . . . Blessed are the pure in heart, for they shall see God.
> — Matthew 5:3-8

While leaving these instructions would have been both the easiest and the most critical part of Jesus' mission, his ultimate goal could not have been accomplished until after his Resurrection. When his personal-soul exploded throughout the entire universe of the Primordial Soul, linking up with all other personal-souls everywhere, this contact would have allowed (if indeed not *forced*) Jesus to consciously experience all the accumulated soul-pain within all those other personal-souls. Inconceivably excruciating as it must have been, going through such a painful ordeal would have tremendously empowered him,[1] for, through it, he would have gained the means to cancel out the debt of all humanity's stored-up soul-pain:

> Behold the lamb of God, who takes away the sins of the world.
> — John 1:29

By experiencing all humanity's built-up soul-pain, Jesus would have been acting as proxy for the whole human race; and, in the process, he would have gained both the power and the right to release people from their past debts to their own personal-souls, by making it possible for them to fulfill those very obligations, through him. By consciously joining their own personal-souls with the Holy Ghost, people would effectively gain all of Jesus' own knowledge and experience, including his afterdeath knowledge and experience of their hidden, unreleased soul-pain, and so be able to credit it as their own, thus canceling out all their own past soul-debt.

---

1 Following his resurrection, Jesus told his disciples, *"All authority in heaven and earth has been given to me."* —Matthew 28:18.

Don't you know that all of us who were baptized into Christ Jesus
were baptized into his death?
                              — Romans 6:3

. . . by his knowledge my righteous servant will justify many; for he
shall bear their iniquities.
                              —Isaiah 53:11

The inherent nature of the human unconscious supports the
possibility of such a merger. While the conscious mind, by its very
nature, always recognizes distinctions between things, the unconscious does not; it is precisely this collective, nondiscriminating
nature of the unconscious which makes it possible for people to
feel empathy and love for one another, since their inner souls do
not instinctively recognize any distinctions between one's own
situation and that of another. Thus, linking up Jesus' soul with any
other could conceivably produce a merging not only of feeling, but
even of experience and sense of identity between the two; the two
personal-souls would, in effect, become one.

I and the Father are one.
                              — John 10:30

On that day you will realize that I am in my Father, and you are
in me, and I am in you.
                              — John 14:20

Such a union of separate souls within the same psyche is not
entirely without historical precedent, at least according to one
report. In the seventeenth-century French mass-possession case
made famous in Aldous Huxley's best seller, *The Devils of Loudun*,
one of the Jesuit priests sent to help the possession victims,
Jean-Joseph Surin, apparently became possessed himself during
the course of the exorcism ritual. Later, in a letter to a friend, Surin
discussed this entrance of a foreign soul into his own psyche,
describing it as a phenomenon virtually identical to that suggested
above, as a unification not only of feeling, but even of experience
and identity between the two:

I find it almost impossible to explain what happens to me during
this time, how this alien spirit is united to mine, without depriving
me of consciousness or of inner freedom, and yet constituting a

103

second "me," as though I had two souls. .... I feel as if I had been pierced by the pricks of despair in that alien soul which seems to be mine. .... I even feel that the cries uttered by my mouth come from both souls at once; and I find it hard to determine whether they are the product of joy or frenzy.[1]

Either Merger or Flood: Reunification and the Wall

If such a merger of multiple souls within one psyche is possible, and Christ's personal-soul were to unite with those of others, this could have the effect of releasing those others from their obligation of reabsorbing and experiencing all the filth of their own ocean of soul-debt themselves, the only option that existed prior to Jesus' sacrifice.[2] By virtue of Jesus' Resurrection, a new option would have been made available, that of letting Christ's experience substitue for our own, but people would have to pay dearly for that privilege, by inviting Jesus' own personal-soul to take up permanent conscious residence within their own psyches. By co-existing within the same psyche, Jesus' righteousness would be able to be credited as their own:

> Go up and down the streets ... look around and consider, search through her squares. If you can find one person [one soul] who deals honestly and seeks the truth, I will forgive this city [this whole person].
> — Jeremiah 5:1

Many, of course, would reject such an offer, opting instead to tough it out alone during life. But those so choosing to remain independent of Jesus' Holy Ghost would not realize that, by rejecting this offer, in effect they would be depending on the wall, the barrier between the conscious and unconscious, to always remain standing.

Of course, it would have been humanity's own ancient decision to repress their souls into unconsciousness which originally created the wall, that barrier which even today separates the conscious from the unconscious in the human psyche. And because the very act of suppressing those memory-bearing souls would have also made them

---

1   T.K. Oesterreich, *Possession: Demonical & Other* (New York: University Books, 1966), 217.
2   Isaiah 65:6-7; Jeremiah 4:18, 10:19; Obadiah 1:15; Joel 3:7.

forget doing it, humanity would have thus discovered, quite by accident, an almost perfect form of self-deception. Not completely perfect, however; if this mental wall should ever break down, all the personal-souls that had been imprisoned by death in the depths of the unconscious would instantly regain their freedom,[1] while their other halves, their living spirits, would find themselves forced to experience vastly greater amounts of soul-pain than even that which they had originally sought to avoid.[2]

> Because you have rejected this message [the input from your own souls] and have relied on oppression and depended on deceit, this sin will become for you like a high wall, cracked and bulging, that collapses suddenly, in an instant.
> — Isaiah 30:12-13

Most people would be blissfully unaware of the swelling flood waters of accumulated soul-pain quietly churning behind that barrier, held back as if by the wall of a dam. If that wall ever broke, all who had failed to take advantage of Christ's offer would suddenly find themselves confronting their entire soul-debt, being forced to reabsorb and consume perhaps thousands of lifetimes' worth of repressed soul-pain all at once:

> The men sitting on the wall [the barrier between the conscious and the unconscious] . . . will have to eat their own filth and drink their own urine [will have to reabsorb their own spiritual waste].
> — Isaiah 36:12

The Terror, the Pit, and the Snare

When people first violated the guidelines written into their souls, it would have been natural for them to have become terrified of the pain they then experienced even though that pain would have been a natural corrective measure. The pain would not have been wrong, having been intentionally designed into the system. Nor would it have been wrong for people to have been terrified of the pain, such fear being part of human nature. But, because that pain would have been the pain of correction, it would have been wrong to flee from it.

---

1   Isaiah 5:5, 26:21.
2   Isaiah 9:18; Lamentations 1:13; Ezekiel 28:18.

> Do not make light of the Lord's discipline, and do not lose heart
> when he rebukes you, because the Lord disciplines those he loves,
> and he punishes everyone he accepts as a son.
> — Proverbs 3:11-12

Both the dividing sword of death and the prison-like pit of hell, then, would have been introduced into human experience not because of people's mistakes, not because of our choices or behavior; it seems, instead, that these ancient scourges were the result of only one thing: humanity's terrified decision to flee from correction, our attempt to escape the justice meted out by our own souls. Were we, by fleeing from the pain we were so terrified of feeling in our own souls, unknowingly digging pits in the back of our own psyches, pits into which we promptly fell at our deaths? By trying to sidestep the system God designed, humanity seems to have brought about conditions the Creator never intended to exist.[1] By trying to go over God's head, we apparently cut off our own.

Any artificially created wall separating the conscious from the unconscious would be sure to fall eventually, and when it did, all those trapped personal-souls would finally be able to climb out of the dark pit of death's unconscious realm. But once they emerged from that pit, returning to full conscious awareness, they would immediately find themselves caught in an even more deadly snare:

> Terror and pit and snare await you, O people of the earth . . .
> whoever flees at the sound of terror will fall into a pit; whoever
> climbs out of the pit will be caught in a snare.
> — Isaiah 24:17-18

They would find waiting for them, on the surface of consciousness, a choice: either voluntarily joining with the Holy Ghost or remaining independent. If they chose independence, they would unknowingly be condemning themselves to a sudden death from within, as all their lifetimes of soul-pain were released. Forced to consciously experience all the accumulated soul-pain from all their past lives all at once, they would be utterly destroyed.

---

1   Perhaps Death and Hell were never intended to exist by God; perhaps it was not He, but the acts of humanity, which created them. If so, death and hell would only be temporary conditions which would cease to exist one day: *"Then death and hell were thrown into the lake of fire."* —Revelation 20:14.

I shall strike down those who live [independent of the Lord] . . .
they will die with a great pestilence. I offer you now a choice
between the way of life and the way of death.
— Jeremiah 21:6-10.

The Primordial Soul: The Stone Never Broken

At the end of such a Day, only those who had sincerely invited
Jesus' Holy Ghost to take up permanent residence within their
psyches would remain; and with that, humanity's spiritual history
would have come full circle.[1]

The stone which the builders rejected has become the capstone.
Everyone who falls on that stone will be broken to pieces, but he
on whom it falls will be crushed.
— Luke 20:17-18

Although people had rejected the guidance of that original soul
in the beginning, when the end finally rolled around again, that
same Primordial Soul would have become permanently re-en-
throned as ruler over all humanity.

Prior to the fall of the wall, all who violated the Primordial
Soul's programming would find themselves stumbling and falling
over that same programming at their deaths, breaking apart into
three separate pieces—a dead body, a shriveled-up personal-soul,
and a living spirit. That moral programming, it seems, was the key
to their spiritual integrity. But when the fall of the wall finally
occurred, that same Primordial Soul over which people had stum-
bled and fallen so many times before would return, newly empowered, to now fall upon them, upon all who had not yet reconciled
themselves to it; this would have the effect of revealing, activating,
and releasing all their dormant soul-pain all at once, crushing them
completely.

Following such an event, Christ's own fully restored personal-
soul, again one with the Primordial Soul from which it originally
sprang, would reside and rule once more from within each survi-
vor's psyche, like a capstone on the top of the pyramid of all
humanity.

---

1   *"Whoever endures to the end will be saved."* — Matthew 10:22.

CHAPTER 6

EVER HEARING BUT NEVER UNDERSTANDING

Division Theory Around the World and Through the Ages

The legend of Egypt's "God of Death" was the origin and continued focus of more than 4,000 years of Egyptian preoccupation with life after death. After Osiris' death, his remains were divided and scattered. But when those pieces were subsequently reunited, he was restored to eternal life.
— The Legend of Osiris

Judeo-Christianity has always claimed to hold a monopoly on religious truth, and (as will be seen) Division Theory at least partially supports that claim. However, the full version of that truth is not to be found in any of the West's official doctrines, but instead remains hidden and mostly unrecognized within its sacred texts; this full truth seems to have been apprehended by only a handful of people over the millennia.

The fresh testimony Division Theory illuminates within these scriptures suggests that Judeo-Christianity was originally based upon the religious implications of humanity's divided psyche. But the West's monopoly on the theological significance of this division was not absolute; in fact, fresh examination of scriptures from other religious traditions indicates that many different faiths have been founded upon that same split in human consciousness.

Many religions contain parallels to Division Theory. In fact, such parallels can be found in the scriptures of most of the world religions, including the more obscure faiths, suggesting that a wide range of cultures once not only acknowledged this split in human consciousness, but also recognized that such a split carried with it profound religious implications. Unfortunately, such insights seem to have been either ignored, overlooked, or forgotten over the course of time. Perhaps, where religion is concerned, worldly success leads to communication failure; by becoming more political and authoritarian, religions run the risk of drifting away from the original visions of their founders. With luck, however, such insights are written down before they can be completely forgotten. Today, multiple parallels to Division Theory can be found within the earliest scriptures of a wide variety of religions; and such parallels, taken together, constitute compelling evidence of a common heritage, all but totally lost in the mists of time.

It is vanity to assume that the religions existing today are the only ones ever to receive valid insights into the nature of life and death. The human race has been around for at least 40,000 years, scientists believe, and archeological evidence indicates that people have always believed in an afterlife, right from the first. And for tens of thousands of years before our present species ever showed up, the other, first Homo sapiens, Neanderthal man, had already been using religious ceremony to bury his dead.[1] Despite all this wealth of religious past, the oldest surviving religious writings date back only 5,000 or 6,000 years; we can only speculate what people actually believed before that because it's all been buried and forgotten under the inscrutable weight of unrecorded history.

Forgotten, yes. But perhaps not entirely lost. As might be expected, the oldest traces of religion, obscure and fragmented though they may sometimes be, contain the best clues to humanity's earliest beliefs. But what might not be expected is that startling similarities are to be found between the religions of widely scattered cultures. Regardless of whether one examines the ancient cultures of China, Persia, Egypt, or Greece, one finds the local faiths repeating the same, curiously familiar story: the after-death division of soul and spirit.

Although separated by thousands of miles, the ancient religions of the pre-Buddhist Chou dynasty of China, the Indo-Iranians of Persia, Egypt's Old Kingdom, and the ancient Greeks all believed that people had not one, but two "souls" which both continued to exist after physical death. Each of these ancient

---

1 Arnold Toynbee, Arthur Koestler, et al, *Life After Death* (New York: McGraw-Hill, 1976), 39, 53, 57, 176.

traditions also claimed that their binary souls possessed two completely different sets of characteristics, and, although those two souls were closely united during life, at death they would completely part, each going its separate way into a different afterlife.

Division Theory in Egypt

The Egyptians believed that besides a physical body everyone also possessed multiple spiritual parts, including two immaterial, potentially immortal "souls": a *ka* and a *ba*. Paralleling Division Theory, these two were intimately connected in life but split apart at physical death.

The ka was a person's double, his unconscious self.[1] Its hieroglyphic symbol was a pair of upraised arms, u-shaped, like a cup waiting to be filled. As the part of a person which possessed all his desires, expectations, and needs,[2] the ka was, in effect, the person's abstract individuality and personality.[3] Thought to be born along with a person, the ka dwelt within one's heart[4] until it was forcefully separated from the body at death. After death, the ka's behavior took on an instinctive, dim-witted character; it was thought to stay in or near the person's tomb, incomprehendingly trying to stay near the body that had been its home in life.[5]

The ka's hieroglyphic "cup," as it turns out, was filled after all—by its other half, the ba, which dwelt within the ka during life.[6] Thought of as the life principle itself, the actual spark of life residing in a living person, the ba had immortal, godlike characteristics.[7] The ba was believed to pre-exist the physical birth of the individual, entering the body at birth and exiting it again at death.[8]

---

1 Joseph Crehan, "Near-Eastern Societies," in Toynbee, *Life After Death*, 116.
2 Christine El Mahdy, *Mummies, Myth, and Magic* (New York: Thames and Hudson, 1989), 12.
3 E.A. Wallis Budge, *The Egyptian Book of the Dead* (New York: Dover, 1967), lxi-lxii.
4 Just as Western culture identifies the heart with the soul, the ka was closely identified with the heart by the ancient Egyptian. E.A. Wallis Budge, *Osiris and the Egyptian Ressurrection*, Vol. II (New York: Dover, 1973), 130-32.
5 El Mahdy, 12.
6 Budge, *Osiris*, 128.
7 Budge, *The Egyptian Book of the Dead*, lxiv.
8 El Mahdy, 13.

Unlike the ka, with which it had been so intimately connected in life, the ba did not remain near the tomb after death. What it reportedly *did* do then—roam the heavens after death, conversing with whatever spiritual beings it ran across[1]—indicates that the ancient Egyptians credited the ba with both intelligence and the power of communication, as well as the spark of life and the power of animation.

Sacred prayers at one's funeral were supposed to reunite the ba with its ka in the next world.[2] The deceased was then transformed into an *aakhu*,[3] ensuring the dead person's continued existence in the after-world. All the prayers in *The Egyptian Book of the Dead* had but one aim, to ensure life after death by assisting the departed to become an aakhu, thus avoiding the ultimate horror dreaded by every Egyptian—dying a second, final, spiritual death.[4]

Transfigured spirits likened to the gods themselves, perfected aakhus were imagined to be radiant, glorious, intelligent, immortal beings shining like the very stars in heaven.[5] But rejoining the ba and ka in the afterlife was itself not enough to become a perfected aakhu; one also had to successfully pass the great judgment.

After death, the aakhu was believed to take a harrowing trip to a place of judgment, where one's heart (associated with the ka) was weighed. Egyptians worried that, after death, their ka might turn against them, testifying against them during this judgment to reveal their sins. If that testimony was poor, if their heart revealed shame and guilt, then their ka would be removed from them forever.[6] This, then, was the ultimate disaster, that "second death" considered far more threatening than the first:

> My heart, my mother; my heart, my mother! My heart whereby I come into being! Let there by nothing to withstand me at my judgment; may there be no resistance against me. . . . May there

---

1 Budge, *Osiris*, 129.
2 El Mahdy, 110.
3 Although Budge tentatively defines the aakhu as a "spirit-soul," it seems unclear whether the aakhu was itself the reunified ka and ba or some sort of spiritual body which contained the reunited ba and ka: *"The exact meaning of the word Khu, or, as it is written in the Pyramid Texts, Aakhu, is very hard to discover, and authorities have differed greatly in their translations of the word, and in their descriptions of what the Khu is."* —Budge, *Osiris*, 132.
4 El Mahdy, 13.
5 Budge, *The Egyptian Book of the Dead*, lxvii.
6 El Mahdy, 154.

be no parting of thee from me in the presence of him who keeps the scales of [of judgment]! Thou art my ka within my body.[1]

Those who did not successfully pass this divine judgment had their ka, or heart, promptly "eaten" by Am-mit, a goddess of the underworld, "She who devours."[2] The early Egyptians were horrified by this possibility, as some of the chapter titles of *The Egyptian Book of the Dead* illustrate:

Chapter XIV. The Chapter of Driving Away Shame From the Heart of the Deceased.

Chapter XXVII. The Chapter of Not Allowing the Heart of a Man to be Taken From Him in the Underworld.

Chapter XLIV. The Chapter of Not Dying a Second Time.[3]

The deceased was apparently directly involved in this judgment process. As in the "life review" so commonly reported by modern near-death experiencers, the ancient Egyptian seems to have expected the judgment experience to force him to recognize his sins and shortcomings by directly confronting him with his past memories:

It is an awful thing for the sinner to be made to recognize the sin which he has committed . . .[4]

If, on the other hand, one's heart was found to be in proper balance with the scales of justice, the person's aakhu journeyed straightaway to heaven[5] to commune forever with the gods. In order to become a shining, glorified, perfected aakhu at death, one would need to possess a perfect state; in fact, tremendous emphasis was put on issues such as wholeness and purity,[6] which were apparently even then the keys to eternal life. And also (or is this the same thing?) the soul, the ka, had to be "satisfied" and "fulfilled" before such perfection was possible:

---

1 A prayer in Chapter XXXb of The Papyrus of Ani, from Budge, *The Egyptian Book of the Dead*, 309.
2 Van Baaren, 119.
3 Budge, *The Egyptian Book of the Dead*, xxxiii-xxxv.
4 Toynbee, 117.
5 El Mahdy, 156.
6 Budge, *The Egyptian Book of the Dead*, lxvii, lix, lxiii, lxix.

Chapter CXXX. The Chapter of Making Perfect the Khu.

Chapter C. The Chapter of Satisfying the Khu.[1]

This final goal of Egyptian theology was also described with different terminology: becoming an *Osiris*. An Osiris (just as the legend of the god Osiris would suggest) was the recombined totality of all the divided parts of a person's spiritual self, glorified and risen into heaven to commune directly and eternally with the Supreme God.[2] Both of these terms—perfected aakhu and Osiris—meant that one had achieved eternal life and eternal happiness, thereafter enjoying a divine existence in heaven.

Division Theory in Persia

The ancient Zoroastrians of Persia, the first people to anticipate the coming of a universal Judgment Day, also embraced a doctrine about a binary human soul. These ancient people, precursors of much of Western thought, credited people with two sides to their spiritual selves, the *urvan* and the *daena*. They believed that the complete unification and reconciliation of these two halves, if achieved prior to physical death, would result in personal immortality.[3] In fact, however, the belief in this two-part soul in Persia is even more ancient than Zoroastrianism itself; Indo-Iranians already believed, prior to Zoroaster's birth, that people possessed two souls; the *urvan*, following death, became imprisoned in the land of the dead, and the *fravashi* was thought to be immortal and unharmed by death.[4]

Zoroaster taught that, after death, all people had to cross the Bridge of the Separator, where "their own soul and their own self shall torment them." Such torment, he taught, would come to all who had been "dwellers in the House of the Lie" during their lives. At this bridge, all souls were thought to be stripped naked; "this ordeal had the effect of separating the dead in some unspecified way."[5]

---

1 Ibid., xxxiv, xli.
2 Ibid., lxx.
3 Julien Ries, "Immortality," in *The Encyclopedia of Religion*, 7:123.
4 Gherardo Gnoli, "Iranian Religions," in *The Encyclopedia of Religion*, 7:279.
5 Brandon, 153.

At some later date after that ordeal, according to Zoroaster, yet another test would have to be endured, a test of "molten metal and fire." At the end of time, Zoroaster believed (as did the Jews and later the Christians and Moslems) that the dead would rise back to life, in order to go through a testing period involving fire. Following this "Last Day" scenario, Zoroaster (again like the Jews and the Christians) believed that all people would "become of one voice."[1]

Division Theory in Greece

Just like the Jews, the Egyptians, and the Persians, the ancient Greeks were partially familiar with Division Theory. Like the neighboring cultures around them, the Greeks credited human beings with three parts to their makeup: a body, a *thymos*, and a *psyche*:

> The thymos was the conscious self, and the psyche something akin to the life principle. To the Homeric Greeks, a human being was only truly a human being when body, thymos and psyche were all functioning properly together as an inter-related whole. Death shattered this living whole: with the dissolution of the body, the thymos was merged with the air, and the psyche, transformed into a shadowy replica of the living person . . . descended into Hades. . . . There, with the wraiths of all the other dead, bereft of self-consciousness . . . [they] lived on in dismal gloom.[2]

Later, as Pythagorean thought entered Greek theology, the doctrine of reincarnation was grafted onto this scenario,[3] bringing it even closer into alignment with Division Theory.

Division Theory in China

During the Chou dynasty of China (1025-256 B.C.), the nobility entertained a strikingly similar notion, believing themselves to be composed of two spiritual halves which parted company at death. One of these, the *hun*, was intelligent, spiritual, masculine, active, and "yang"-like and always returned to enter the presence of God after death. The other half of the self, the *p'o*, was considered only semiconscious, more earthy, feminine, emotional, passive, and more

---

1   Ibid., 163.
2   Ibid., 81.
3   Ibid., 89.

"yin"-like; after death, it was always inescapably doomed to an eternal imprisonment in a murky, underground land of the dead.[1]

Division Theory in Modern Religions

Although none of our current religions incorporate a binary spiritual self into their doctrines, the ancient Jewish tradition that people are composed of a body, soul, and spirit was inherited by both Christianity and Islam. And similarly conceived was India's early Vedic belief that all people are made up of three parts: a body, an *asu* (the life force), and a *manas* (the seat of internal feeling, located in the heart),[2] an ancient belief which has since evolved into the modern Hindu doctrine that all people are made up of a body, a "subtle body," and a spirit.[3]

These religions still technically possess the terminology needed to differentiate between two separate spiritual components, but this duplication is generally considered irrelevant, devoid of any significance to modern theology. Today, people of the West commonly treat the terms "soul" and "spirit" as if they were interchangeable. Nevertheless, the terminology does exist within each of these traditions—and that terminology carries with it the implicit suggestion that the concept of a binary soul was once a fundamental element of those religions' earliest belief systems.

The inclusion of such binary soul doctrines within traditions as diverse as the Egyptian, the Chinese, the Persian, the Indian, the Greek, and the Judeo-Christian strongly suggests that these now-dissimilar faiths may be but faint echoes of what was once a single, world-spanning religion.

Buddhism is one of the few world religions that does not contain such binary soul terminology; Buddhism denies the existence of any soul, so it obviously can't believe in a double soul. This is one of the most interesting curiosities about Buddhism—it subscribes to the doctrine of reincarnation, but it does not believe that there is any soul which does that reincarnating. Division Theory provides a perfectly reasonable explanation for this apparent inconsistency. Buddhism holds that there is no self, no personal component possessing any

---

1   Seidel, 124-27.
2   Ries, 133.
3   Sibajiban Bhattacharyya, "Indian Philosophies," in *The Encyclopedia of Religion*, 7:166.

functional identity which reincarnates; instead, what does reincarnate, according to Buddhism, is merely an impersonal spark of living consciousness which is passed from life to life like a flame being passed from one candle to another.[1]

This is precisely what Division Theory envisions! Division Theory agrees that the soul, the only component of a person containing any memory or sense of identity, does not reincarnate, but merely descends into a deep unconscious state. It is the conscious living spirit, which, as Buddhism insists, is utterly devoid of any sense of identity, that returns to live again in another body. True, Buddhism does not contain a two-soul system, but Buddhism's vision of the truth, although perhaps incomplete, is not inconsistent with the universal vision; and Buddhism and Division Theory appear to describe the same phenomenon.

The Buddhist *Tibetan Book of the Dead*, available to the West only in the past fifty years, provides some parallels to Division Theory in its vision of people being overwhelmed by the unconscious after physical death. In the book's Foreword, Lama Anagarka Govinda observes, "If through some trick of nature, the gates of an individual's unconscious were suddenly to spring open, the unprepared mind would be overwhelmed and crushed."[2] Yet the *Tibetan Book of the Dead* teaches that just such a "trick of nature" is exactly what happens at death.[3]

If, as the evidence suggests, the split-mind religious belief was widespread at one time, it has long since been abandoned and forgotten by the major religions; the most recent record of this belief still being widely regarded as significant in a civilized society can be found in the writings of Aristotle, who briefly mentioned it in *On The Soul*, written more than 2,300 years ago.[4]

Division Theory in Primitive Religions

Although the larger religions no longer focus on such a belief, many smaller ones still do. It seems that smaller, more isolated groups have been more successful in keeping this idea alive;

---

1   Ries, 127.
2   Evans-Wentz, lii.
3   Ibid., 34-35.
4   Aristotle, *On the Soul*, Book II (New York: Penguin Books, 1986), 413b.25; 430a.15-20.

primitive cultures in every part of the world, from the Americas to Africa, from Asia to Australia to the Solomon Islands—cultures that are utterly separated in every other way—have in common the doctrine that people possess two souls.

This binary-soul doctrine is widespread throughout North American Indian tradition, found in over a dozen different tribal cultures in the U.S. and Canada.[1] In South America, the Mbua of Brazil[2] and the Waica of the Amazon basin[3] profess it as well. In Africa, this belief is shared by the Ewe of Togo and the Bambara of Mali.[4] In Eurasia it's found in the religions of the Khanty and the Mansi of the Ob River region, the Samoyed of Europe and Siberia, the Tunguz of the Yenisei River, and the Yukagir of Siberia.[5]

It can only be assumed that either these peoples independently arrived at the same conclusion or each inherited this doctrine from the same source.

Identical beliefs are also shared by the Mossi of Burkina Faso in West Africa,[6] the Melanesians of the Solomon Islands, the Eskimos of the Arctic,[7] and the Guarani-Apapocuva of South America.[8] However, all these peoples' religions parallel Division Theory even more closely; they believe not only in binary souls, but also that those souls divide at death, with each separate soul-unit then experiencing a different sort of afterlife.

And, of all the traditional beliefs of all the peoples on earth today, those of the Australian Aborigines and the Luba of Zaire most closely mirror Division Theory: the people of both cultures believe that one of their two soul units goes on to reincarnate after death, while the other becomes trapped in a fixed unconscious realm.[9]

In many of the cultures among North American Indians, Australian Aborigines, and African tribesmen, one of two spiritual units is identified as the source of life and consciousness, while the other is associated with the unconscious and the feelings. In such

---

1 Ries, 127.
2 Riviere, 13:428.
3 Ries, 128.
4 Riviere, 429.
5 Ries, 128.
6 Riviere, 428.
7 Toynbee, 43, 48-50.
8 Otto Zerries, "South American Religions: An Overview," in *The Encyclopedia of Religion*, 13:497.
9 Toynbee, 40; Ries, 124.

cases, the "feelings" unit is always the one believed to experience afterlife as a prisoner in a "world of the dead." Many of these cultures also believe in reincarnation;[1] the doctrine of rebirth seems, if anything, even more universal than that of the binary soul itself; both doctrines repeatedly appear among the most ancient beliefs of every continent.

If belief in Division Theory indeed was once widespread, perhaps humanity's current religions also contain other hidden bits and pieces of such a world-embracing theological vision. By examining modern religions through the lens of Division Theory, a curious relationship between Hinduism-Buddhism, Judeo-Christianity, and Taoism comes into focus, a relationship which seems to spotlight a common origin between them all. Hindu-Buddhist tradition seems to attribute to people the qualities of the conscious spirit, and to God those of the unconscious soul, while Judeo-Christianity does the exact opposite, identifying Man with the unconscious soul and God with the conscious spirit.[2] Meanwhile, Taoism seems to have chosen a third path, one that focuses on the primal relationship between the conscious spirit and the unconscious soul, never identifying God or Man with one or the other. The obvious implication is that, while these religions all ended up focusing on but one aspect of the whole spiritual picture, they all began by trying to describe an identical vision: the original division of human consciousness.

The Original Vision of Hinduism

Some of the most fundamental tenants of Hinduism, as found in their Upanishads, seem upon close examination to be based on the premise of Division Theory:

> Like two birds of golden plumage, inseparable companions, the individual self [the subjective, feeling soul] and the immortal self [the objective, impersonal spirit] are perched on the branches of the selfsame tree. The former tastes of the sweet and bitter fruits of the tree; the latter, tasting of neither, calmly observes.
> — The Mundaka Upanishad[3]

---

1   Long, "Reincarnation," 265.
2   See Chapter 7: A Tapestry Folded in Half.
3   *The Upanishads, Breath of the Eternal*, trans. by Swami Prabhavananda and Frederick Manchester (Hollywood: Vedanta Society of Southern California, 1948), 46-47.

The first aspect of the Self [the conscious, objective spirit] is . . . awake . . . conscious only of external objects. . . . He is the enjoyer of the pleasures of the senses. The second aspect of the Self [the unconscious, memory-laden soul] is . . . dreaming, and conscious only of his dreams. In this state he is the enjoyer of the subtle impressions on his mind of the deeds he has done in the past.
— The Mandukya Upanishad[1]

Likewise, in another ancient Hindu scripture, the Laws of Manu, this fundamental division is again addressed, but the author of this treatise recognized that these two halves of the self split apart at death, with only one of the parts then going on to reincarnate:

. . . man is not a simple, but a complex being: "That substance which gives a power of motion to the body, the wise men call . . . the 'knower of the field' or . . . the vital spirit. . . . Another internal spirit called . . . the great soul, attends the birth of all creatures embodied, and thence in all mortal forms is conveyed a perception either pleasing or painful. These two, the vital spirit and reasonable soul, are closely united . . ."[2]

This text later suggests that it's only the "vital spirit" and not the "reasonable soul" which reincarnates, but never describes whatever eventually happens to this soul after death. The whole religion of Hinduism seems to have eventually solidified around the "spirit-reincarnation" theme, while the fate of the other half of the self, the soul, was never accounted for.

The Vision of Swedenborg

Surprisingly, certain forms of Christian doctrine do support Division Theory, perhaps most obviously in Swedenborgian theology. Emmanuel Swedenborg founded one of the newest and most controversial branches of Christian thought. His mystic visions into the worlds of the afterlife were given a cool public reception in the eighteenth century; yet today his vision seems to

---

1 Ibid., 50.
2 *The Laws of Manu*, trans. by G. Buhler in *The Sacred Books of the East*, vol. xxv (Oxford, 1886), as quoted with added commentary by Evans-Wentz in *The Tibetan Book of the Dead*, 47 n. Manu is Hindu mythology's parallel to Judaism's Adam—the first human. *The Laws of Manu* are credited as scriptures of the highest authority by Orthodox Hindus.

fall right in line, offering yet another parallel to Division Theory. The idea of an after-death split of human consciousness was fundamental to Swedenborg's teachings; and this vision—while odd to the people of his age—can now be recognized as fully consistent with those of many others who came before him. According to Swedenborg, the human psyche splits apart after death, and the two parts go on different paths; but from his point of view, the soul enters an unconscious existence, while the other part, the conscious spirit, becomes lost and is thereafter unaccounted for.

On the division of consciousness, Swedenborg wrote in *Heaven and Hell*:

> Man has both discernment [unconscious value-judgment] and intention [conscious free-will decision making] . . . discernment alone does not constitute a person, nor does intention alone; rather it is discernment and intention together (p. 344).

> [People have] two "thoughts," one more outward [conscious] and one more inward [unconscious]. . . . these two thoughts are separate. . . . people take precautions to prevent the more inward from flowing into the more outward and somehow becoming visible (pp. 420-21).

On the separation of the conscious spirit from the unconscious soul after death, Swedenborg wrote:

> A person's . . . state after death is called "the state of his more inward [unconscious] elements." . . . the more outward things he was involved in [conscious of] . . . go to sleep (p. 420).

> The outer or natural [consciousness] becomes dormant. . . . his more outward [conscious] elements . . . are parted after death . . . and go to sleep (pp. 422-23).

> Man has something that angels [the dead] do not: . . . his more outward elements . . . all the elements of his natural or outer [consciousness], and . . . insights and data (p. 237).

On the unconscious soul's inability to think rationally or make new decisions once the conscious spirit has been taken away after death, he wrote:

. . . in the other life they lose their faculty of logical thought (p. 382).

. . . bringing [certain] things . . . out to . . . consciousness was not allowed (p. 382).

. . . after death a person can no longer be re-formed by teaching the way he could in the world, because his [conscious mind] is then stilled and is incapable of being opened (pp. 397-98).

No one in the spirit world is allowed to think [for themselves] (p. 419).

From these brief excerpts from Swedenborg's writings, it's clear that he was describing the same vision of an after-death division of human consciousness that had been recognized by so many others before him. These quotes also make it increasingly obvious that Hinduism and Christianity are but two sides to the same story; Hinduism reports on reincarnation, the fate of the spirit after death, while Christianity reports on heaven and hell, the fate of the soul.

Science's Vision of the Psyche

When the ancient text *The Tibetan Book of the Dead* was made available to the West, Carl Jung immediately declared it to be a psychological analysis of the death experience. Jung realized that the twentieth-century's new science of psychology had uncovered qualities and patterns within the human psyche that closely parallel ancient Tibetan doctrine.[1] In fact, some of the most fundamental elements of Jung's psychology seem to duplicate perfectly the universal prophetic picture. One of the pioneers of modern psychoanalytic theory, Jung came to the disturbing conclusion that powerful forces out of the distant past can have distinct and possibly even autonomous existences within the human unconscious, in an area he labeled the "collective unconscious."[2] The contents of this level of the mind, according to Jung, originate in humanity's very distant past, instead of in the individual's present life experience. Jung felt that this "collective unconscious" is

1 Evans-Wentz, 53.
2 Jung, *The Structure and Dynamics of the Psyche.*

filled with huge amounts of psychic remains, patterns and impressions originating from remote ages in human history. While he never specifically proposed that those unconscious elements were the personal-souls of people's earlier incarnations, the idea that such previous souls might still exist within some deeply unconscious level of the mind would be fully consistent with Jung's vision. Jung distinguished:

> . . . three psychic levels: (1) consciousness, (2) the personal unconscious, and (3) the collective unconscious. The personal unconscious consists . . . of all those contents that became unconscious either because they lost their intensity and were forgotten or because consciousness was withdrawn from them (repression). . . . The collective unconscious . . . the ancestral heritage of possibilities of representation, is not [from the] individual . . . and is the true basis of the . . . psyche . . . . The collective unconscious . . . appears to consist of . . . primordial images.[1]

In describing this collective unconscious as containing many "primordial images" which together form an "ancestral heritage," Jung closely approximates the vision of Division Theory; if people's previous personal-souls truly were buried in the deepest parts of the unconscious, they would be exactly what Jung described: primordial images (early memories) and an ancestral heritage (one's truest ancestors would be his own previous selves).

Modern Psychology and Division Theory

Recent advances in psychological theory are drawing Jung's insights even closer in line with Division Theory. Swiss psychologist Arno Gruen, for example, has suggested that the division of the human mind into consciousness and unconsciousness corrupts human integrity, implying that this split in the human psyche, despite being commonplace, is totally unnatural. And once again, Gruen parallels Division Theory by insisting that this split can and should be repaired, even though such a rejoining of the conscious and unconscious would inevitably be very unpleasant:

> Human development may follow one of two paths: that of love [the soul] or that of power [the spirit]. The way of power, which is central in most cultures, leads to a self that mirrors the ideology of domination. This is a fragmented, split self that rejects suffering and helplessness [the

---

1   Jung, *The Structure and Dynamics of the Psyche*, para. 321, pp. 151-52.

spirit rejects the soul because the soul feels pain]. . .
Autonomy is that state of integration in which one lives in full harmony
with one's feelings and needs [integration of spirit and soul].[1]
. . . having access to life-affirming emotions, to feelings of joy,
sorrow, pain—in short, to a sense of being truly alive—is essential
for the development of autonomy . . .[2]

Gruen explains that this split typically occurs at a very early
age, when a person first confronts the necessity of having to submit
to a greater authority:

> . . . the feeling of utter defenselessness will be repressed and split
> off from the growing self. . . . children will block out everything
> reminiscent of the situation in which they experienced these
> feelings, thus reducing their capacity for empathy and,
> consequently, their humanness. In this manner, entire parts of
> their . . . self will be split off from consciousness.[3]

Division Theory in Philosophy

In the arena of philosophy too, Division Theory has long been
anticipated. In the fifth century B.C., Plato related a story already
thought quite ancient in his day, a legend about a primordial "fall"
from unity into multiplicity. Seven centuries later, Origen apparently placed such stock in this creation legend that he placed it at
the center of his teachings.[4] A thousand years later, Saint Bernard
of Clairvaux taught his students that the specific purpose of the
many exercises and observances of Christian life were to make
people aware of their own inner state of division.[5] St. John of the
Cross, four hundred years after Bernard, taught that all dicotomies
and dualities—such as subject-object, male-female, or even con-
scious-unconscious—are no longer real or meaningful for a soul
who has achieved divine union.[6]

---

1 Arno Gruen, *The Betrayal of the Self* (New York: Grove Press, 1986), 1.
2 Ibid., 9.
3 Ibid.
4 E. Glenn Hinson, "Origin," in *Great Thinkers of the Western World*, ed. by Ian P. McGreal (New York: HarperCollins, 1992), 64.
5 M. Basil Pennington, O.C.S.O., "Saint Bernard of Clairvaux," in *Great Thinkers of the Western World*, 93.
6 Mary E. Giles, "Saint John of the Cross," in *Great Thinkers of the Western World*, 167.

In recent centuries, philosophers have expounded on the early ideas of division, often using the notion of a foundational division as a framework to assist them in their efforts to define the essential nature of reality. Immanuel Kant focused on the division between *phenomena* and *noumena*,[1] while William Blake addressed the distinction between *imagination* and *reason*.[2] It was the *subject-substance* dicotomy that got Georg Wilhelm Friedrich Hegel's intellectual juices flowing,[3] and the *will-idea* polarity for Arthur Schopenhauer.[4] *Being-in-itself* contrasted with *being-for-itself* in the work of Jean-Paul Sartre,[5] while to Paul Tillich *existence* wrestled with *essence*.[6] And the famous *I-Thou* relationship was the key to understanding the universe for Martin Buber.[7]

Furthermore, Blake, Hegel, Sartre, and Tillich all specifically endorsed the theory that an original primordial unity suffered an ancient, catastrophic rupture. Blake went so far as to claim that all subsequent divisions and dicotomies, whether in objective existence or merely subjectively apparent to the human mind alone, were the direct consequences of the primordial fall and rupture.[8]

Hegel named this original unity *spirit* and its divided halves he identified as *subject* and *substance*. He viewed their division as part of a profound metaphysical circle, spiraling ever-upward. Upon dividing apart, Hegel maintained, the two halves begin struggling to reunite, eventually doing so at a more mature, more advanced level of being. This newly reformed unity then divides once more, repeating the cycle endlessly. While the unity's two halves are divided, Hegel believed, they are tormented by the need to end the division; and the ultimate reunion of the two halves is inevitable. But the reunion of the halves would not be achieved merely by returning to their earlier states; rather, the reunited unity

---

1   Frank N. Magill, ed., *Masterpieces of World Philosophy* (New York: HarperCollins, 1990), 327.
2   Marjean D. Purinton, "William Blake," in *Great Thinkers of the Western World*, 316.
3   Magill, 351.
4   Magill, 359.
5   Magill, 607.
6   Lawrence F. Hundersmarck, "Paul Tillich," in *Great Thinkers of the Western World*, 498.
7   Magill, 529.
8   Purinton, 316.

would posses a hard-won new quality, a new state of being, a new immediacy,[1] as if the unity, although infinite, would be able to grow, progress, even evolve, through the agonizing, self-confrontative process of division and reunion—the process, in other words, of living and dying.

These celebrated philosophers tried—and perhaps even succeeded—in grasping and relating genuine glimpses of the divided unity that is our reality. All their approaches may indeed be correct—although necessarily incomplete—perspectives of the ultimate nature of our divided reality. Just as we have seen that the field of psychology has perceived part of the picture, as did the ancient Hebrews, Egyptians, Persians, Hindus, Greeks, Buddhists, and Christians, the world's philosophers also have recognized but part of the whole picture.

The Babel Compromise

> The word of the Lord came to me: "Son of man, there are two women, daughters of the same mother. They became prostitutes in Egypt. . . . The older was named Oholah, and her sister was Oholibah. They were mine. . . . Oholah is Samaria, and Oholibah is Jerusalem."
> — Ezekiel 23:1-4

It cannot be a coincidence that the oldest religions known to humanity all believed that people were composite creatures which split apart at death into three separate elements: Egypt's body, ba, and ka; the ancient Greeks' body, thymos, and psyche; the Chinese body, hun, and p'o; the Indo-Iranians' body, urvan, and fravashi; the Zoroastrians' body, urvan, and daena; Vedic Indians' body, asu, and manas; and the Hebrews' body, soul, and spirit.

The earliest traditions of each of these religions date far back into the unknown depths of time. The Greeks consistently asserted that their own creed had come from the most ancient of sources. The traditions in the Jewish scriptures are likewise thought to be ancient, dating back to at least 4,000 B.C.[2] The Zoroastrianism and the Hinduism of today are thought to have originally evolved from

---

1 Magill, 352.
2 *The Thompson Chain-Reference Bible* (Indianapolis: B.B. Kirkbride Co., Inc., 1983), 1512.

the same source, splitting apart millennia before Christ;[1] both the original Persian religion which Zoroaster revised into Zoroastrianism and the pre-Hindu Vedic religion of India descended from a single earlier, now wholly lost Indo-Iranian faith.[2] And not only is Egypt's *Book of the Dead* also supposed to date at least that far back, but even this ancient work is thought to have been but a copy of another, even more ancient tradition. Most historians agree that the Egyptians' religion, during the great Pharoahic dynasties, was already a blurred and barely comprehended descendant of another far older faith which even then was almost entirely lost in the mists of time. The material in *The Egyptian Book of the Dead* must have originated during an extremely early point in Egyptian culture, historians argue, because by the time the great Pharaohs started to have copies of it placed in their tombs, neither they nor the priests who transcribed the words seem to have fully understood the meaning of what they were writing.[3]

It seems clear from existing evidence that a single creed may have once enveloped much of the earth. Since these faiths were already in full bloom at the beginning of recorded history, and since they contained striking theological parallels to one another, it can only be concluded that some earlier master, mother faith, of which no direct historical evidence remains, pre-existed all these later religions. Such a mother religion must have suffered some severe setback, for the present world religions all appear to have degenerated far from this primordial religious vision, completely forgetting the original concept of Division Theory, leaving behind only the faintest traces of its original form and substance.

But what could possibly have been responsible for the deterioration of the common vision of all these faiths? What would have caused each of them to fail to pass on the great vision they had inherited from that mother religion? The answer may found in what is perhaps the Hebrew scriptures' single most repetitive theme: its admonitions not to follow after strange gods. The Jews are thought to be one of the first peoples to follow monotheism, the belief in the existence of only one, all-powerful God. However,

---

1 R.C. Zaechner, *The Dawn and Twilight of Zoroastrianism* (London: Oxford, 1961), 39-40.
2 Ibid., 70-2, 119-20.
3 Budge, *The Egyptian Book of the Dead*, xvii, xii, xxii.

many historians feel certain that the earliest form of the ancient Egyptian religion also recognized but one, all-powerful, unknowable God.[1] And Zoroastrianism and possibly even Hinduism are also thought to have originally started out as monotheisms.[2] But each of these other religions apparently bowed to forces pressuring them to compromise, eventually accepting and assimilating the local gods. At first, it seems, they became creeds with only one full-fledged deity, but also with many other near-Gods, lesser but still divine beings; but as time wore on, all these religions (except Judaism) dropped, or forgot, all distinctions entirely, becoming full-fledged polytheisms.

In their eagerness to disseminate their religious doctrine, the enthusiastic followers of this early mother religion apparently saw fit to violate the integrity of its message, allowing the local populations to hold onto their familiar local gods while simultaneously bringing them into the fold of Division Theory. If so, they would have been prostituting the purity of this mother religion, selling it at a price:

> I gave you my solemn oath and entered into a covenant with you, declares the Sovereign Lord, and you became mine. . . . But you trusted in your beauty and used your fame to become a prostitute. You lavished your favors on anyone who passed by and your beauty became his. . . . You took [what I] gave you, and you made for yourself male idols [gods of other religions] and engaged in prostitution with them. . . . You engaged in prostitution with the Egyptians, your lustful neighbors. . . . You engaged in prostitution with the Assyrians, too. . . . Then you increased your promiscuity to include Babylonia . . .
> — Ezekiel 16:8,15,17,26,28-29

But, unlike true prostitution, that price would not have been paid by the people who came to the religion, but by the religion itself. The people who were promulgating this ancient mother religion would have quite literally been bribing the populations around them, in effect saying "If you come into our religion, we will compromise and accept your gods":

---

1   Budge, *The Egyptian Book of the Dead,* cxxviii.
2   Brandon, 152; *Bhagavad-Gita (Song of God),* trans. by Swami Prabhavananda (New York: New American Library, 1972), 6, 15.

127

You adulterous wife! You prefer strangers to your own husband! Every prostitute receives a fee, but you give gifts to all your lovers, bribing them to come to you from everywhere for your illicit favors. So in your prostitution you are the opposite of others; no one runs after you for your favors. You are the very opposite, for you give payment and none is given to you.
— Ezekiel 16:32-34

The evidence, then, suggests that people once tried to build a worldwide religion. Wanting to provide all people with an "eternal name," a permanent memory of one's identity and past which could be successfully transferred from one life to the next, they built a huge, monolithic religion specifically designed and structured to teach people how to honor the integrity of their psyches, so their personal-souls would not be "dispersed" and lost at physical death. But in their understandable enthusiasm to spread this doctrine as widely as possible, they foolishly violated the integrity of that religion by agreeing, for the sake of expediency, to absorb the familiar local gods of each population center into that religion's master doctrine. Unfortunately, while such a compromise tactic would indeed have allowed such a religion to spread quickly at first, it would have eventually weakened and diluted that great mother religion until it finally collapsed upon itself, breaking up into many dissimilar local off-shoots that could no longer relate to one another; the original message, meanwhile, would have become increasingly lost in the confusion:

There was a time when all the world spoke a single language and used the same words . . . [People] said, "Let us build ourselves a . . . tower [a religion] with its top in heaven and make an [eternal] name for ourselves, or [our souls] will be dispersed . . ." The Lord came down to see the . . . tower which they had built, and he said, "Here they are, one people with a single language, and now they have started to do this . . . Come, let us go down there and confuse their language, so they will not understand what they say to each other." So the Lord dispersed them . . . there the Lord made a babble of the language of the whole world.
— Genesis 11:1-9

But, in one little corner of the world, this unfortunate development not only seems to have been understood, but also was apparently expected to change again one day; the Hebrew prophecies include clear and unmistakable references to a coming time when all people would again join as one in their faith and understanding and worship.[1] Those ancient Hebrew prophets insisted that there would once again be a single worldwide religion on earth; this was to come at the time of the end, a time when even Zoroaster himself recognized that all humanity would "become of one voice."

And now Division Theory has been rediscovered.

---

1   Isaiah 59:19.

CHAPTER 7

A TAPESTRY FOLDED IN HALF

The Divided Theologies of East and West

God sets us nothing but riddles.
—Fyodor Dostoevsky[1]

Although they wear a myriad of disguises, there are essentially only two schools of theology today, the Eastern and the Western, and each explains a great deal about the nature of reality and human experience. Most people in both the East and the West, upon learning how their native doctrines go about explaining the vagaries of life and existence, are satisfied, believing these explanations have made proper sense. The East's strongest card seems is its faith that the vagaries of fate in this life are actually Divine Justice; the strongest card of the West is its faith that total perfection and complete salvation can be acquired immediately following this life.

Both sides, however, are incomplete, failing to provide answers to some rather critical questions. Division Theory offers perfectly sound resolutions for these failings, showing how these "partial" theologies could be true simultaneously and how the wisdom of each compensates for the blind spots of the other.

A Question of Fate

Western theology has a giant, towering blind spot when it comes to explaining the varieties of human experience: why are

---

1   Fyodor Dostoevsky, *The Brothers Karamazov*, as quoted by Seldes in *The Great Thoughts*, 111.

different people given different fates? Where is God's justice if people are given only one chance and one life to live, but find that this chance is dramatically unequal from person to person, with some people born into favorable circumstances, others into unfavorable circumstances? Where is God's justice when some lives are wonderful and others are horrible? Where is justice when the infants born into these circumstances are supposed to be completely equal, none even the slightest bit more deserving than another? Why should some experience horrible and unremitting tragedy from birth, though they do not seem to deserve it, while others receive great, sometimes even glorious privileges from birth, though they also do not seem to deserve them? Where is God's justice if we are all born but once, and at birth are each no more virtuous or deserving than another, yet we are allotted vastly different lives? How can those who subscribe to such a belief system ignore the logical conclusion to which it leads: that any God responsible for such a system would have to be fundamentally unjust and simply could not truthfully claim to love all His people equally?

The West argues, of course, that outer circumstances are not important, that the only valid concern is whether or not one lives in such a manner as to enter heaven at death; but this argument breaks down: no one can deny that there are those whose births strongly encourage them to live Christian lives, while others' births strongly if not totally prohibit them from even considering Christian lives. Conventional Western thought—rooted in Judeo-Christianity—doesn't reconcile this discrepancy, but Division Theory does. By showing how Eastern reincarnation theology interfaces perfectly with Western heaven-hell theology, Division Theory introduces the concept of *karma* into the Western theological scenario.

Karma is the Eastern idea that the circumstances of our lives are dealt to us justly, based on our own past behavior in previous lives. If we behaved well in the past, then our present lives hold positive circumstances and opportunities, the consequences of that earlier good behavior. If we lived wrongly in the past, then we are confronted by the difficult and unpleasant consequences of those wrong actions in our present lives.

Karma explains how the varying circumstances found in the real world can be recognized as divine justice in action; Western theology, on the other hand, lacking any similar doctrinal mechanism, is incapable of identifying divine justice in progress in this world at all and can only hope to see it operating in the afterlife. Division Theory's ability to incorporate the concept of karma into Judeo-Christian doctrine produces a greater ability to explain the actual variety of circumstances found in life.

A Question of Justice

The book of Job is perhaps the most confusing of all the Holy Scriptures, for what is not stated in Job seems to be the key to everything else. The whole book of Job is a great mystery which has been discussed and argued over throughout history; now, however, Job's distressing question may finally have been answered.

In the text, God showers his loyal servant Job with great and miserable tragedies, even though, by both God's and Job's own admission, he has done nothing in his life to deserve such bitter punishments. When Job protests to his Creator for justice, God replies by asking Job if he understands the mysteries of heaven, all the secrets that God knows. Does Job know everything about the universe, God asks? Does he know about things that happened long before Job was born? No? Then don't accuse your Creator of injustice, God replies!

Ultimately, what God seems to have been saying was: (1) Job had done nothing wrong in his life to deserve these sorrows; (2) but God knows much that Job did not; and (3) God adamantly denied behaving unjustly.

And there the book ends, Job humbled but still in the dark about why all those terrible scourges happened to him, serving through the centuries as an example of great faith in the midst of trouble. But the reader is left wondering, as Job must also have been, about the true disposition of God's justice.

Division Theory, after all these centuries, finally offers an intellectually honest, cogent answer to Job's question: if God's justice is perfect, yet Job didn't do anything in that life to deserve the fate he received, then Job must have done something to deserve those punishments at some point in time prior to his life as Job. God seems to be hinting this when he goes on and on about how there is so much that Job doesn't know. Was God hinting that Job really did deserve the punishment, but due to long-ago matters that Job was no longer aware of and which God had no intention of revealing to him?

This seems the only answer to Job's question that does not violate the concept of a just and honorable God. Logic dictates that Job's offense, whatever it was, must have occurred prior to his life as Job. God's hints that the answer was to be found in matters beyond Job's awareness support this conclusion; in fact, in one place God actually says that Job was alive thousands of years ago at the dawn of the world:

> [God answered Job] . . . Where were you when I laid the earth's foundation? . . . Who marked off its dimensions?
> . . .
> . . . Surely you know, for you were already born! You have lived so many years!
> — Job 38:4-5,21

This passage has often been explained away in traditional Western theology as an example of God's sarcasm, but, indeed, are we to understand that the infinitely perfect Creator and Lord of the Universe indulges in anything as lowly and petty as sarcasm?

The only possible answer to Job would seem to be this: Job lived and sinned in an earlier life; and in order for this to be so, reincarnation must indeed be a functioning condition within the Judeo-Christian universe.

A Question of Memory

Eastern reincarnation theology fails to answer why people forget their past lives. What would be the point, the West asks, of living eternally, life after life after life, if people were meant to forget each life after they live it? If people are supposed to be learning something, gaining wisdom through all these multiple incarnations, any ability to learn would be stymied by this tendency to forget. For all practical purposes, people lose their immortality when they lose their memories, so this would be really no better than just living one life and then, at death, truly and utterly ceasing to exist.

Division Theory offers a reasonable explanation for this dilemma, pointing out, first, that this splitting of soul from spirit, this forgetting of all past memories at death, seems to have been an accident which God had not intended to happen, brought about by humanity's own regretful actions. Second, Division Theory, through the Judeo-

Christian prophecies, suggests that all those past lives are not truly lost, but will all be returned to us during Judgment Day.

Thus, Division Theory yields a theology superior both in logic and justice to either Eastern or Western theology alone; it seems the whole truth was here all along, just divided in two.

A Paradox

There is a basic paradox in the traditional explanation of Christianity, a paradox fundamental to the whole modern concept of the religion; yet, due to a sort of embarrassed confusion over the issue, this paradox is not usually discussed.

> Can the believing husband in Heaven be happy with his unbelieving wife in Hell?
> Can the believing father in Heaven be happy with his unbelieving children in Hell?
> Can the loving wife in Heaven be happy with her unbelieving husband in Hell?[1]

Christianity insists above all else that people should love their enemies, genuinely caring for and being concerned about those who do evil. Such caring people, its texts inform us, who actually do love their enemies and really feel for those who do evil, will be the ones who enter the Kingdom of Heaven, where full satisfaction is promised. The "wicked," however, will not enter heaven and won't be found there. In other words, while believers are enjoying great comfort in heaven, they are accutely aware that the wicked people, those whom they tried so hard to learn to love, who had in fact become their true "loved ones," would be experiencing severe discomfort in hell.

The paradox is—how could heaven be heavenly to Christians if the wicked, those they have purposely and consciously chosen to love, in fact ordered to love, are separated from them and known to be in great distress? If this is the expected end result, then why are Christians instructed to create these bonds of love in the first place? How could believers find happiness in heaven if they knew their loved ones are miserable in hell?

---

1   Jonathan Edwards, *Discourses on Various Important Subjects* (1738), as quoted by Seldes in *The Great Thoughts*, 118.

Doesn't such a plan defy reason? Heaven is supposed to hold the fulfillment of all needs and desires, yet, in order to get to heaven, are we instructed to develop those very needs and desires which are most certain to remain unfulfilled there? The orthodox tradition has no explanation for this breach of logic; when its teachers are confronted with this paradox, they often mumble some indistinct reply that "people in heaven will be happy in spite of knowing their loved ones are in hell." But such is not a satisfactory answer. As it has done with so many other mysteries, however, Division Theory's breakdown of religious reality into soul and spirit provides a resolution to this dilemma.

The key to this mystery lies in the fact that the spirit never dies; it's never destroyed, never lost, never abandoned. This spirit is the vital immediate living self, the source of all choice and conscious thought. Those in heaven would never need to suffer grief for their lost loved ones, because those loved ones would still be right there with them! All that could possibly be lost, according to Division Theory, would be the contents of the evil ones' personal-souls, the memories and "sense of identity" from evil past lives. Their true selves, their living spirit, would never be lost, although the memories of poor past experiences might. Thus, those in heaven would need to feel no sense of disappointment at the fate of their loved ones, for those loved ones would be, indeed, still alive and quite well off, and everything anyone ever found to love in them would still be there.

Once again, the paradoxes of religion disappear once we return to the original focus of religion—the division of the human psyche.

Conscious God/Unconscious God

Each of the world's primary religious traditions identifies the characteristics of one of the two halves of the mind with human beings, while the opposite form of consciousness is identified with the deity. In the East, people tend to be associated with the conscious spirit, while the deity is associated with the unconscious soul; in the West, people are associated with soul, and the deity with spirit.

In Eastern religions, people are identified almost exclusively with the active, rational, passionless, objective conscious spirit which reincarnates over and over, while the subjective, sensitive, feeling soul is largely ignored or denied. In fact, people are so strongly encouraged to identify exclusively with the one and not the other that they are actively discouraged from displaying any of the attributes of the unconscious soul. For example, in Hinduism's *Bhagavad-Gita,* the god Krishna instructs a follower to struggle against giving in to his soul's feelings of compassion and love for his own friends and family:

> Arjuna: "What is this crime I am planning, O Krishna? Murder most hateful, murder of brothers!"
> Krishna: "Arjuna, is this hour of battle the time for scruples and fancies? . . . What is this weakness? It is beneath *you.*"[1]

In these Eastern religions which credit people with the attributes of the conscious spirit, their concept of deity is often polarized more toward the unconscious soul. The East's Buddha, for example, like the West's Heavenly Father, is generally conceived of as all-pervading and blissful; but, unlike Him, Buddha is conceived of as formless, characterless, nonjudgmental, and, in some schools of Buddhist thought, virtually "self"-less, extinguished, a non-being being who may or may not be responsible for the existence of the world but definitely doesn't express himself through history or interact in the affairs of men. And, according to the tenets of Eastern mysticism, this sort of deity may be approached only by achieving the subtlest unconscious inner meditative state.

In the West, it's just the opposite: people are primarily credited with the attributes of the unconscious soul, while the deity is perceived as having the opposite attributes of the conscious spirit. In Judeo-Christianity, the truest essence of an individual is thought to be his unconscious side, his sensitive and subjective "heart and soul," his "innermost self," his moral conscience, brotherly love, and emotional nature. This polarization is so severe that Western religions have sometimes required their followers to identify exclusively with the unconscious soul, completely denying the conscious spirit. In fact, for a long time Christianity's official policy was to discourage people from critically examining their own religion, teaching that reason, logic, and science, all basic functions of the conscious mind, were the ultimate enemies of their faith:

---

1   *Bhagavad-Gita,* 34-35.

Reason is the greatest enemy that faith has; it never comes to the aid of spiritual things, but—more commonly than not—struggles against the divine word, treating with contempt all that animates from God. Whoever wants to be a Christian should tear the eyes out of his Reason.
— Martin Luther[1]

The image of the West's deity is also similarly polarized, seen as possessing the classic attributes of the conscious spirit but not so much those of the soul. The "Great and Terrible God of Israel," for example, is generally portrayed as a very definite, objective, conscious, active, impersonal, judgmental, fully formed individual living being who most definitely does observe and express Himself in history and the affairs of men.

The world's two primary religious traditions seem to be observing the same picture from opposite perspectives;[2] how likely is it that this is merely coincidence?

Left- and Right-Brain Signatures in the Hebrew Prophecies

One of the greatest curiosities of the Jewish scriptures is that those prophets who came from the northern kingdom of Israel prophesied differently than did the prophets of the southern kingdom of Judah. That difference seems to be defined by Division Theory. The prophets from the northern kingdom received their prophecies as visions; but the prophets of the southern kingdom received theirs as words. It is as if in the north the unconscious soul functioned as a receiver; but in the south it was the conscious spirit that relayed the message.

---

1 Martin Luther, *Table Talk*, as quoted by Seldes in *Great Thoughts*, 254.
2 "*When the primitive world disintegrated into spirit and nature, the West rescued nature for itself. It was prone to a belief in nature, and only became more entangled in it with every painful effort to make itself more spiritual. The East, on the contrary, took mind for its own, and by explaining away matter as mere illusion (maya), continued to dream in Asiatic filth and misery. But since there is only one earth and one mankind, East and West cannot rend humanity into two different halves. Psychic reality exists in its original oneness, and awaits man's advance to a level of consciousness where he no longer believes in the one part and denies the other, but recognizes both as constituent elements of one psyche.*" — C.G. Jung, *Modern Man in Search of a Soul*, trans. by W.S. Dell and Carey F. Barnes (New York: Harcourt, Brace, 1933), 191.

The northern prophets primarily reported visual, right-brain type information; the southern prophets primarily related verbal, left-brain type information. The northern prophets "saw visions of the Lord," but, for the southern prophets, "the word of the Lord" was what came to them.

Thus, even the style of Israel's prophets reflected the secret truth of their religion—that it had to do with the division of consciousness of the human mind.

Yahweh's Wife

> As soon as Jesus was baptized . . . the Spirit of God descend[ed] like a dove and light[ed] on him. And a voice from heaven said, "This is my Son, whom I love; with him I am well pleased."
> — Matthew 3:16

The hypothesis that Western religion's original focus was on the division of the psyche would clear up a long-standing mystery about the earliest days of Judeo-Christianity. According to historians, the texts found in the Bible were all written sometime after 800 B.C., and many questions exist about the forms Israel's religion took prior to that time.

At the time of the earliest texts, a single theme was being repeated with great force and urgency: "Hear, O Israel, the Lord thy God, the Lord is One!" This message apparently held great relevance to the Israelites of that age; with these words, those earliest texts repeatedly reaffirm the singularity and unity of their deity. Such a fervent concern seems the earmark of an internal doctrinal issue for the Judaism of that era, and as such must be contrasted against the better-known doctrinal issue of that same age—the falsity of other gods. Whereas most of the problems Israel had with its religion back then seem to have revolved around keeping its people from following strange gods, this curious doctrinal manifesto would indicate that some Israelites did in fact not think that their God, Yahweh, was "One." In fact, considering the force of their objections, there must have been some fairly influential elements within that early Jewish culture that held that their God was, in some way, multiple, or perhaps divided in some fashion!

Another mystery, seemingly connected, is the recent archaeological discoveries concerning the Canaanite goddess Asherah:

Some Israelites appear to have thought that Yahweh had a wife, like the other gods: archaeologists have recently unearthed inscriptions dedicated "To Yahweh and his Asherah." King Manasseh (687-420) . . . actually put up an effigy to Asherah in the Temple . . . most Israelites were devoted to Asherah and some thought she was Yahweh's wife . . .[1]

But instead of any Biblical passages suggesting that Asherah was Yahweh's mate, we find only the message repeated: "Hear, O Israel, the Lord thy God, the Lord is One!" There are references to an Asherah in the early texts, but instead of being identified as Yahweh's mate, this female deity was presented as one of the "foreign gods" the Israelites disobediently followed.

Yet at one time Yahweh probably was believed to have had a consort. The Canaanite's supreme god, El, was believed to have a wife, named Asherah; and, at one time, this same Canaanite High God El seems to have been directly identified with Israel's Yahweh:

Abram said . . . "I have raised my hand to Yahweh, El, creator of heaven and earth . . ."
— Genesis 14:22

It is highly likely that Abraham's God was El, the High God of Canaan. The deity introduces himself to Abraham as El Shaddai (El of the Mountain), which was one of El's traditional titles. Elsewhere he is called El Elyon (The Most High God) or El of Bethel. The name of the Canaanite High God is preserved in such Hebrew names as Isra-El and Ishma-El.[2]

Is it possible that, immediately prior to the era in which the Biblical texts were written, Judaism more directly recognized the Primordial Division? Is it possible they associated the conscious spirit with Yahweh, the male God of Israel, and the unconscious soul with Asherah, a female Israelite Goddess largely unknown to the modern era? And if so, could a religious reform have occurred at some later point, in which "the powers that were" concluded that the concept of division was being over-emphasized, instead of the need for unity? And, thinking this, did they then throw out all

---

1 Karen Armstrong, *A History of God* (New York: Alfred A. Knopf, 1994), 47, 52.
2 Ibid. 14.

references to Israel's female Goddess, intending to focus exclusively on the male figure by repeating a new slogan designed to turn attention away from Division—"The Lord is One"?

Although any direct references to Yahweh's female counterpart have since been lost, the Biblical texts have not completely lost sight of the binary nature of Israel's God; repeated references to Yahweh's two parts, His soul and spirit, remain intact within the Hebrew Bible. And such references are consistent with the usage of these terms throughout the rest of the Biblical texts: the spirit is presented as capable of action, intention, and thought, while the soul is presented as the source of feeling, memory, and sense of identity.

The Spirit of God is repeatedly described as initiating and inducing thought and action throughout the Bible, but God's feelings and sense of identity somehow remain apart. Indeed, when the Spirit of God descended onto Jesus at his baptism, the famous voice from God which said "This is My Son, with whom I am pleased" was not heard coming from that spirit settling upon Jesus, but instead came from afar, from heaven. Why? Perhaps because, like us (who are "made in God's image"), God also has both soul and spirit, and, like us, it is His soul which possesses both His sense of identity (My Son) and His feelings (whom I love).

Throughout the Bible, the phrase "Spirit of God" is used again and again, but always when God is thinking, communicating, or acting. And as if to emphasize that God's sense of identity did not sit with His spirit, but with His soul, He even sometimes referred to His own spirit in the third person:

The Lord said to Moses . . . "I have filled him with the Spirit of God, with skill, ability, and knowledge . . ."
— Exodus 31:1-3

God's spirit functioned verbally, communicating His intellect to others; the "Word of God" always came from His spirit, never His soul:

Then the Lord . . . put the Spirit on the seventy elders. When the Spirit rested on them, they prophesied . . .
— Numbers 11:25

The Spirit of the Lord spoke through me; his word was on my tongue.
— 2 Samuel 23:2

He gave him the plans of all that the Spirit had put in his mind . . .
— 1 Chronicles 28:12

God's spirit acted, behaving as the source of His power, strength, and vitality:

Then the Spirit of the Lord came upon Gideon, and he blew a trumpet . . .
— Judges 6:34

The Spirit of the Lord came upon him in power so that he tore the lion apart with his bare hands . . .
— Judges 14:6

God's spirit was even understood to be the source of life itself:

Then you, my people, will know that I am the Lord, when I open your graves and bring you up from them. I will put my Spirit in you and you will live. . .
— Ezekiel 37:13-14

But when God is presented as experiencing feeling and emotion, it is not His spirit, but His soul which is referred to:

The Lord examines the righteous, but the wicked and those who do violence his soul hates.
— Psalms 11:5

Hear the word of the Lord . . . Your New Moon festivals and your appointed feasts my soul hates. They have become a burden to me; I am weary of bearing them.
— Isaiah 1:14

But in discarding references to Yahweh's female counterpart, did this prehistoric religion take a wrong turn? By allowing people to forget that there were two sides to a person's inner self, did they make it even more difficult for people to achieve that unity between those two parts which they so strongly urged?

When this change in religious policy first took place, Israel's priests would have probably had some sort of prehistoric "town crier" travel their dusty streets, endlessly intoning "Hear, O Israel: The Lord thy God is One!" to encourage all Israel to seek that

same unity of self which Yahweh Himself possessed and represented. But if the populace was thereby allowed to forget that there
actually were two parts, soul and spirit, that needed to be brought
together to achieve that unity, what good would it be to cry "unity,
unity," if no one knew any longer just exactly what the things were
that needed to be joined together?

CHAPTER 8

THE GOSPEL OF DIVISION

The Outlawed Knowledge of Those Closest to the Truth

A man said to [Jesus], "Tell my brothers to divide my father's possessions with me."
He said to him, "O man, who has made Me a divider?" He turned to His disciples and said to them, "I am not a divider, am I?"
— The Gospel of Thomas 72

Very little was known about the early Christian cult known as the *Gnostics* (Greek: the "knowers") until the twentieth century; a cache of their writings was only just discovered in Nag Hammadi in 1945, and it wasn't until 1977 that any translations were published.[1] From the rise of the Papacy's political clout during the Roman Empire until these rediscovered scriptures were published in 1977, all that the world knew about the Gnostics was what the admittedly hostile Roman church had to say about them. But with the publication of this large collection of original Gnostic works, a new door has been opened toward understanding the mysterious theology of the Gnostics, providing new insights into an obscure yet pivotal chapter in the earliest days of the Christian church. Scholars are uncertain exactly when these new scriptures were first written, but some place their origins in the same time frame as when the Gospels themselves were first committed to paper.[2]

---

1   James M. Robinson, translators' director, *The Nag Hammadi Library in English* (San Francisco: Harper & Row, 1977).
2   Elaine Pagels, *The Gnostic Gospels* (New York: Random House, 1979), xvi-xvii.

Gnosticism was an intrinsic element of the earliest appearances of Christianity; scholars openly admit that even the Gospel of John betrays some Gnostic influence.[1] The politically powerful Roman church, however, eventually condemned the Gnostics because they wouldn't conform to the demands of Rome. Century upon century, the Roman church ruthlessly continued to repress Gnosticism.[2]

But such repression of Gnosticism may now be difficult to continue, due to the rediscovery of these Nag Hammadi texts. These unexpected new sources of information about early Christian history and doctrine have been intensely studied since their publication, but much in these texts has proven to be just as cryptic and incomprehensible as any of the most obscure passages in the Bible. Although they have been available for study for several years, the meaning of these new scriptures has largely remained an unbroken riddle to the world.

That is, until Division Theory is tried as a key; just as it seemed to unlock the riddles of the Bible, it also appears to unlock the secrets of the Gnostics.

• The Gnostics knew that the self is binary in nature, differentiated into soul and spirit:

> . . . without the soul the body does not sin, just as the soul is not saved without the spirit. But if the soul is saved when it is without evil, and the spirit is also saved, then the body becomes free from sin. For it is the spirit that quickens the soul . . .
> — The Apocryphon of James 11:38-39, 12:1-6

• It has long been known that the Gnostics' theology was dualistic. These Nag Hammadi scriptures repeatedly refer to humanity's spiritual nature as dualistic, variously describing it as the relationship between man and woman, male and female, or husband and wife:

> Whereas in this world the union is one of husband and wife—a case of strength complemented by weakness—in the aeon the form of the union is different, although we refer to them by the same names.
> — The Gospel of Philip 76:6-9

---

1   See John 15:15; I John 2:27.
2   *New Catholic Encyclopedia* (New York: McGraw Hill, 1967), VIII: 524.

When Eve [the contents of the unconscious mind] was still in Adam [the conscious mind], death did not exist. When she separated from him death came into being. If he again becomes complete and attains his former self, death will be no more.
— The Gospel of Philip 68:22-26

For they [the soul and spirit] were originally joined to one another when they were with the Father before the woman [the unconscious soul] led astray the man [the conscious spirit], who is her brother. This marriage [gnosis] has brought them back together again and the soul [the woman, the unconscious] has been joined to her true love, her master [the man, the spirit, the conscious mind] . . .
— The Exegesis on the Soul 133:4-9

• It has also been long known that the Gnostics believed in the reincarnation of the spirit:

He [Jesus] has ascended, and he has given us a pledge and promised life to us all and revealed to us children [other incarnations] who are to come after us, after bidding us love them, as we would be saved for their sakes.
— The Apocryphon of James 15:35; 16:2

• They believed that the self became divided by death; they even believed that Jesus himself had to go through this division when he died on the cross:

"My God, my God, why, O Lord, have you forsaken me?" It was on the cross that he said these words, for it was there that he was divided.
— The Gospel of Philip 68:26-29

On the day you were one you became two. But when you become two, what will you do?
— The Gospel of Thomas 11

For such [death] is the judgment which had come down from above. It has passed judgment on everyone; it is a drawn sword, with two edges, cutting on either side.
— The Gospel of Truth 25:35-26:4

• They believed that, after death, the separated soul usually became trapped in a permanent unconscious existence:

Before Christ, some came from a place they were no longer able to enter [consciousness], and they went where they were no longer able to come out [the unconscious]. Then Christ came. Those who went in he brought out, and those who went out he brought in.
— The Gospel of Philip 68:17-22

• The Gnostics believed that most people travel vainly through lifetime after lifetime, making no progress, continually losing all their previous selves and souls:

Jesus said, "The Kingdom of the Father is like a certain woman who was carrying a jar full of meal. While she was walking on a road, still some distance from home, the handle of the jar broke and the meal emptied out behind her on the road. She did not realize it; she had noticed no accident. When she reached her house, she set down the jar and found it empty."
— The Gospel of Thomas 97

An ass which turns a millstone did a hundred miles walking. When it was loosed it found that it was still in the same place. There are men who make many journeys [lifetimes], but make no progress toward a destination. When evening [death] came upon them, they saw neither city nor village, neither creation nor nature, power nor angel [they were in the isolation of the soul's afterlife]. In vain have the poor wretches labored.
— The Gospel of Philip 63:11-21

• They believed their old personal-souls still existed within them:

Does not that which is yours exist within you? Yet, while you are in this world, what is it that you lack? This is what you have been making every effort to learn.
— The Treatise on Resurrection 47:12-16

• They seem to have viewed their religion in the same way that people today view psychology:[1]

We are its [the unconscious'] slaves. It takes us captive, to make us do what we do not want, and what we do want we do not do.[2] It is powerful because we have not recognized it [because it remains

---

1 Pagels, 123.
2 Compare with Romans 7:15-20.

hidden, being unconscious]. While it exists it is active. Ignorance [being unconscious of something] is the mother of all evil.
— The Gospel of Philip 83:26-31

• The Gnostics believed that they had to achieve a reunion of consciousness with all their previous personal-souls before they could enter the "Kingdom of Heaven":

[Jesus said,] You who have joined the perfect, the light [consciousness] with the Holy Spirit, unite the angels with us also, the images [one's previous souls]. Do not despise the lamb [the soul which was slaughtered at death], for without it, it is not possible to go in to see the King [God]. No one will be able to go in to the King if he is naked [if he is not "clothed" with all his own past souls].
— The Gospel of Philip 58:11-17

[Jesus said,] "Verily I say unto you, no one will ever enter the kingdom of heaven at my bidding, but only because you yourselves are full. . . . therefore I say to you, become full and leave no space within you empty."
—The Apocryphon of James 2:28-33; 3:34-37

Then, if one has knowledge [gnosis], he receives what are his own and draws them to himself.
. . . consuming . . . death by life.
. . . Raise up those who wish to rise, and awaken those who sleep.
— The Gospel of Truth 21:11-15; 25:15-19; 33:6-8

Light the light within you. Do not extinguish it. Raise your dead who have died, for they have lived and died for you. Give them life. They shall live again. Knock upon yourself as upon a door, and walk upon yourself as upon a straight road.
— The Teachings of Silvanius 107:14-33

If he is undivided, he will be filled with light, but if he is divided, he will be filled with darkness. . . . When you see your likeness [your own soul], you rejoice. But when you see your images [your previous souls] which came into being before you, and which neither die nor become manifest, how much you will have to bear!
— The Gospel of Thomas 61 & 84

- The Gnostics believed they knew what had to be done:

If the woman [the soul] had not separated from the man [the spirit], she would not die with the man. His separation became the beginning of death. Because of this, Christ came to repair the separation which was from the beginning, and again unite the two, and to give life to those [personal-souls] who died as a result of the separation and unite them. But the woman is [only] united to her husband in the bridal chamber [while in the physical body]. Indeed, those who have united in the bridal chamber will no longer be separated. Thus Eve [the soul] separated from Adam [the spirit] because she was never united with him in the bridal chamber.
— The Gospel of Philip 70:9-22

- They believed that conscious recognition was a fundamental step in this "holy quest":

Since the deficiency came into being because the Father was not known, therefore when the Father is known, from that moment on the deficiency will no longer exist. As with the ignorance of a person, when he comes to have knowledge his ignorance vanishes of itself, as the darkness vanishes when light appears, so also the deficiency vanishes in the perfection.
— The Gospel of Truth 24:28-25:3

. . . You saw the spirit . . . you became spirit. You saw Christ, you became Christ. You saw the Father, you shall become Father . . . you see yourself, and what you see you shall become.
— The Gospel of Philip 61:27-35

- They believed they had to make the unconscious conscious:

Jesus said, "Blessed are they who have been persecuted within themselves [feeling the pain within their own souls]. It is they who have truly come to know the Father.
. . . That which you have will save you if you bring it forth from yourselves. That which you do not have within you [that which you remain unconscious of] will kill you if you do not have it within you.
. . . Every female [unconscious personal-soul] who will make herself male [conscious] will enter the Kingdom of Heaven."
— The Gospel of Thomas 69,70,114

- And in order to do this they also had to make the conscious self temporarily unconscious:

> Once more I reprove you, you who are: become like those who are not, that you may be with those who are not.
> — The Apocryphon of James 13:14-17

> The Lord . . . said, "Verily I say unto you, none will be saved unless they believe in my cross. But those who have believed in my cross, theirs is the kingdom of God. Therefore become seekers for death, like the dead who seek for life, for that which they seek is revealed to them . . . none of those who fear death will be saved; for the kingdom of death belongs to those who put themselves to death."
> — The Apocryphon of James 6:1-18

- This passage seems to explain something that has confused Biblical students for ages. When Jesus rose Lazarus back up from the dead, his disciples behaved as if they had been taught that to die, as Lazarus did, would be a very profitable act for them:

> [Jesus] told them plainly, "Lazarus is dead, and for your sake I am glad I was not there, so you may believe. But let us go to him." Then Thomas (called Didymus) said to the rest of the disciples, "Let us also go, that we may die with him."
> — John 11:14-16

This scripture has never seemed to make any sense; numerous explanations have been offered for it, but none that really seemed right. But if experiencing the unconsciousness of the dead soul's reality is necessary for salvation,[1] as these Gnostic scriptures say, then this passage suddenly makes perfect sense.

- The Gnostics believed that what had to be done was to reunite the conscious and unconscious halves of the human mind:

> Jesus said to them, "When you make the two one, and when you make the inside like the outside, and the outside like the inside, and the above like the below, and when you make the male and the female one and the same, so that the male not be male nor the female female . . . then you will enter the Kingdom."
> — The Gospel of Thomas 22

---

1 Compare with Isaiah 22:14.

• Although most of the teachings contained in this Gnostic literature was lost in the Roman church's persecution, a little of their doctrine somehow managed to seep into the official canon, as in this remarkable parallel passage clearly stating that Jesus' purpose was to reunite the soul and spirit:

> For he himself [Jesus] is our peace, who has made the two one [the soul and spirit reunited] and has destroyed the barrier. . . . His purpose was to create in himself one new man out of the two, thus making peace, and in this body to reconcile both of them . . .
> — Ephesians 2:14-16

• These Gnostic scriptures have more to say about this concept, suggesting that "making the two one" was not only Jesus' purpose, but also in some fashion the key to his powers; and the same passages also suggest that this potential is available to all:

> Jesus said, "If two make peace with each other in this one house [body], they will say to the mountain, 'Move away,' and it will move away. . . . When you make the two one, you will become the sons of man, and when you say, 'Mountain, move away,' it will move away."
> — The Gospel of Thomas 48 & 106

> What the father possesses belongs to the son, and the son himself, so long as he is small, is not entrusted with what is his. But when he becomes a man his father gives him all that he possesses.
> — The Gospel of Philip 60:1-6

• The Gnostics believed that, after achieving "gnosis," uniting the soul and spirit within them, they would no longer experience death; for them, the usual splitting of the soul and spirit would no longer occur at the demise of the physical body:

> Whoever finds the interpretation of these sayings will not experience death.
> — The Gospel of Thomas 1

> The heavenly man has many more sons than the earthly man. If the sons of Adam are many, although they die, how much more the sons of the perfect man, they who do not die but are always

begotten. The father makes a son, and the son does not have the power to make a son. For he who has been begotten has not the power to beget, but the son gets brothers for himself, not sons [when one reincarnates and remembers, the new incarnation is recognized as a fellow self (brother-brother relationship), not as an earlier generation (father-son relationship)].
                                                — The Gospel of Philip 58:17-26

• The Gnostics believed they understood the warnings of the Hebrew prophecies, believing that, one day, all the dead unconscious personal-souls would come flooding back into the conscious world, and every one would have to step out of the way to allow these other selves to return:

Mary said to him, "Whom are your disciples like?" He said, "They are like children who have settled in a field [the conscious mind] which is not theirs [alone]. When the [other] owners of the field [the personal-souls of one's previous incarnations] come, they will say, 'Let us have back our field.' They [the disciples] will undress [take off the body, entering the unconscious world] in their presence in order to let them have back their field and to give it back to them."
                                                — The Gospel of Thomas 21

• By being willing at that time to abandon the physical body without fear, apprehension or shame, the Gnostics believed they would actually come face to face with Christ himself:[1]

His disciples said, "When will you become revealed to us and when shall we see you?" Jesus said, "When you disrobe without being ashamed and take up your garments [bodies] and place them under your feet like little children and tread on them. Then will you see the Son of the Living One, and you will not be afraid."
                                                — The Gospel of Thomas 37

These passages suggest that the Gnostics held a rather more sophisticated theology than has been generally believed. However, some of the scanty impressions which have trickled down through history about them—that they believed in reincarnation, followed a form of dualistic theology, and believed in magical powers—do seem to be substantiated through these Nag Hammadi scriptures. But, by comparing these ancient scriptures to the discoveries made

---

1   As also promised in Revelation 22:4.

this century with the new, modern science of psychology, we've learned more about the belief systems of these earliest Christians than we ever knew before: we've learned that their long-lost theology (which, dawning on this planet at virtually the same instant in history that Jesus did, may represent the original, purest form of Christianity) was based on the division of the human psyche.

It was, in fact, Division Theory itself.

One might argue that if not for this cache of Gnostic literature, the Roman church's campaign to erase Gnosticism from the face of the earth might have succeeded and Division Theory might never have been rediscovered. But the ideas that were the foundation of Gnosticism, however—just as all ideas which contain truth—have been rediscovered over and over again in history: here in 800 B.C. China, there in 400 B.C. India, again in the first-century-A.D. Roman Empire, and perhaps again and again in the future.

CHAPTER 9

JUDGMENT DAY

Past Lives and the Resurrection of the Dead

Hear the word of the Lord, you scoffers. . . . You boast, "We have entered into a covenant with death, with the grave we have made an agreement. When an overwhelming scourge sweeps by, it cannot touch us, for we have made a lie our refuge and falsehood our hiding place." So this is what the Sovereign Lord says: ". . . hail will sweep away your refuge, the lie, and water will overflow your hiding place. Your covenant with death will be annulled, your agreement with the grave will not stand. . . . The understanding of this message will bring sheer terror. The bed is too short to stretch out on, the blanket too narrow to wrap around you. The Lord will rise up . . . to do his work, his strange work, and perform his task, his alien task."
—Isaiah 28:14-21

If reincarnation is true, belonging to the same reality the Judeo-Christian scriptures describe, it raises a very interesting question: how would this truth affect the classic prophecy about the "raising of the dead" during Western religion's Judgment Day scenario? Biblical prophecy maintains, of course, that during Judgment Day all the world's dead will be returned to physical life. But if reincarnation is true, multiple numbers of personal-souls would belong to each living spirit; such souls would obviously be unable to return to life in separate bodies, since they would secretly share common identities. What form then would such a Universal Resurrection have to take if reincarnation is a reality?

Marrying the doctrine of reincarnation with Western religion effects a startling transformation, yielding a hybrid theology far more potent than the mere sum of its parts would suggest. As might be expected, such a union would profoundly alter the core and substance of Western religion. What might not be expected, however, are the interesting changes it produces in the interpretation of certain scriptures, pointing out, as it were, an entirely new level of meaning within those revered works.

If reincarnation did not belong in Western theology, then inserting it should decrease the level of coherent meaning within the Judeo-Christian scriptures; if it weren't meant to fit into the picture, trying to force it in should only make things more confusing. Instead, however, such an addition appears to *increase* the level of coherent meaning in these books, clarifying, in fact, many passages which previously seemed cryptic and incomprehensible. If, as Division Theory suggests, the Eastern doctrine of reincarnation is true, it requires the West to completely re-evaluate its traditional interpretations of some of the most pivotal scriptural prophecies.

One of the most obvious differences between East and West is Judeo-Christianity's fabulous collection of prophecies, predictions purported to be of great significance to all humanity. In comparison, Eastern religions are lacking in this area, counting far fewer predictions among their own exalted works.

The Western prophecies largely focus around a single event, known variously as Armageddon, Judgment Day, or The Great and Terrible Day of the Lord, when the divine plan for humanity is to be brought to a dramatic conclusion. The Christian world expects Jesus to return at that time, and the Jewish world holds similar hopes for its own long-awaited Messiah. But by far the most bizarre element of this prophecy holds that all of humanity's dead, all the way back to the beginning of time, are, somehow, to be returned to physical life during this period:

> He will destroy the shroud that enfolds all peoples, the sheet that covers all nations; he will swallow up death forever . . .
> — Isaiah 25:7-8

> . . . the bed is too short to stretch out on, the blanket too narrow to wrap around you.
> — Isaiah 28:20

During this event, these prophecies promise the "defeat of all evil," followed by an era completely devoid of misery, grief, and death, in which all humanity will have become "one with God."

This Judgment Day scenario was consistently described in the most horrible and dramatic terms by the Old Testament prophets. Throughout their many books, they returned to this topic again and again, as they repeatedly described an event with the same basic elements:

- Judgment Day was to be the dramatic conclusion of a divine plan to establish a Kingdom of Heaven on Earth.
- It was expected to put all humanity into great confusion.
- It was supposed to be a time of great testing, when only the most faithful would survive.
- It was to include the greatest human strife in history, when horrible natural and supernatural phenomena would occur.
- It was to somehow involve the raising of the dead back to physical life, to be judged and then either punished or rewarded.
- It was to be the ultimate war of good vs. evil.
- It was to result in the elimination of all evil from the face of the earth.

The Undecipherable Passages

Despite the diminishing influence of religious thought in the West, the descriptions of the Last Day as prophesied in the Bible are deeply ingrained in our culture and therefore are familiar to almost anyone in the West today; but while a general consensus exists concerning the interpretation of the more famous Judgment Day prophecies, certain others seem designed only to elicit dissent and confusion. Many lesser-known scriptural passages regarding Judgment Day seem terribly odd and confusing and don't seem to make any sense at all; and no one has been able to successfully incorporate their peculiar details into the conventional framework of Judgment Day. Although vivid descriptions of the Last Day scenario are sprinkled generously throughout the Western scriptures, the meaning of many of the specific details within these prophecies seem cryptic, almost purposely so:

> I will make boys their officials, mere children will govern them.
> — Isaiah 3:4

... And a child will lead them.
— Isaiah 11:6

The Lord himself will give you a sign: The virgin will be with child and she will give birth to a son, and will call him Immanuel. He will eat curds and honey when he knows enough to reject the wrong and choose the right. But before the boy knows enough to reject the wrong and choose the right, the land of the two kings you dread will be laid waste.
— Isaiah 7:14-16

Say to them, This is what the Lord, the God of Israel says: "Every wineskin should be filled with wine." And if they say to you, "Don't we know every wineskin should be filled with wine?" then tell them, This is what the Lord says: "I am going to fill with drunkenness all who live in this land, including the Kings who sit on David's throne, the priests, the prophets, and all those living in Jerusalem. I will smash them one against another, fathers and sons alike, declares the Lord."
— Jeremiah 12:12-14

This is what the Lord says: "Cries of fear are heard—terror, not peace. Ask and see: Can a man bear children? Then why do I see every strong man with his hands on his stomach like a woman in labor, every face turned deathly pale? How awful that day will be! None will be like it."
— Jeremiah 30:5-7

The Lord will create a new thing on earth—woman will surround man.
— Jeremiah 31:22

The people will be food for the fire; no one will spare his brother. On the right they will devour, but still be hungry; on the left they will eat, but not be satisfied. Each will feed on the flesh of his own offspring.
— Isaiah 9:19-20

Just as you drank on my holy hill, so all the nations will drink continually; they will drink and drink and be as if they had never been.
— Obadiah 16

Children as governors and leaders? A land of two kings destroyed during Jesus' childhood? Filled wineskins? Drink and cease to exist?

Forced universal drunkenness? Men bearing children? Woman surrounding man? An unquenchable cannibalistic lust for siblings and children? Although incredibly bizarre, these passages apparently refer to events which are also scheduled to occur during Judgment Day; but how they could possibly fit into that scenario has never been understood.

These truly peculiar statements and many others like them have consistently made mockeries of Man's attempts to fully decipher the West's literature of "divine revelation."

Faced with such bizarre passages, would-be interpreters have been throwing their hands up in defeat for millennia. Biblical students are always free, of course, to blame any perceived lack of interpretive vision on "divine will," falling back on the passage of Isaiah 29:10-11, where it's suggested that the full picture and meaning of these Last Day prophecies was purposely withheld from human understanding.[1] Yet, in other passages, the scriptures also insist that such matters eventually will be explained.[2]

These passages, however, are not isolated or extraneous statements at all; rather, since they are repeated over and over throughout the Judgment Day prophecies, they obviously represent some sort of previously unrecognized, fundamental themes within the greater Last Day scenario.

The Key to the Mystery Scriptures

Division Theory brings to light a textual undercurrent which runs through these Western scriptures, a hidden theme which cannot be detected unless one is already familiar with its premise: that one half of humanity's binary being reincarnates after death, while the other half is cast off into a fixed heaven-hell realm. Through the lens of this premise, many of the most bizarre and inscrutable passages in the Western scriptures seem to be instantly resolved, in turn drawing the whole enigmatic Judgment Day prophecy into sharp focus. Division Theory offers

---

1 There is an ancient tradition of the existence of deeper mystical or spiritual meaning hidden beneath the surface of the Holy Scriptures. (Howe.) For Biblical references of deeper meanings being kept out of sight, see Isaiah 8:16; Daniel 12:4,9.
2 Jeremiah 23:20; Habakkuk 2:3.

explanations for how each of the seemingly nonsensical passages listed above could actually make perfect sense, showing them to be not merely plausible, nor merely logical, but, if the Division Premise is correct, literally inevitable events in the scenario's unfolding.

Bizarre Prophetic Themes

Many of these cryptic themes, making no sense whatsoever within the conventional vision of Judgment Day, recur throughout Western scriptures. These themes include: a winepress;[1] drunkenness;[2] cannibalism of neighbors, family, offspring, and even self;[3] violation of the temple;[4] a wall being built, standing, and being broken down again;[5] exiles going into exile through a hole in a wall[6] and prisoners coming out of confinement through a break in a wall;[7] shame being revealed;[8] an army of locusts attacking, invading, and consuming people;[9] all humanity being stricken by madness;[10] widespread multiple possession by evil spirits;[11] melting of

---

1 On the theme of the winepress, see Isaiah 63:3; Lamentations 1:15; Revelation 14:19-20, 19:21.

2 On the theme of drunkenness, see Isaiah 19:14, 51:21, 63:6; Jeremiah 48:26, 51:7,37-39, 57; Lamentations 4:21; Ezekiel 23:32-34; Obadiah 1:16; Nahum 1:10, 3:11; Habakkuk 2:16; Zechariah 9:15; Revelation 18:2-3.

3 On the theme of cannibalism, see Isaiah 9:19-21, 49:26; Jeremiah 5:17, 19:9; Lamentations 2:20, 4:10; Ezekiel 5:10; Micah 3:2-3; Proverbs 1:10-19.

4 On the theme of the violation of the Temple, see Jeremiah 5:19, 51:51; Ezekiel 7:24, 9:7, 24:21; Daniel 9:26-27, 12:11-12; Micah 4:11; Matthew 24:15.

5 On the theme of building and tearing down a wall, see Isaiah 25:4, 30:12-13; Jeremiah 49:27; Amos 7:7; Ezekiel 13:5, 10-15.

6 On the theme of exiles going into exile through a hole in a wall, see Ezekiel 8:7-10, 12:5-12.

7 On the theme of prisoners coming out of confinement through a hole in a wall, see Jeremiah 51:44-45.

8 On the theme of shame being revealed, see Isaiah 47:2-3; Jeremiah 13:26, 48:37; Ezekiel 16:37; Hosea 7:1; Micah 1:11; Nahum 3:5.

9 On the theme of locusts attacking men, see Isaiah 33:4, 40:22; Jeremiah 51:14; Joel 1:2-4, 2:25; Amos 7:1.

10 On the theme of all mankind being struck by madness, see Isaiah 29:9; Jeremiah 51:7; Zechariah 12:4, 14:12; Deuteronomy 28:26; 2 Thessalonians 2:11; Revelation 18:2-3.

11 On the theme of universal multiple possessions by evil spirits, see Isaiah 4:1, 16:3-4; Jeremiah 30:6, 51:14; Ezekiel 9:7, 22:23; Matthew 12:39-45, 23:27.

hearts;[1] release of captives and prisoners;[2] the universal experience of inner pain "like a woman in labor";[3] shaving of heads and beards;[4] the saving and losing of people's personal "vines and fig trees";[5] and, last but not least, a heavenly army not being called to "come down from heaven," but rather to "wake up."[6]

Such bizarre themes seem completely out of place within the conventional interpretation of the Judgment Day prophecies,[7] a popular but secular interpretation which seems to focus more on political concerns than spiritual ones. This conventional vision tends to revolve around the political interactions of various leaders, nations, and armies, all of which group together against the political state of Israel. Jesus then returns, still wearing his A.D. 33 body, and, leading his army out of the sky, triumphantly defeats the evil earth army.

Variations on themes such as this are rampant in the West today, and while they are not entirely without scriptural support,[8] they invariably have no ready explanation for the myriad references to cannibalism, the wall, the drunkenness, the locust army, or any of the other peculiar recurring themes found in these scriptures. The persistence of these themes within the Judgment Day prophecies demands that they also be recognized as fundamental, if indeed not pivotal, elements within the overall scenario.

---

1   On the theme of hearts melting, see Isaiah 13:7; Ezekiel 21:7.
2   On the theme of the release of captives and prisoners, see Isaiah 42:7, 49:9, 61:1; Zechariah 9:11.
3   On the universal experience of labor-like pain, see Isaiah 13:8, 21:3, 26:18, 33:14; Jeremiah 4:19, 6:24, 13:21, 49:24, 50:43; Hosea 13:13; Psalm 48:5-6.
4   On the theme of shaving heads and beards, see Isaiah 7:20, 15:2; Jeremiah 41:5, 48:37; Ezekiel 7:18.
5   On the theme of personal vines and fig trees, see Isaiah 36:16; Jeremiah 5:17, 8:13; Micah 4:4; Zechariah 3:10.
6   On the theme of waking up, see Isaiah 26:19, 51:9,17, 52:1; Daniel 12:2; Joel 1:5; Ephesians 5:14.
7   Hal Lindsey, *The Late Great Planet Earth* (New York: Zondervan Publishing House, 1979), 32-33, 48-60.
8   See Ezekiel 38, 39.

The Raising of the Dead

This is the key. The Universal Resurrection of the dead scheduled to occur during Judgment Day[1] gives Division Theory the ability to distill sense from all those cryptic passages. From the perspective of Division Theory, the raising of people from the dead becomes a much more plausible, comprehensible, and significant phenomenon because, in order to come back to life, all those long-dead unconscious personal-souls would have to be re-united with their original conscious spirits. Those living spirits, of course, might have since reincarnated hundreds, perhaps even thousands, of times and thus would have produced hundreds or even thousands of other personal-souls, all of which would then also be trying to reunite with that same original living spirit. There would suddenly be a very large number of unconscious personal-souls all trying to reconnect to a single, suddenly very bewildered conscious spirit, in each and every person alive on earth.

From the perspective of Division Theory, it is precisely such an event that the Bible describes in its Judgment Day prophecies,[2] covering it in stunning, meticulous detail, showing every reaction from each group of participants: Christ, the living, the personal-souls from hell, and the personal-souls from heaven.

If the premise of Division Theory is correct, and all the world's dead personal-souls were to simultaneously rise, mentally resurfacing into their own reincarnated selves, bringing with them all their separate identities and memories, a horrible inner psychological battle would begin in each living person. All of those reawakened personal-souls would desperately struggle against one another as each sought to regain its control over the mind and body, each demanding complete, unconditional access to the individual's entire supply of consciousness and strength. A terrible psychological war would begin within each living person, and this insane battle would break out inside every living person on the planet at the same time.

---

1   On the theme of raising from the dead, see Isaiah 25:7-8, 26:19,21, 28:15-20, 33:1, 41:1,4, 42:7, 61:1; Jeremiah 5:15-16, 8:4, 51:44,49; Ezekiel 16:53-55, 37:12-14; Daniel 12:2; Hosea 13:14; John 5:26-29.

2   The method of interpretation of the Holy Scriptures is not as hard and dry as some would like to portray it. No less a religious personage than Martin Luther once said, "*I acknowledge no fixed rules for the interpretations of the Word of God.*" —*An Open Letter to Pope Leo X*, as quoted by Seldes in *The Great Thoughts*, 253.

As bizarre as such a scenario might seem, it would explain a number of those mysterious prophetic themes:

- The dead personal-souls, upon reawakening, would become drunk and giddy with life after having been "dry" so long.
- Each person in whom this in-rush of personal-souls was occurring would effectively go mad, being suddenly possessed by multiple personalities.
- People would vividly experience within their bodies and minds the agony which had been stored up and amplified while all their dead personal-souls had been in hell.
- The dead personal-souls would be able to return only after the barrier between the conscious and unconscious, the wall, had somehow been either removed or destroyed.
- Hundreds or perhaps even thousands of invading dead personal-souls would suddenly surface in each living person's mind, swarming around inside their psyches like locusts, consuming from all sides and leaving nothing to remain.
- The personal-souls reawakening into the conscious living world would be those "prisoners and exiles" who were to be rescued.
- The theme of the cannibalism of siblings and offspring would refer to the bizarre fact that the resurfaced personal-souls, who would be consuming and draining off the life energy of the conscious spirit, would be the old incarnations, the spiritual ancestors, of the living people in whose bodies and minds they would be reawakening. These life-starved personal-souls, once they found life available again, would attack and consume it ravenously, ruthlessly, and it wouldn't make a shred of difference to them that they were eating away the life of their own spiritual offspring, their own reincarnated selves. They would stop at nothing to seize life once they saw it again within their reach. The prophecies describe these reawakening personal-souls as an invading army, the "most ruthless of all nations."[1] Such terminology seems particularly appropriate, since these long-lost personal-souls, truly knowing what it means to be dead, would be in a position where it's either them or us.

When considered from the fresh perspective of Division Theory, the meaning of these themes and others become both

---

1   Ezekiel 28:7.

easily recognizable and highly relevant. In fact, testing Division Theory by applying it to the Judgment Day prophecies produces truly phenomenal results. Not only do many of the Bible's bizarre themes and cryptic passages instantly resolve into obvious sense, but they also all fit gracefully together, producing a narrative which is not only coherent and logical, but indeed, perhaps for the first time in the history of Western religion, a Judgment Day narrative which is theoretically plausible, because for the first time it is founded in scientific realities with which we are familiar.

On the Return of the Souls

As the dead were raised, they would bring with them all their separate identities and memories, and also the agony of hell. As souls suddenly reconnected with their lost conscious spirits, in whichever particular incarnations they happened to be at that moment in time, all those then living on the earth would suddenly become completely overwhelmed by the countless number of personalities and forgotten memories of previous lives that would be simultaneously surfacing within each of their minds.[1] The pain that each of these souls had been suffering in hell would also still be inside them and would also surface into conscious awareness along with them:

> At this my body is racked with pain, pangs seize me, like those of a woman in labor; I am staggered by what I hear, I am bewildered by what I see. My heart falters, fear makes me tremble; the twilight I longed for [death, unconsciousness] has become a horror to me. They set the tables, they spread the rugs, they eat, they drink!
> — Isaiah 21:3-5

> Be stunned and amazed, blind yourself and be sightless; be drunk, but not from wine, stagger, but not from beer.
> — Isaiah 29:9

> This is what the Lord, the God of Israel, said to me: "Take from my hand this cup filled with the wine of my wrath and make all the nations drink it. When they drink it, they will stagger and go mad."
> — Jeremiah 25:15-16

---

1 See Isaiah 29:9, 49:21; Jeremiah 30:6; Joel 1:2-4.

If the wall separating the conscious world from the unconscious world were somehow suddenly severed, all of humanity's dead personal-souls, whether trapped in hell or waiting in heaven, would be set free once again on the earth:[1]

> The sea will rise over Babylon [the land of the unconscious dead] . . . and make him spew out what he has swallowed . . . the wall of Babylon will fall. Come out of her, my people! Babylon must fall because of Israel's slain, just as the slain in all the earth have fallen because of Babylon. Babylon's thick wall will be leveled.
> — Jeremiah 51:42,44,49,58

The sudden release of the personal-souls imprisoned by death would be like an invading army of countless locusts, buzzing around and within every human mind:

> The Lord Almighty has sworn by Himself: "I will surely fill you with men, as with a swarm of locusts, and they will shout in triumph over you."
> — Jeremiah 51:14

> Your plunder, O nations, is harvested as by young locusts; like a swarm of locusts men pounce on it.
> — Isaiah 33:4

> When he opened the Abyss, smoke rose from it like the smoke from a gigantic furnace . . . and out of the smoke locusts came down upon the earth . . . they were told to harm only those people who did not have the seal of God on their foreheads. . . . During those days men will seek death, but will not find it.
> —Revelation 9:2-4,6

People will wonder where all these other selves came from and will ache to be rid of them and their pain:

> We were with child, we writhed in pain, but we gave birth to wind . . . we have not given birth to people of the world.
> — Isaiah 26:18

> Can a man bear children?
> — Jeremiah 30:6

---

1 On the captives being released from subconscious prisons, see also Zechariah 9:11; Psalm 126:1.

The least of you will become a thousand.
— Isaiah 60:22

People would feel violated in the worst possible way, for their very inner minds and bodies would have been attacked, overrun, and occupied:

> We are disgraced . . . and shame covers our faces, because foreigners have entered the holy places of the Lord's house [the body, which Jesus identified as the true "Temple of the Lord"].
> — Jeremiah 51:51

> This is what the Sovereign Lord says: "I am about to desecrate my sanctuary—the stronghold in which you take pride, the delight of your eyes, the object of your affection [the human body]."
> — Ezekiel 24:20

The living would experience exactly what the personal-souls felt, all the agony of their inner hells:

> Oh, my anguish, my anguish! I writhe in pain. Oh, the agony of my heart! My heart pounds within me, I cannot keep silent. For I have heard the sound of the trumpet.
> — Jeremiah 4:19

> The sinners . . . are terrified; trembling grips the godless: "Who of us can dwell with the [inner] consuming fire? Who of us can dwell with [inner] everlasting burning?"
> — Isaiah 33:14

After being dead and cut off from life for so long, the released personal-souls, like empty cups eager to be filled, or like starving men rushing toward water, would race toward the light of consciousness, quickly becoming intoxicated with life stolen from the living. Having little faith in promises of salvation, such evil personal-souls would believe this was their only chance to regain life and would jump at it eagerly.

> Say to them, "This is what the Lord, the God of Israel, says: Every wineskin [soul] should be filled with wine [the living spirit]." And if they say to you, "Don't we know that every wineskin should be filled with wine?" then tell them, "This is what the Lord says: I am going to fill with drunkenness all who

live in this land. And I will smash them one against the other, fathers and sons alike . . ."
— Jeremiah 13:12-14

You will drink your sister's cup ["sister" is a symbol for one's feminine "other half," the soul], a cup large and deep: it will bring scorn and derision, for it holds so much. You will be filled with drunkenness and sorrow, the cup of ruin and desolation, the cup of your sister . . . you will drink it and drain it dry . . .
— Ezekiel 23:32-34

Babylon [the unconscious realm of the dead] will be a heap of ruins, a place where no one lives. Her people all roar like young lions. But while they are aroused, I will set a feast for them, and make them drunk, so that they shout with laughter. . . . I will punish Bel in Babylon, and make him spew out what he has swallowed. . . . Come out of him, my people!
— Jeremiah 51:37-39,44-45

The souls released from the realm of death would feast on the very life-force of the living, feasting on their own spiritual off-spring, their own reincarnated selves:

I will make your oppressors eat their own flesh; they will be drunk on their own blood, as with wine . . .
— Isaiah 49:26

I will make them eat the flesh of their own sons and daughters, and they will eat one another's flesh during the siege imposed on them by the enemies who seek their lives.
— Jeremiah 19:9

The unconscious personal-souls risen from hell would be able to completely surround, submerge, and overcome people's conscious spirits and will power:

The Lord will create a new thing on earth—woman [the unconscious] will surround man [the conscious].
— Jeremiah 31:22

And I saw a beast coming out of the sea [the unconscious]. . . . One of the heads of the beast seemed to have a fatal wound, but the fatal wound had been healed [that which had once been dead had

since come back to life]. . . . He was given power to make war
against the saints and to overcome them.
                    —Revelation 13:1,3,7

The Biblical passages suggest that all the souls of the dead from
the beginning of time would be released from their unconscious
captivity to rejoin their conscious living spirits,[1] their other halves
still alive on earth, regardless of whether they were from heaven
or hell:

> No one will get away, none will escape. Though they dig down
> to the depths of the grave, from here my hand will take them.
> Though they climb up to the heavens, from there I will bring
> them down.
>   — Amos 9:1-2

> They [the conscious spirit and unconscious soul] will never again
> be two nations or be divided into two kingdoms.
>   — Ezekiel 37:22

The world of the unconscious would awaken; life would re-
enter the dead, and the dead would subdue the living:

> The days are coming when the reaper [death] will be overtaken by
> the plowman [life], and the planter [consciousness] by the one
> treading grapes [unconsciousness].
>   — Amos 9:13

The first to break through the walls of death, Jesus is portrayed
as leading an army of dead personal-souls back out through the
same opening, into the world of the living:

> None of these [dead souls] will be missing, not one will lack her
> mate [her conscious half]. For it is his [God's] mouth that has given
> the order, and his spirit will gather them together.
>   — Isaiah 34:16

> I am planning disaster against these people, from which you
> cannot save yourselves. . . . One who breaks open the way will
> go up before them; they will break through the gate [between

---

1 On the souls returning to their original spirits, see Isaiah 13:14; Jeremiah
   5:16.

the conscious and the unconscious] and go out. The king will pass
through before them, the Lord at their head.
— Micah 2:3,13

The unconscious is portrayed as a river that will overflow its
banks, flooding into the conscious world:

Because this people has rejected the gently flowing waters of
Shiloah [the unconscious Holy Ghost] . . . the Lord is about to
bring against them the mighty flood waters of the River [the entire
unconscious]. . . . It will overflow all its channels, run over all its
banks and sweep on into [the conscious world], swirling over it,
passing through it, and reaching up to the neck. Its outspread
wings will cover the breadth of your land, O Immanuel! Raise the
war cry, you nations, and be shattered!
— Isaiah 7:6-8

Hail will sweep away your refuge, the lie, and water will overflow
your hiding place.
— Isaiah 28:17

The Sequence of the Return

The Biblical prophecies suggest that this opening of the vaults
of the unconscious, releasing all those personal-souls imprisoned
there, would, instead of happening all at once, occur in three
distinct stages:

On that day, they shall raise a lament three times told, saying, "We
are utterly despoiled—the property [bodies] of the Lord's people
changes hands. He takes it from me! He assigns our fields to
traitors!"
— Micah 2:4 NEB

The prophecies describe this three-phase release in various
other ways, as three woes,[1] a sword striking three times,[2] hair being
shaved and divided into three portions, and people being separated into three groups which would each be dealt with differently
during Judgment Day.[3]

---

1   Revelation 8:13.
2   Ezekiel 21:14.
3   Ezekiel 5:1-12.

The First Phase: The Locusts

The first two emissions from the unconscious would come from hell. The first emission would release hell's souls, and the second would release something even more evil. The first emission would seem like a mental invasion of locusts:

> And I saw a star that had fallen from the sky to the earth. The star was given the key to the shaft of the Abyss. When he opened the Abyss, smoke rose from it like the smoke from a gigantic furnace. . . . And out of the smoke locusts came down upon the earth and were given power. . . . They were told . . . to harm . . . people. . . . They were not given power to kill them, but only to torture them . . .
> — Revelation 9:1-5

The beginning of this period, when the dead would first begin to be felt and heard, would be quiet and subtle; people would barely perceive their presence within:

> . . . you will speak out of the ground; your speech will mumble out of the dust. Your voice will come ghostlike from the earth; out of the dust your speech will whisper.
> — Isaiah 29:4

All the living would be completely amazed that these past selves were raising back into consciousness, who had been long dead and thought to exist no longer:

> And I saw a [many-headed] beast coming out of the sea [out of the unconscious]. . . . the beast seemed to have a fatal wound, but the fatal wound had been healed [the beast had returned from the dead]. The whole world was astonished and followed the beast.
> — Revelation 13:1-3

Seeming to anticipate today's New Age fascination with spiritual "channeling," these prophecies foresee the people of the world all seeking to bring forth these personal-souls from the unconscious realms, looking forward to meeting their former selves. People would waste no time in bringing up these old personal-souls, eager to find out about their various past lives, along with any other mysterious, exciting, or otherwise entertaining revelations these apparently immortal personal-souls might be able to offer:

> Tell us what the former things were, so we may consider them and know their final outcome. Or declare to us the things to come, tell us what the future holds, so we may know that you are gods. Do something, whether good or bad, so that we will be dismayed and filled with fear.
> — Isaiah 41:22-23

The Second Phase: Hell

Following these developments, the second emission from the unconscious would occur. As all the reawakened souls from hell became stronger and more numerous throughout the world, more and more people would go completely mad, having been taken over by swarming hordes of famished unfamiliar other selves bubbling up from inside their own minds. However, as humanity raised up these old souls from hell, it would find that something else had also risen up along with them—the central omnipotent authority that had dominated these dead souls while they were in their unconscious prison. In the Last Day, according to Division Theory's perspective on these prophecies, the living would become possessed not only by the reawakened souls from hell, but also, through them, by the "ruler" of hell as well. Humanity would thus become possessed by pure evil.[1] So, while the first phase would have seen the dead emerging back into the real world, the second would see the full awakening of evil in humanity's collective psyche.

At first, this underlying influence would be able to only partially function through the risen dead souls, still unable to fully control them and operate through them. Thus, at first, its power to do harm to the living through the risen dead would remain limited:

> They [the risen dead] were not given power to kill them, but only to torture them . . .
> — Revelation 9:5

---

1 Evil which, through the natural effects of the unconscious, had coalesced and congealed inside these dead souls during their unconscious imprisonment and had then carefully remained hidden inside them as they rose back up to living consciousness. See Appendix A: Fruit of the Division.

But later, as it gained more strength, this universal evil psychic influence would boldly command all to call up their past selves. Those who refused this command would effectively be put to death, being forced down into the unconscious themselves, utterly submerged out of conscious reality altogether:

> Then I saw another beast coming up out of the earth [out of the grave]. . . . He exercised all the authority of the first beast on its behalf, and made the earth and its inhabitants worship the first beast, whose fatal wound had been healed . . . he deceived the inhabitants of the earth. He ordered them to make a [mental] image in honor of the beast who was wounded by the sword and yet lived [instructing people to reawaken their past souls by concentrating upon mental images of them]. He had the power to bring this image of the first beast fully to life, so that it could speak [to fully awaken and re-animate the old souls, thus allowing them to speak and act once more], and cause all who refused to worship the beast to be killed.
> — Revelation 13:11-12,14-15

> The sixth angel poured out his bowl on the great River Euphrates [the unconscious], and its water was dried up [its contents, the souls, were let out] to prepare the way for the kings of the East [the rulers of hell]. Then I saw . . . spirits of demons . . . go out to the kings of the whole world . . .
> — Revelation 16:12-14

Upon discovering that these old personal-souls, when reawakened, were fiendishly evil and finding out that, once begun, the process of bringing those souls back to life would then automatically continue by itself, humanity would find itself betrayed from within, possessed by multitudes of former selves who then refused to give the body back:

> Look at the nations and watch—and be utterly amazed. For I am going to do something in your days that you would not believe, even if you were told. I am raising up the Babylonians [the occupants of hell], that ruthless and impetuous people, who sweep across the whole earth to seize dwelling places [bodies] not their own.
> — Habakkuk 1:5-6

These passages describe how those unfortunates foolish enough to willingly bring up their old dead personal-souls would then find that they had been betrayed, losing all control over their own minds and bodies. Once this happened, they would find themselves in a living death, trapped in a body and mind they could no longer control, unable to do anything except scream silently within themselves:[1]

> I waste away, I waste away! Woe to me! The treacherous betray!
> With treachery the treacherous betray!
> — Isaiah 24:16

Review of the Judgment Day Scenario

This vision of multiple possession during Judgment Day is certainly an unfamiliar picture to modern Western religion, but perhaps it shouldn't be. Jesus testified about the coming day when the dead would rise up from within people's own minds; Christ characterized Judgment Day as a time when the living would be invaded by large groups of "unclean spirits":

> A wicked and adulterous generation asks for a miraculous sign! But none will be given it except the sign of Jonah. For as Jonah was three days and nights in the belly of a fish, so the Son of Man will be three days and three nights in the heart of the earth.
> — Matthew 12:39-40

These passages have long been recognized as referring to Jesus' own Resurrection. But he may have also been discussing resurrection in general, because the dialogue that directly follows in this discourse clearly refers to the events of the Last Day, when all the generations of the dead would rise back up as well:

> The men of Nineveh will stand up [rise up from the dead] at the judgment [along] with this generation and condemn it.
> — Matthew 12:41

Immediately after this clue that he was, indeed, speaking of the Last Day scenario, Christ continued his dialogue, offering additional details on the actual events scheduled to occur during Judgment Day's Universal Resurrection:

---

1 See also Jeremiah 4:31; Lamentations 5:2; Isaiah 19:4; Matthew 24:9.

> When an unclean spirit comes out of a man [as happens
> naturally at death], it goes through arid places [hell] seeking
> rest and does not find it. Then it says, "I will return to the house
> [the person] I left." When it arrives, it . . . goes and takes with
> it seven other spirits more wicked than itself, and they go and
> live there. And the final condition of that man is worse than the
> first. That is how it will be with this wicked generation [during
> Judgment Day].
> — Matthew 12:43-45

In a different passage, Jesus offers still another confirmation
that people's old dead personal-souls still exist somewhere inside
them:

> Woe to you. . . . You are like whitewashed tombs, which look
> beautiful on the outside but on the inside are full of dead men's
> bones and everything unclean."[1]
> — Matthew 23:27

The Last Chance

During the horrors of the first two phases, many would probably call on their Maker, begging for salvation. And, according to
the perspective of Division Theory, they would be granted just
such a chance. Once the personal-souls from hell were brought
back to consciousness, reconnected with their original living spirits, they would be provided with an invaluable opportunity that
could only be characterized as the grace of God. Reawakening
these long-dead personal-souls would serve a profoundly noble
and loving purpose; in being raised, all these long-dead personal-
souls would be given, for one last precious time, the opportunity
to make new decisions, to change their minds, and thus an opportunity to turn to God and be saved. The same promise was offered
to everyone: "All who call upon the name of the Lord will be
saved"[2]; but, once dead, all the lost personal-souls who hadn't been

---

1 Although this passage is, on its surface, a diatribe on hypocrisy, in it Jesus
  compares living people (specifically the innerly divided) to innocent-looking
  containers concealing the remains of the dead. Any such statement by Jesus
  is of interest to the student of Division Theory; since Jesus' mission and
  message so profoundly revolved around the issue of death, it is highly doubtful
  that he would have used any death imagery lightly.
2 Joel 2:32.

willing to call on their Maker while alive were made constitutionally incapable of changing their minds to call on Him then. However, upon reuniting with their conscious spirits, these personal-souls would once again possess the conscious mind's capacity of free will, and would thus no longer be the unwilling slaves of evil, but could instead choose to repent and turn to God. So, from the perspective of Division Theory, the reason for raising up the evil dead is so they would receive one last chance to reconsider God's offer; and, once conscious again, many souls probably would then cry out in their distress and pain, begging for salvation from the Great Immortal God:

> "In those days, at that time," declares the Lord, "the people of Israel and Judah together [soul and spirit reunited] will go in tears to seek the Lord their God. They will ask the way to Zion and turn their faces toward it."
> — Jeremiah 50:4-5

Unfortunately, the baser pleasures that would also come with receiving conscious life again would probably blind many of the reawakened dead to this greater gift of free will, and multitudes would probably blindly forfeit this precious last chance to "See with their eyes, and hear with their ears, and understand with their hearts, and turn, and be healed."[1]

The Third Phase: Heaven

From the perspective of Division Theory, the final confrontation does not really seem like an attack at all, although the personal-souls still loyal to hell would be likely to see it that way.[2] When the third and final unconscious emission, coming from heaven, entered the conscious world, all the storehouse of heaven would be completely emptied, and all of its personal-souls would leave there to return to the world of living earthly consciousness:

> When he opened the seventh seal, there was silence in heaven . . .
> — Revelation 8:1

---

1   Isaiah 6:10.
2   Proverbs 28:1.

Once the heavenly personal-souls, carrying the Holy Ghost within them, leave heaven to re-enter the conscious world,[1] then the hellish ones, who would have been having such a good time in the physical world again, would suddenly discover that they couldn't tolerate the presence of these new intruders from heaven.[2] Their very proximity would cause the hellish personal-souls excruciating pain, like "a woman in labor."[3] The personal-souls from hell would then face an unpleasant choice[4]—either returning forever back into the unconscious world or literally burning into nothingness from the divine radiance of the Holy Ghost within each of the newest returning personal-souls.

The divine army would be awakened;[5] the personal-souls waiting in heaven would be called to leave the realm of the unconscious[6] to return and rejoin their living spirits:

> Depart, depart, go out from there! Touch no unclean thing! Come out of it and be pure, you who carry the vessels [the Holy Ghost] of the Lord. But you will not go in haste or in flight; for the Lord will go before you; the God of Israel will be your rear guard.
> — Isaiah 52:11-12

> Awake, awake! Clothe yourself [re-enter your bodies] with strength, O arm of the Lord; awake, as in days gone by [when you lived before], as in generations of old.
> — Isaiah 51:9

The end would come like a tidal wave;[7] just as when all the water flows out from the shore for a brief moment only to then suddenly return in a gigantic wave, so too the personal-souls faithful to the Holy Ghost would briefly leave during the rapture,[8] only to be

---

1   Ephesians 5:14.
2   Psalm 5:4-5.
3   The souls who have "transplanted themselves" into the conscious world from the subconscious will experience great pain when they are approached by God's presence (see Isaiah 17:10-11).
4   See Jeremiah 21:8.
5   For other passages on Jesus coming to reawaken his church from their dispersion in the subconscious realms, see The Song of Songs 2:8-13; Isaiah 52:1, 60:1.
6   See also Isaiah 48:20, 49:9; Jeremiah 50:8, 51:6,45; Hosea 11:10; Revelation 18:4.
7   Isaiah 8:6-9.
8   See Appendix B: Rapture by Death.

multiplied a thousandfold[1] upon their return, having been increased by all the others who'd also been waiting in heaven for that same ultimate moment:

> The end will come like a flood.
> — Daniel 9:26

The heavenly personal-souls would then awake, returning to full consciousness from their long stays in their unconscious heaven:[2]

> This is what the Lord Almighty, the God of Israel says: "When I bring them back from captivity, the people ... will once again use these words: ... 'At this [God's call], I awoke and looked around. My sleep had been pleasant to me.'"
> — Jeremiah 31:23-26

> The ransomed of the Lord will return. They will enter Zion [the conscious world] singing; everlasting joy will crown their heads. Gladness and joy will overtake them, and sorrow and sighing will flee away.
> — Isaiah 35:10

As soon as heaven's personal-souls re-emerged into consciousness, the hellish ones would flee back into the unconscious. Unable to tolerate co-existence with the Holy Ghost, they would voluntarily abandon their feasts of the conscious life, beating a hasty retreat back to the darkness:[3]

> A thousand will flee at the threat of one, at the threat of five you will all flee away.
> — Isaiah 30:17

> Therefore this is what the Sovereign Lord says: "My servants will eat, but you will go hungry; my servants will drink, but you will go thirsty; my servants will rejoice, but you will be put to shame."
> — Isaiah 65:13

---

1 Isaiah 60:22.
2 For other passages on the awakening of the church from the subconscious realms, see Psalm 73:20, 126:1; Isaiah 29:7-8; Jeremiah 31:21.
3 See also Psalm 9:17; Isaiah 17:12-14, 22:3-4, 29:7-8, 47:5; Joel 2:20; Nahum 1:8; 2 Thessalonians 1:9; 2 Peter 2:17.

The wicked dead would face an unpleasant choice: either voluntarily abandon their claims to the conscious spirit and return to unconsciousness, or be utterly destroyed:

> This is what the Lord . . . says [to the evil personal-souls]: "I am about to turn against you the weapons of war that are in your hands [the use of the unconscious as a weapon] . . . and I will gather them [those heavenly personal-souls still left in the unconscious] inside this city [the living conscious body]. . . . See, I am setting before you the way of life and the way of death. Whoever stays in this city [body] will die . . ."
> — Jeremiah 21:4,9-10

The scriptures point out that the wicked dead would never have a chance, as this entire scenario had all been planned right from the beginning, and that God would make sure that the evil personal-souls would all return to hell:

> The Virgin Daughter of Zion [the souls of heaven] despises and mocks you . . . toss[ing] her head as you flee . . . you have said, . . . "I have ascended the heights . . . the utmost heights [of full consciousness] . . . I have dug wells in foreign lands [other's bodies] . . ." Have you not heard it? Long ago I ordained it. In days of old I planned it; now I have brought it to pass. . . . Because you rage against me and because your insolence has reached my ears, I will put my hook in your mouth, and I will make you return by the way you came.
> — Isaiah 37:22-29

This extreme judgment, worse than death, would condemn the evil dead to an eternal unconscious existence, cut off forever from conscious life, with no further chances of salvation:[1]

> Do not weep for the dead, or mourn his loss [for they will get a second chance], rather, weep bitterly for him who is [permanently] exiled [into the unconscious], because he will never return nor see his native land again.
> — Jeremiah 22:10

---

1   See also Psalm 5:10, 9:5-6; Isaiah 41:11-12, 48:18-19; Jeremiah 8:3,13, 30:16; Hosea 9:2, 13:3; Joel 1:10.

They will be punished with everlasting destruction [permanent
exile from the living spirit] and shut out from the presence of the
Lord and from the majesty of his power . . .
— 2 Thessalonians 1:9

Takers of the Last Chance

The raising of the evil dead would have a purpose, according to
Division Theory: so that they could be provided one last chance for
salvation. Once raised, they could then take God up on His ever-present offer, that "All who call on the name of the Lord will be saved."
However, the perspective of Division Theory on these prophecies
indicates that God offers some very peculiar instructions to those who
would take Him up on this offer, instructions requiring, perhaps not
so surprisingly, nothing less than an ultimate act of faith. God's
instructions to them seem to be to simply allow the rest of the clamoring
reawakened masses to push them back down into the unconscious
realm of death once more.[1] If only they restrain their natural instinct
to fight for survival by entering the fray,[2] these prophecies suggest, if
only they can keep from desperately fighting to stay "above surface"
mentally, they will be instantly pushed down by all the others also
struggling for consciousness and life. As Gandhi understood, the way
of heaven is always the way of nonviolence, even if it means giving up
everything dear and precious:

> I tell you, do not resist evil. If someone strikes you on the right
> check, turn to him the left also. And if someone wants to sue you
> and take your tunic, let him have your cloak as well. If someone
> forces you to go one mile, go with him two miles. Give to the one
> who asks of you, and do not turn away from the one who wants to
> borrow from you.
> — Matthew 5:39-42

Once a personal-soul rose up, these prophecies suggest, and
then acknowledged and called on God, it could resubmerge and

---

1   On the raised dead who choose Christ and then voluntarily return to the
    subconscious realms, see Ecclesiastes 4:11; Micah 4:9; I John 3:16;
    Revelation 2:10-11, 7:9-14.
2   *"We are more wicked together than separately. If you are forced to be in a crowd,
    then most of all you should withdraw into your self."* —Seneca the Younger,
    Eqistolae Morales, as quoted by Seldes in *The Great Thoughts,* 376.

safely wait in the unconscious realms until the horrors of Judgment Day were over:

> Go, my people, enter your rooms and shut the doors behind you; hide yourselves for a little while until his wrath has passed by.[1]
> — Isaiah 26:20

This would be an ultimate act both of repentance and of good will, giving up one's own life for others, and would be rewarded as an act of faith:

> If you spend yourself in behalf of the hungry, and satisfy the needs of the oppressed, then your light will shine in the darkness, and your night will become like the noonday.
> — Isaiah 58:10

> Blessed are the meek, for they will inherit the earth.
> — Matthew 5:5

> In repentance and rest is your salvation, in quietness and trust is your strength.
> — Isaiah 30:15

These scriptures contain repeated suggestions that such a voluntary descent into death, the same sacrifice Jesus made, would be required of all people:[2]

> [Jesus said] . . . you will drink the cup I drink and be baptized with the baptism I am baptized with.
> — Mark 10:39

> Whoever finds his life [as when they are raised from the dead], will lose it, and whoever loses his life for my sake will find it.
> — Matthew 10:39

---

1 Notice how this reference in Isaiah, written long after the Egyptian exile, seems to predict a second Passover.

2 For other indications that God will require everyone to undergo this baptism, this immersion, into the subconscious, see Isaiah 30:15, 50:10, 57:1-2; Joel 1:14; Matthew 16:25, 20:23, 24:9; Mark 8:34-45, 10:39; Luke 17:33; John 11:25-26, 12:25-26, 15:13; Acts 9:16; I Peter 5:10; I John 3:16; I Timothy 3:12; I Corinthians 15:22.

> If anyone would come after me, he must deny himself and take up
> his cross and follow me. For whoever wants to save his life will lose
> it, but whoever loses his life for me will find it.
> — Matthew 16:24

The cross Jesus had to bear was the voluntary death; he died to help the rest of us. But he emphasized over and over again that anyone who wanted to enjoy the benefits his sacrifice gained would have to follow him and take up his cross. The earliest Christian martyrs believed this even included taking up the cross of voluntary death. But Jesus neither chose nor preached intentional self-destruction. What Jesus did promote was the selfless giving of oneself for the ideals of love and integrity; and he stated quite clearly that this path needed to be walked to the very end—to death itself, if necessary. As he did, so must we all; this was the bottom line of his statement for the world.

How many today are willing to walk this path of love to its bitter end? Perhaps many would like to think they would if they had to, but most are grateful, and fairly confident, that they'll never be faced with such a decision. According to Division Theory, however, we'll all have to. We'll all be forced to, ultimately. Even those already dead, who have not yet made this voluntary passage from life to death, would be resurrected just to have the chance to volunteer for it!

In the land of the dead, lost personal-souls would have been waiting endless ages with but one thing on their shriveled little minds: returning to life. In their grinding misery they would ask one question endlessly: "When? When will we finally be released from this eternal night of the unconscious?"

When Jesus descended into that pit and preached to those there, he brought his message of hope, but mixed with this was also a warning: "You'll get to come out, but you will have to go back in again." They would rise again, he told them, but following this would come yet another stay in the pit. He further emphasized that they could ask all they wanted, but when the time came and they rose back to life, they would still have to return to the depths once more, at least temporarily:

> Someone calls to me from Seir, "Watchman, what is left of the
> night? Watchman, what is left of the night?" The watchman

replies, "Morning is coming, but also the night. If you would ask, then ask; and come back yet again."
— Isaiah 21:11-12

Knowing this final test was coming was permitted; knowing about it wouldn't keep it from coming, and they'd still have to rely on their own faith when it arrived. As will we all.

While certainly requiring great faith, such a return to the unconscious would be far more than merely a test of that faith; it would also be a security measure, placing people in the only safe place left during Judgment Day:[1]

"I will sweep everything from the face of the earth," declares the Lord. "The wicked will have only heaps of rubble when I cut off man from the face of the earth" . . . In the fire of his jealousy the whole world will be consumed, for he will make a sudden end of all who live in the earth.
— Zephaniah 1:2-3,18

The heavens will disappear with a roar; the elements will be destroyed by fire, and the earth and everything in it will be laid bare.
— 2 Peter 3:10

The scriptures seem to warn that, yes, this path would be frightening and somewhat painful, but they would survive:

How awful that day will be! None will be like it. It will be a time of trouble for Jacob, but he will be saved out of it. . . . "I am with you and will save you," declares the Lord. "Though I completely destroy all the nations [of souls] among which I scatter you, I will not destroy you. I will discipline you but only with justice; I will not let you go entirely unpunished."
— Jeremiah 30:7,11

Whether a personal-soul had been faithful since its original life or had only just recently turned to God as one of the resurrected dead, its reward would be the same:

---

1   For other passages describing people finding Christ's assistance and security once they've submerged into the unconscious depths, see Psalm 124:1-5, 143:9; Proverbs 28:12, 22:3; Isaiah 43:2, 50:10; Jeremiah 6:1; Zechariah 10:11; Matthew 10:23.

The workers who were hired about the eleventh hour came and each received a denarius. So when those came who were hired first, they expected to receive more. But each one of them also received a denarius. When they received it, they began to grumble against the landowner . . . But he answered one of them, saying, "Friend, I am not being unfair to you. Didn't you agree to work for a denarius? Take your pay and go. I want to give the man who was hired last the same as I gave you."
— Matthew 20:9-11,13-14

As those from heaven came back, God would announce to the newly reformed personal-souls hiding in the unconscious that the horrible two-stage siege was over, and would call them to wake up to full consciousness also, be part of the heavenly return,[1] and watch the wicked flee back to the depths of the unconscious realms:

Awake, awake! Rise up, O Jerusalem, you who have drunk from the hand of the Lord, the cup of his wrath, you who have drained to its dregs the goblet that makes men stagger. . . . These double calamities have come upon you—who can comfort you? . . . Therefore hear this, you afflicted one, made drunk, but not with wine. This is what your Sovereign Lord says . . .: "See, I have taken out of your hand the cup that made you stagger; from that cup, the goblet of my wrath, you will never drink again. I will put it into the hands of your tormentors [the evil dead] who said to you, 'Fall prostrate that we may walk over you.' And you made your back like the ground, like a street to be walked over."
— Isaiah 51:17,19,21-23

Upon returning to full consciousness, the personal-souls from heaven, who had been unconscious for ages, would awaken in bodies only to find others surfacing there also, all incarnations of one another.[2] With the help of the Holy Ghost, they would all be able to recognize and accept one another as valid extensions of themselves, yet they would be surprised and overwhelmed, having been completely unaware of the existence of these other parts of their histories and selves:

Zion [heaven's personal-souls waiting in the unconscious] said, "The Lord has forsaken me, the Lord has forgotten me." [But God

---

1   See also Song of Songs 5:2-5; Psalm 18:4-19; Isaiah 11:12, 13:4-5.
2   Isaiah 43:5.

says,] "Can a mother forget the baby at her breast and have no compassion on the child she has borne? Though she may forget, I will not forget you! . . . Your sons [souls of later incarnations, later generations of the self] hasten back, and those who laid you waste [the wicked personal-souls] depart from you. Lift up your eyes and look around; all your sons gather and come to you. As surely as I live," declares the Lord, "you will wear them all as ornaments; you will put them on, like a bride. Though you were ruined and desolate and your land laid waste [though dead, unconscious, and bodiless], now you will be too small for your people [your own past-selves], and those who devoured you will be far away. The children born during your bereavement [the personal-souls of your later incarnations] will yet say in your hearing, 'This place is too small for us; give us more room to live in.' Then you will say in your heart, 'Who bore me these? I was bereaved and barren; I was exiled and rejected. Who brought these up? I was left all alone, but these—where have they come from?' "

— Isaiah 49:14-15,17-21

God would explain just exactly what He had done, replacing evil personal-souls in bodies with good ones:[1]

Since you are precious and honored in my sight, and because I love you, I will give men in exchange for you, and people in exchange for your life. Do not be afraid, for I am with you. I will bring your children from the East and gather you from the West . . .

— Isaiah 43:4-5

I will give their wives [personal-souls] to other men and their fields [bodies] to new owners.

— Jeremiah 8:10

The scriptures defend this plan of juggling bodies, souls, and spirits, saying, basically, that it's God's creation and He can do as He pleases with it:

This is the word that came to Jeremiah from the Lord: "Go down to the potter's house, and there I will give you my message." So I went down to the potter's house, and saw him working at the wheel. But the pot he was shaping from the clay was marred in his

---

1 See also Proverbs 21:18; Isaiah 35:10.

hands, so the potter formed it into another pot, shaping it as seemed best to him. Then the word of the Lord came to me: "O house of Israel, can I not do with you as this potter does?" declares the Lord. "Like clay in the hands of the potter, so are you in my hand, O house of Israel."
— Jeremiah 18:1-6

The result of all this juggling of consciousness and unconsciousness, bodies and souls and spirits, is that all the living would, through the Holy Ghost, be reunited with God, and the imperfect human "ego" which humanity has zealously served for so long would finally be properly subordinated by the conscious remembrance of God:[1]

Woe to that wreath [the ego of the conscious spirit], the pride of Ephraim's drunkards, to the fading flower, his glorious beauty, set on the head of a fertile valley [the unconscious] . . . that wreath, the pride of Ephraim's drunkards will be trampled underfoot [by the flood of souls]. That fading flower [consciousness] . . . will be like a fig ripe before harvest—as soon as someone sees it and takes it in his hand, he swallows it [describing the resurrected souls fighting over the available consciousness]. In that day the Lord Almighty will be a glorious crown, a beautiful wreath for the remnant of his people [suggesting that the living Spirit of God would itself provide the consciousness that sits on each soul].
— Isaiah 28:1,3-5

This juggling of bodies and souls and spirits, repairing the ancient fracture of the human psyche, would effectively fulfill all justice and therefore all the promises of the Bible. And in the process, it would have created the perfect situation for people to live in. No longer would there be any death of personality, but instead, when people's bodies wore out, they could discard them and instantly reincarnate into new bodies, maintaining full awareness of their past histories and identities:[2]

Every man will sit under his own vine [the long string of his own past history] and under his own fig tree [his own past

---

1 See also Isaiah 28:1-6, 33:18; Ezekiel 37:27; Revelation 3:10, 21:7, 22:4.
2 On people becoming able to remember the thread of their past histories and maintain their sense of identity with their past and future selves and incarnations, see Zechariah 3:10; John 3:16; Revelation 3:5.

personal-souls and identities], and no one will make them afraid . . .
> — Micah 4:4

To them I will give within my temple and its walls a memorial and a name better than sons and daughters [better than unknowingly reincarnating as subsequent generations of separate individuals]; I will give them an everlasting name [a remembrance of their same identity throughout all time, reincarnating into subsequent generations as the same individual].
> — Isaiah 56:5

No longer would any evil or selfishness remain in the human heart, because that interface which was placed between the Primordial Soul and everyone's psyches 2,000 years ago, the Holy Ghost, would have finally become fully conscious. Such a restored communicative link with the Primordial Soul would function as a guide for all their thoughts and actions:[1]

"This is the covenant I will make with the house of Israel after that time," declares the Lord. "I will put my law in their minds and write it on their hearts. I will be their God, and they will be my people. No longer will a man teach his neighbor or a man his brother saying, 'Know the Lord,' because they will all know me, from the least of them to the greatest . . ."
> — Jeremiah 31:33-34

The entire story and sequence of events of Judgment Day seems to be outlined in the book of Amos, in his story of the locusts, the fire, and the plumb line:

This is what the Sovereign Lord showed me: He was preparing swarms of locusts [the evil dead] after the king's share had been harvested [after the rapture] and just as the second crop was coming up. When they [the locust-souls] had stripped the land clean [utterly wiping out all life in humanity], I cried out, "Sovereign Lord, forgive! How can Jacob survive? He is so small!" So the Lord relented [suggesting that the locust-souls will not entirely wipe out all human life]. "This will not happen," the Lord

---

1 On God setting up a controlling influence over the minds and actions of humanity, see Isaiah 29:21, 34:11; Ezekiel 36:26-27; Joel 2:28; Hosea 10:11; Zechariah 1:16.

said. This is what the Sovereign Lord showed me [would take place next]: The Sovereign Lord was calling for judgment by fire; it dried up the great deep [emptying out the unconscious] and devoured the land [this is the pain the evil personal-souls felt as the Holy Ghost approached them]. Then I cried out, "Sovereign Lord, I beg you, stop! How can Jacob survive? He is so small!" So the Lord relented. "This will not happen either," the Sovereign Lord said [suggesting that the inner fire will not utterly destroy everything, either]. This is what he showed me [would happen next]: The Lord was standing by a wall that had been built true to plumb [Christ], with a plumb line in his hand. And the Lord asked me, "What do you see, Amos?" "A plumb line," I replied. Then the Lord said, "Look, I am setting a plumb line among my people Israel; I will spare them no longer."

— Amos 7:1-8

CHAPTER 10

MORNING IS COMING, BUT ALSO THE NIGHT

The Dawn of Collective Consciousness

Whether you turn to the right or to the left, your ears will hear a voice behind you, saying, "This is the way; walk in it."
— Isaiah 30:21

Many religions seem to have been, at one time or another, at least partially familiar with what I am calling Division Theory; but only two traditions, Judeo-Christianity and Zoroastrianism, were apparently able to perceive that the story was not yet complete, that this ultimate drama still had more changes scheduled to occur.

The evidence suggests that many ancient religions recognized that death threatened to divide the soul from the spirit, and a few even recognized what individuals need do to prevent such a tragedy. But knowledge of the origin of this state of affairs seems to have been entrusted only to Israel, and glimpses of the conclusion Judgment Day would bring to this story of humanity's divided consciousness seem to have been exclusively entrusted to Israel and Zoroaster.

The first change in this state of affairs since the Primordial Division would have been Christ's Resurrection. None of the world's other religions anticipated such an eventuality, never foreseeing any further changes taking place in the nature of death as they knew it. They assumed, reasonably enough, that physical death would always threaten to divide soul from spirit and that, once such a division had occurred, it would be completely irreversible, permanently condemning the soul to a netherworld existence exiled from the living spirit.

Because of that assumption, it has been hard for older religions, even Judaism itself, to accept Christianity's revolutionary message that a change indeed has taken place, that a new situation has arisen since those earlier times. Such religions often seem fixated on the belief that the information they originally received was not only accurate, but also complete. Of course, those religions, when first formed, faithfully described the nature of human mortality at that point in time. But introducing a savior capable of effecting a systemwide repair of the Division into this cosmic drama would have vastly changed the entire situation, making possible new alternatives which those other religions never considered.

Christ's death and Resurrection would not, by themselves, have repaired the Primordial Division; it would merely have facilitated such a repair in the future. So long as Jesus' soul remained dormant, below conscious awareness in the minds of humanity, the Primordial Division would only continue to grow wider.

The Gnostic texts contain repeated assertions that the reunion of souls and spirits could be achieved only while in a physical body:

> If the woman [the soul] had not separated from the man [the spirit], she would not die with the man. His separation became the beginning of death. Because of this, Christ came to repair the separation which was from the beginning, and again unite the two, and to give life to those who died as a result of the separation and unite them. But the woman is [only] united to her husband in the bridal chamber [while in the physical body].
> — The Gospel of Philip 70:9-22

Jesus' stated objective was to "release captives and prisoners" and to "seek and save what was lost," and after his soul exploded throughout the universe, forcibly penetrating into and merging with all other souls everywhere, he would have found himself in precisely the situation he needed to be in to effect that objective. He could then use his own spirit, his own consciousness, to raise all the lost dead souls of humanity, by raising them back to conscious awareness within himself! However, at least according to the scriptures of the Gnostics, he would need to occupy a physical body himself in order to accomplish such a feat. The canonical scriptures concur, predicting that Jesus would return to earth again in a physical body at the very time just such a Universal Resurrection was supposed to occur.

The conventional Western position, however, is that during Jesus' Second Coming he will spontaneously reappear full grown, hovering in the air wearing the same physical body he had in A.D. 33. As mentioned earlier, this view conflicts with the suggestion, in Mark 2:19-22, that just as new wine must be poured into new wineskins, new life must also be poured into a new body. Traditional Western theology never solved the riddle of why Jesus seemed to switch topics halfway through this discourse, changing from wedding guests fasting to wine and wineskins; but if, as Division Theory proposes, reincarnation is true and Jesus knew it, then this passage could very well have been a discussion of a single topic, that of Jesus' departure and coming return. If so, this passage suggests that Jesus will return by reincarnating into a new baby body, instead of regenerating the same adult body he had when he was crucified. This interpretation drastically changes many long-held assumptions about his Second Coming.

Perhaps not coincidentally, his reincarnation could in and of itself cause the Universal Resurrection, and he wouldn't even have to be aware he was making it happen! Although his spirit would be physically alive once again, Jesus' personal-soul would still be linked to all the unconscious souls of the rest of humanity, as it had been ever since his Resurrection, and once he discovered such alien material hidden within his own unconscious, his own integrity would naturally, and quite innocently, compel him to seek it out.

And as all this material rose up to consciousness in him, it would do so in us as well.

Discovering the hidden presence of humanity's unconscious souls deep within his own is all it would take to flood consciousness into them; this, of course, would reawaken them, releasing an army of long-lost personal-souls into every human mind. Simply by consciously noticing their existence, Jesus' spirit would, in effect, be mentally drawing these personal-souls up out of the murkiest, foggiest, cloudiest depths of humanity's psyches, riding upon the "clouds" of the unconscious. [If the kingdom of heaven is within you (Luke 17:21), doesn't it stand to reason that the clouds of heaven upon which Jesus is prophesied to return (Matthew 24:30) will be as well?] And everyone would witness this wonder at the exact same moment:

At that time they will see the Son of Man coming on a cloud with power and great glory.
— Luke 21:27

For as lightning that comes from the East is visible even in the West, so will be the coming of the Son of Man.
— Matthew 24:27

And the Glory of the Lord will be revealed, and all mankind together will see it.
— Isaiah 40:5

Like dawn spreading across a mountain, a large and mighty army comes, such as never was of old, and never will be in ages to come. . . . the Lord thunders at the head of his army, his forces are beyond number.
— Joel 2:2,11

Thus, the integrity which saved Jesus from the clutches of death in A.D. 33 would, upon his reincarnation, free the rest of humanity's souls from the same pit.

And a Little Child Will Lead Them

If Jesus were to reincarnate after his soul had been linked to all others, the extraordinary scenario described above not only would be likely to occur, but also would do so while he was still a young child:[1]

Now learn this lesson from the fig tree: When its branch [Jesus is called The Branch] is still tender [young], and its leaves have appeared [once a new life-cycle has begun], you know that summer is near. Even so, when you see all these things [once Jesus has begun a new life-cycle and is still young], know that it [Judgment Day] is near, right at the door.
— Matthew 24:32-33

From infancy, of course, his mind would slowly grow toward full conscious awareness, not becoming capable of clear objective

---

1 The Aramaic word *talya* signifies "boy," "young man," and "servant," as well as "lamb." —*New Catholic Encyclopedia*, VIII:339. Therefore, in John 1:29, John the Baptist might have actually been saying "There is God's little boy, who takes away the sins of the world."

thought until he was at least a few years old. However, during those early years before he reached that full awareness, while his unconscious imagination still dominated his thought processes, the human race would probably experience some very peculiar phenomena. His child's imagination would be likely to randomly spark temporary contacts with different unconscious souls within his own, momentarily flooding them with partial consciousness. While the effect such episodes would have on the general population seems beyond anyone's ability to anticipate, a certain prophecy does promise that:

> Your sons and daughters will prophesy, your old men will dream dreams, your young men will see visions. Even on my servants, both men and women, I will pour out my Spirit . . . before the coming of the great and dreadful day of the Lord.
> — Joel 2:28-31

Having Jesus' Resurrection catapult his perfect soul into forced unconscious union with all humanity's imperfect souls would provide an elegant solution to humanity's Primordial Division. Once Jesus' soul began, 2,000 years ago, to recognize and compensate for humanity's unconscious failings, it would have effectively melded to people's personal-souls. By completing what people would not complete, by drinking to the bitter dregs the cups they themselves had filled but then refused to drink, Jesus would have effectively, and quite irrevocably, connected himself to all people. He would have tied all humanity to himself by the ties of debt: psychic, mental, unconscious debt. After all, nothing forges stronger ties between people than shared pain and hardship. By joining, even substituting for us, in the experience of such inner pain, Jesus would have shared in a very real part of our lives and would have thus come to partake even of our very identities.

As soon as that reincarnated Christ-child finally reached the age of awareness, the very act of consciously exploring his own psyche would draw all humanity's lost personal-souls to consciousness;[1] all our souls would pop right up behind his own,[2] like a string of floats tied on a fishing line.

---

1 This reunion is beautifully illustrated in Song of Songs 3:1-4. See also Isaiah 51:14.
2 John 12:32.

As Jesus' soul exploded out of the unconscious back into the conscious world, all the undead hellish personal-souls still holding on to their precious renewed life would be instantly destroyed, as a "holy fire" suddenly erupted inside them when all their dormant soul-pain suddenly became activated:[1]

> And pain will seize them when they shall see that child of woman sitting on the throne of his glory.
> — Enoch 62:5

Because all humanity's personal-souls would be connected with Jesus' own, when he pulled them all back up to consciousness they would be not only rising from the dead to reunite with their own conscious spirits, but also simultaneously blinking into consciousness in Jesus' mind as well. At that time, Jesus, a living person, a little boy, would suddenly find himself consciously connected with all humanity,[2] able to psychically peer into the minds and hearts of everyone on the planet, to communicate with them, to influence them, and to judge them:

> He will not judge by what he sees with his eyes, or decide by what he hears with his ears; but with righteousness he will judge the needy, with justice he will give decisions for the poor of the earth . . .
> . . . a little child will lead them.
> — Isaiah 11: 3-4,6

> I will put my law in their inward parts, and I will write it in their hearts; and I will be their God, and they will be my people.
> — Jeremiah 31:33

Such a child would possess the ability to instantly communicate with anyone; indeed, he would always know what everyone was thinking:

> Whether you turn to the right or to the left, your ears will hear a voice behind you, saying "This is the way; walk in it."
> — Isaiah 30:21

---

1 Isaiah 33:14; Lamentations 1:13; Ezekiel 28:18.
2 Ezekiel 37:27; Joel 2:28; Luke 13:20-21, 17:20-24; I Corinthians 3:16; Ephesians 1:10, 5:31-32; Colossians 1:20.

Before they call I will answer; while they are still speaking I will hear.
— Isaiah 65:24

A little child would have instantly become the most important and powerful person on earth;[1] since he would be able to see through everyone's eyes, and everyone would be able to see through his, his opinion and perspective would become the undisputed standard for the whole world:

The law will go out from Zion, the word of the Lord from Jerusalem. He will judge between the nations, and will settle disputes for many peoples.
— Isaiah 2:3-4

As Zoroaster had foreseen, humanity would have truly become "all of one voice." In fact, with Jesus peering out through every human mind, an evolutionary leap for the entire human race, a fundamental change in the very nature of human identity itself, would have occurred:

The Lord will be king over the whole earth. On that day there will be one Lord, and his name the only name.
— Zechariah 14:9

The next step in the evolution of the human race would have been reached, the next generation of the family of man. As a son is to his father, so the new human race would be to that species which had preceded it. Just as Jesus was not just called a man, but

---

1 Yet another long-hidden prophecy about Jesus' return to inherit his Father's kingdom while a young child is found in Ecclesiastes 4:13-15: *"Better a poor but wise youth [Christ] than an old but foolish king [the human ego] who no longer knows how to take warning. The youth may have come from prison [the subconscious realm of the dead] to the kingdom, or he may have been born in poverty within his kingdom [Christ can be accepted, 'reborn' into people's souls now, before he comes to power, while he is still 'in poverty,' or they may accept Christ once they've risen from the dead 'come from prison']. I saw that all who lived and walked under the sun followed the youth [Christ reborn as a young child], the king's successor. There was no end to all the people who came before them [all the followers of the boy-king, Christ, upon his Second Coming, will recall all their previous lives which had 'come before them']."* The following line, Ecclesiastes 4:16, refers of course to the event also mentioned in Revelation 20:7, but then, that's another story.

rather the Son of Man, so our entire species would no longer be the same humanity it had been, but instead would be the next generation, or offspring, of mankind itself.

Most importantly, after having been alienated from it for untold ages, since the original "fall" when humanity first pushed the soul away from the spirit, the Creator would have finally returned to His true Temple:

> The Lord you are seeking will return to his temple . . .
> — Malachi 3:1

> Don't you know that you yourselves are God's temple?
> — I Corinthians 3:16

> The kingdom does not come visibly, nor will people say "here it is" or "there it is," because the kingdom of God is within you.
> — Luke 17:20-21

All Things Judged Useful

> May the table set before them become a snare; may it become retribution and a trap. May their eyes be darkened so they cannot see, and their backs be bent forever.
> — Psalm 69:22-24

Once the Universal Resurrection was completed and multiple personal-souls had returned to rejoin with each living spirit, all people would, for the first time ever, be able to review the long thread of their personal histories as they had traveled from life to life to life through all the ages of humanity. Yet large gaps would probably remain in this reassembled memory, because some of the hellish "locust" personal-souls, who had contained the memories for the years of their lifetimes, would have been burned to destruction. The Jewish scriptures seem to have anticipated this, however, containing a curious promise that while people would find that some of the years of their past had been taken away, God would somehow make up for this:

> I will repay you for the years the locusts have eaten . . . my great army that I sent among you.
> — Joel 2:25

On Judgment Day, when the hellish personal-souls try to flee back into the relative safety of the unconscious, when "the wicked return to the grave" (Psalms 9:17), what then? Would they be able to escape God's Justice, able to escape feeling their inner pain? Would their only punishment simply be to return to the world of the dead?

Perhaps not; Jeremiah (chapters 50 and 51) suggests that God would pursue the evil personal-souls when they flee back into the unconscious world of the dead and completely devastate it. If so, would this mean that all the hellish personal-souls would be completely destroyed, actually ceasing to exist?

Throughout the Bible, the punishment of the wicked is described in four ways: (1) everlasting death and destruction, (2) the eternal experience of great burning pain, (3) "banishment," and (4) "slavery."

It seems clear that God captures the hellish souls, which would cause the wicked to fully experience all their stored pain:

> Your hand will lay hold on all your enemies, your right hand will seize your foes. At the time of your appearing, you will make them like a fiery furnace. In His wrath the Lord will swallow them up and His fire will consume them.
> — Psalm 21:8-9

However, apparently they would not be destroyed completely, ceasing to exist, for other passages suggest that they are to be, in some sense at least, still "alive," still existing, not utterly annihilated:

> Let them go down alive to the grave.
> — Psalms 55:15

> Multitudes who sleep in the dust of the earth will awake: some to . . . shame and everlasting contempt.
> — Daniel 12:2

> Depart from me, you who are cursed, into the eternal fire prepared for the devil and his angels.
> — Matthew 25:41

> They will be punished with everlasting destruction and shut out from the presence of the Lord and from the majesty of His power . . .
> — 2 Thessalonians 1:9

The wicked do not seem destined for extermination, but instead are apparently to be permanently banished from the world of the living, condemned to deep unconscious existences, ejected forever from human awareness:

> Evil men are no longer remembered.
> — Job 24:20

> Banish them for their many sins.
> — Psalm 5:10

> Those who turn to crooked ways the Lord will banish with the evildoers.
> — Psalm 125:5

Why this extreme punishment? If God just terminated their existence entirely, wouldn't that provide complete retribution, yet not seem so cruel? Why would it be better to keep them existing if only to eternally experience pain? Is God not a merciful God?

Or, on the other hand, might there be there some reason these evil ones, deserving as they are, *must* continue to exist as "eternal sacrifices"? What if they could be useful? Might they yet serve their Creator in some way? Why shouldn't they serve God's purposes if it is possible for them to do so?

> Why should there be such a waste of the badness in men?
> — *Tao Te Ching*, 62

> Let the punishment of criminals be useful. A hanged man is good for nothing, and a man condemned to public works will serve the country, and is a living lesson.
> — Voltaire[1]

Some passages suggest that the evilness of the wicked is never to be forgotten by God, being kept forever before His awareness and memory:

> May their sins always remain before the Lord.
> — Psalm 109:15

---

1 Voltaire, "Civil Law," in *Philosophical Dictionary*, 1764, as quoted by Seldes in *The Great Thoughts*, 435.

But why should this be? Why would God want these evils to be constantly remembered? Could it be something as simple as—

Since the world points up beauty as such,
There is ugliness too.
If goodness is taken as goodness,
Wickedness enters as well.
For is and is-not come together;
Hard and easy are complimentary;
Long and short are relative;
High and low are comparative;
Pitch and sound make harmony;
before and after are a sequence.
— *Tao Te Ching*, 2

Perhaps this "evilness" must be remembered, so it won't be repeated—and so it can help to differentiate from the "good." If so, this would fulfill that ancient prophecy, the very first prophecy in the Bible:

When you eat of [the tree of the knowledge of good and evil] your eyes will be opened, and you will be like God, knowing good and evil.
— Genesis 3:5

Although the wicked would never again be remembered as actual individual persons, perhaps both the evil that they did, and the soul-pain which that evil brought, would be consciously re-called, but only dimly so, as if from an old bad dream. After Judgment Day, each person on earth might retain an indistinct yet undeniable inner "feeling" about those evils and pains without any detailed recollection of any actual past experiences or individuals involved. While the evilness and pain might be recalled on a semi-conscious level, the actual names and personalities would forever remain fully shut out from conscious awareness:

He punishes them for their wickedness where everyone can see them.
— Job 34:26

You have rebuked the nations and destroyed the wicked; you have blotted out their names for ever and ever. . . . Even the memory of them has perished.
— Psalm 9:5-6

You will surely forget your trouble, recalling it only as waters gone by.
— Job 11:16

There could be more than simple punishment going on in such a scenario; the evil souls would find themselves being used as a comparative example in the human psyche. They would end up, in effect, chained into slavery in the unconscious side of the human mind, on display as the "evil" that must exist to give meaning and flavor to the "good" that is its opposite. And contrasting good with evil would make good seem far more vividly excellent!

Dimly, as if through a fog, the living would be able to sense the burning regret and burning desire for life and happiness that forever consumed the wicked. And the living would be unconsciously feeling this great desire while at the same time consciously possessing the fulfillment of that desire, life. Thus, they would be filled with tremendous joy and satisfaction, because nothing brings more joy than to both feel great desire and possess its fulfillment. It seems that God is planning to use the "bad" to "fill to overflowing" the cups of the "good."

Under Division Theory's scenario, then, all created beings, even the wicked, would indeed "bow down before God" and serve Him; either freely or in bondage, all would submit to the Creator and do His will:

All the ends of the earth will remember and turn to the Lord and all the families of the nations will bow down before him. . . .
All who go down to the dust will kneel before him—those who cannot keep themselves alive.
— Psalm 22:27,29

The wicked would have become eternal slaves to God, laborers in the unconscious side of the human mind, providing by the natural power of contrast the joy that the living would feel after Judgment Day:

They glean in the vineyards of the wicked. Lacking clothes [lacking a body], they spend the night [death] naked; they have nothing to cover themselves in the cold.
. . . Lacking clothes, they go about naked; they carry the sheaves [the feelings of the soul], but still go hungry. They . . . tread the

197

winepress [of human feeling and emotion], yet suffer thirst [for the feelings of life].
— Job 24:6-7,10-11

I will punish the King of Babylon and his nations . . . for their guilt . . .
. . . they themselves will be enslaved . . .
— Jeremiah 25:12,14

May the praise of God be in [the saints'] mouths, and a double-edged sword [cutting the soul from the spirit] in their hands, to inflict vengeance on the nations and punishment on the peoples, to bind their kings with fetters, their nobles with shackles of iron, to carry out the sentence against them.
— Psalms 149:6-8

They will become eunuchs [impotent slaves] in the palace of the King of Babylon [in the unconscious world].
— Isaiah 39:7

Enslavement and Punishment: Leviathan, the Devil

Division Theory's story of the enslavement and utilization of the souls of the wicked seems to also be repeated in the Bible's references to Leviathan. This may be another name for the devil; it's interesting that the scriptures use this particular term, for the original Hebrew word *leviathan* contains an important facet of meaning which has new significance under Division Theory: in Hebrew, *leviathan* referred to an "intertwined, united serpent."[1] In light of Division Theory's suggestion that the devil may be the composite, or "intertwining" of all the evil souls in the collective unconscious, the ancient Hebrew belief that the leviathan was an evil creature composed of many parts all "intertwined together" stands as yet further evidence that much genuinely valid information actually was deposited within these ancient scriptures.

The Bible describes this monster as a multiple-headed, fire-breathing sea serpent [the sea of the unconscious?], with eyes like rays of light, with smoke [from the fire of hell?] pouring from his nostrils. And it "looks down on all who are haughty; he is king over

---

1 For more on the Leviathan-devil connection, see Appendix A: Fruit of the Division.

all that are proud" (Job 41:34). This statement seems to be the final, crucial clue that decisively identifies this Leviathan as the devil, for Satan is also described as a serpent who is also king over all the proud of the earth.

On the Last Day, according to these scriptures, it will be this Leviathan which will be punished by God (Isaiah 27:1), crushing its many heads and using them to nourish others (Psalm 74:14). The Creator is to pull in this Leviathan with a hook, and then this monster is supposed to speak, begging for mercy! It is to make an agreement with God, consenting to become the Almighty's slave for life, becoming, in fact, the Creator's docile "pet"! (Job 41:1-5)

Once again the Bible seems internally consistent, concurring from every angle. After the Last Day, the wicked would not only be imprisoned in eternal pain—not only would they be permanently banished from the world of the living—but they would actually become willing slaves working in the secret realms, helping to unconsciously provide the living with a more complete sense of joy, happiness, and fulfillment! A truly perfect God, of course, would be so efficient He'd waste nothing, not even the evil in men!

> Even the darkness will not be dark to you; the night will shine like the day, for darkness is as light to you.
> — Psalm 139:12

This twist of making the wicked provide for the good is not as big a surprise as it might seem; actually, anything less would seem imperfect justice, for, in the process of becoming "evil," the hellish souls must have, at some point, wronged others, so they would owe them recompense.

Still, by utilizing such clever strategies, God seems to reveal a crafty streak; just as Division Theory suggests He used death to destroy death, He may also intend to use "evil" to provide an increased sense of fulfillment for the "good."

Change in the Nature of Personal Identity

Would Division Theory's vision of the Last Day, when people's past-life souls merge back together into a single unit connecting with the spirit, mean that our sense of personal identity would be lost? Not necessarily—rather than feeling a sense of loss, one could feel a sense of increase. Although all the personal-souls to survive Judgment Day would be awakening to discover that they were sharing their body with many others, instead of looking at one another and thinking to themselves "I am less than I thought," the reunited Primordial Soul/Spirit could recognize these personal-souls as various chapters of its own past, identifying each as parts of itself. Nothing would be lost.

When scientists came to realize that our planet was but an infinitesimally small piece of a far greater galaxy, did that decrease the substance or importance of any molecule in our world? No: one is made from the other. So, instead of feeling belittled by such a discovery, one could feel infinitely enlarged: "My God! I am so much *more* than I thought!"

> Then you will say in your heart, "Who bore me these? I was bereaved and barren; I was exiled and rejected. Who brought these up? I was left all alone, but these—where have they come from?"
>
> — Isaiah 49:21

AFTERWORD

Is this Division Theory really true? I don't know. There has come no blinding mystical revelation saying that it is; I've seen no visions, heard no voices imparting this as God-given fact. Within my mind there remains doubt.

I wonder, however, if this doubt is not born of my expectation that such mysteries as these would never be solved. Matters of religion, matters of the Bible, and even matters of psychology and the unconscious are mysteries that many assume will never be answered. After all, they've remained unanswered for thousands and thousands of years, have they not? Have I become—has humanity become—so used to having no answer for these matters that, when an answer appears that does fit, I remain unconvinced simply because we've all had it drilled into us that "there is no answer for such things"?

Division Theory seems to work. It acts exactly the way a correct answer is supposed to act—it puts all the pieces together and it makes sense out of all of it.

What would it take to know for sure, to be absolutely certain that Division Theory is true? What would it take to get that deep-down "certainty in the gut" that it's true?

This, of course, is the question of faith. But faith is not what many people think it is. It's not knowing something you can't prove; it's making a conscious choice to believe something you realize you do not know for sure.[1] There are a great many in the world today who get this definition mixed up. There are many religious leaders, for instance, who teach interpretations of these ancient prophecies as if they were not interpretations at all, but

---

1 *"Doubt is not the opposite of faith; it is one element of faith."* — Paul Tillich, *The Dynamics of Faith* (New York: Harper, 1957), 22.

indisputable truths. Many of their statements are based on loose or shaky interpretations of isolated passages, yet they teach as if those explanations and scenarios are the only ones anyone has ever perceived in those pages, totally disregarding the fact that the reason we have scores of different churches and denominations is precisely because people *can't* agree on those writings!

So, with this in mind, I cannot say "I absolutely know for certain that Division Theory is true." God has not personally descended in all His glory to convince me of it. But its logic seems not only sound, but actually delightful to behold, as some ancient holy man might have said. And in my soul, I feel that Division Theory is on the right track. So, in both in my conscious and my unconscious I find confirmation of Division Theory; both my head and my heart tell me they are willing to accept it.

I do not know. But, knowing I do not know, I have examined it, and I have shared this examination process with the world through this book. And after the examination, while still not knowing, I find that it pleases me immensely to choose to believe in Division Theory. I have chosen to believe it; I have chosen to have faith in it.

If Division Theory is correct, what then? Division Theory provides a new base of support for the Judeo-Christian tradition, a base that makes it far more attractive to the scientifically-minded. It makes the claims of the Judeo-Christian tradition less fantastic and impossible, by founding them in scientific realities with which we are already quite familiar. Division Theory thus defends and promotes the evangelistic roots of Christianity, acting to draw in many who otherwise could not believe.

How does Division Theory change Christianity? In its truest sense, it does not. If Division Theory does anything, it restores Christianity to its original form and repoints it in its original direction, by washing away all the erroneous changes and indignities which that tradition has suffered over the last 2,000 years.

How does Division Theory refocus Christianity? By restoring the emphasis on personal integrity and wholeness. How does one reacquire one's integrity and wholeness? Only by nurturing the development of a living, dynamic relationship with the soul of Christ sleeping deep inside one's own soul. We have damaged ourselves through the Primordial Division, Division Theory says, and do not possess the capacity to correct that damage on our own. Our integrity and wholeness are lost to us, and so long as they are, neither we nor this world we live in will know any lasting peace.

We must awaken the sleeper within each of us. As we follow the love-based guidance of the sleeping Christ within, he awakes ever further in our consciousness, allowing us to become one with him and therefore one with the Primordial Soul with whom he himself is one.

This message is not new.

What demands would Division theory place on us? It would require us to examine ourselves, to diligently seek out, identify, and reunify all places in life where we've been dividing ourselves, our ideals, and our actions. We could no longer allow ourselves to pray on "praying Sunday" for justice for the oppressed, mercy for widows and orphans, for food for the hungry, hospitality for the stranger, care for the sick, and so on, and then vote on "voting Tuesday" against all these things. It would require us to take full responsibility for the fruit of our actions; no longer could we invest our money in (give our power to) whichever business or organization seems likely to return a high profit without concerning ourselves with what that business might do with our money. By giving our money (our power) to others to do with as they please, we become co-owners of that business, and so share not only in whatever profit or loss that business experiences, but also in whatever guilt or shame it brings upon itself. Under Division Theory, the investor could no longer divorce his ideals, which might be against tobacco, alcohol, or oil, for example, from his business, which might view the promotion of that tobacco, alcohol, or oil as financially advantageous. If the investors of today had true Christ-like integrity, they could not allow their money to support matters to which they were morally opposed.

If the voters of this world had integrity, they would not allow corporations to do evil without being held personally responsible. As it is, a corporation can perform virtually any despicable act and the people comprising that corporation cannot be held personally responsible. As it is, tobacco executives (and shareholders) can promote smoking and lung cancer, alcohol executives (and shareholders) can promote drinking and alcoholism, oil executives (and shareholders) can promote environmental disaster, without fear of ever being held personally responsible for these crimes against their human family and their earthly home. Anyone who invests in a company is just as responsible as the executive who gives the actual orders, for they have willingly thrown in with them, allowing their own financial influence to be used in this way.

This is division, and it is killing our planet and rotting our culture. We can no longer afford to think in one way and act in another (or allow our money to act in another in our name). We must resolutely fight against division wherever we find it—in our souls, in our families, in our societies, in our business, and, not least of all, in our politics. We must fight against division with passion and determination, but most of all with the integrity that comes from Christ. Division is the Great Lie, father of the devil, and from it no good can come. We must identify the fruit of this lie, rooting it out and exposing it, for a lie can survive only in darkness and shadow. And we must remember most of all that the only way to truly fix the problem is from the bottom up, attacking it at its root—the division within each of our psyches.

This is why Jesus came.

Truth can never be told so as to be understood and not be believed.
— William Blake[1]

For a long time now, religious scholars have bemoaned the loss of Christ's religion, the original religious vision that he had and tried to share with us. Those who thoroughly study the history of early Christianity, examining all of what is known about those first years, tend to accept what their lesser informed church counterparts would be aghast at hearing—that much of the real gist of the message of Jesus Christ seems to have been lost in the mists of time.

Had the doctrines of Jesus been preached always as pure as they came from his lips, the whole civilized world would now have been Christian.
— Thomas Jefferson[2]

Jesus' message fell victim to the political battles in church and government during those early centuries A.D., battles which ultimately shaped what history would and would not be able to pass on about Jesus and his message.

What little was left, after all these battles, seems minuscule compared to what his whole original message must have con-

1 William Blake, Note-Book, 1793, as quoted by Seldes in The Great Thoughts, 45.
2 Thomas Jefferson, Letter to Benjamin Waterhouse, June 26, 1822, as quoted by Seldes in The Great Thoughts, 208.

tained. If it hadn't been such an important treasure that humanity lost, the whole absurd drama over the fate of the original Christian scriptures would be laughable. Here we have the man whose teachings changed history, yet all we were able to save of those precious teachings, in the New Testament, amounts to not much more than a single hour of his thoughts.

That's some serious editing!

But with the 1940s discovery of the original Gnostics' scriptures left at Nag Hammadi, which in turn led to this rediscovery of Division Theory, that original vision may have been at least partially reassembled.

Was the message that ended up in the Bible wrong, or even misleading? Not really. But an awful lot seems to have been left out; one of the key points, about the undesirability of the soul-spirit split, was utterly lost. How important was this key point? Well, it might have been important enough to have made the difference between Christianity remaining holy and spiritual in form and content and it becoming what we actually got, an unholy Christianity which encouraged men to go off on bloody Crusades, a "Christian" church which understood so little of its own message that it once actually sold "forgiveness of sins" for cold hard cash.

It could've made all the difference in the world.

Perhaps it still can.

FRUIT OF THE DIVISION

Ghosts, the Devil, and the Collective Unconscious

The truth? The truth, Lazarus, is perhaps something so unbearable, so terrible, something so deadly, that simple people could not live with it.
— Miguel De Unamuno[1]

All we have, all we know, all we experience, is hopelessly tainted and distorted by the Primordial Division.[2] That early event seems to have become the centerpiece of our entire universe, around which all else was built, and now, no matter where we look, we see only reflections of that defining moment. Since that dark dawn, our experience of life has been, at its worst, a fierce battle between opposing elements; at its best, a grim struggle to achieve balance.

It started with the alienation of spirit and soul and led quickly to the separation of conscious from unconscious, objective from subjective, male from female. From there it went on to distinguish light and darkness, day and night, even life and death. Today, every facet of our existence reflects that primordial defining event; since we are ourselves divided, the lens through which we see and experience the world is as well.

> . . . there is a vast outer realm and an equally vast inner realm; between these two stands a man, facing now one and now the other, and according to his mood or disposition,

---

1 Miguel De Unamuno, *The Tragic Sense of Life*, Ch. VI, as quoted by Seldes in *The Great Thoughts*, 426.
2 Which is exactly what Western religion has been saying about humanity's "fall from grace" for at least 2,500 years.

taking the one for the absolute truth by denying or sacrificing the other.[1]

Thus, we find ourselves endlessly engaged in fights: head vs. heart, intellect vs. emotion, logic vs. intuition, left brain vs. right brain, form vs. substance, objective vs. subjective, science vs. art, career vs. family, work vs. play, responsibility vs. freedom, sex vs. love, law and order vs. right and wrong, prosecution vs. defense, white vs. black, West vs. East, capitalism vs. communism, corporation vs. individual, machine vs. human, opportunity vs. security, Republican vs. Democrat, state vs. church, reason vs. faith, urban vs. rural, rock vs. country, IBM vs. Apple, Coke vs. Pepsi, Ford vs. Chevy, and on and on.

Although the fight comes in many guises and has many names, when we look closely we see it's always actually the same fight again and again. Everywhere we look, in every endeavor, every face, every circumstance, we confront the same ancient division. No matter which way we turn, we run right back into ourselves and that same damned ancient choice. We chose our fate; that choice *became* our fate, and now we have to live it each and every day. On our good days we realize the only way to win is to find some balance between the two sides; on our worst, we identify with one side exclusively and try to grind the other into dust.

We still have more bad days than good ones.

The Division rules. We gave it that right and that power. We sold these things, giving away our birthrights, and in return we received only dust—all that remains of all we have been, in the graveyards of tens of thousands of years.

No, that's not entirely true. The Division did give us something more. For all we gave away to the Division, it did give us more than just dust.

It gave us the devil, too.

According to popular imagination, the devil is a horrible looking creature, red, horned, tailed, and ugly, and he alone is responsible for both all earthly and all spiritual troubles that the human race has ever had to suffer. He is the only enemy anyone has ever had or ever will have; all troubles anyone ever had were painstakingly crafted by him, and all this is due to his relentless, all-consuming passion to make us miserable.

---

1   Jung, *Modern Man in Search of a Soul,* 120.

What rot! Yet, in the midst of all this nonsense lies a very important and genuine truth.

The devil is a less-than-prominent figure in the Old Testament, but his role expands in the New Testament. What is perhaps most curious is that he is portrayed, not as *a* tempter, but as *the* tempter of people. When it seems clear to the reader that a passage is describing a person being tempted by his own ego, these texts state unequivocally that it is the devil which is tempting them. When, after having just received the Spirit of God and all the power that implies, Jesus went into the desert to confront the ambitions of his own ego, the Bible states that the devil tempted him. When Peter's ego swelled so strong he dared to rebuke Jesus (Matthew 16:23, Mark 8:32), Jesus actually called Peter "Satan." And in another place, Jesus also calls another disciple, Judas, "a devil" as well (John 6:70); He doesn't say Judas "had" a devil, or even that he was "possessed by" a devil, but that he actually *was* a devil. Imagine that.

Jesus once told a crowd of people that they all were the children of their "father, the devil" (John 8:44), and they wanted only to do his bidding. And in other cases the devil is described as "entering" someone, who would then (from the perspective of the reader, at least) give in to the temptation to do something or other (as in Luke 22:3).

And Jesus himself, perhaps the only human ever to completely overcome and subordinate his own ego, testified that he saw Satan "fall like lightning from heaven."

If the devil is not the human ego, it certainly seems that he does all his work through it!

In the conscious world, a certain psychological element known as the human ego seems to be fundamentally related to the spiritual world's "devil," the legendary master of hell. Moreover, it is self-evident that those most likely to end up in that hell would be the people who, while alive, always treated their own egos as their "masters."

Could this be? Could the devil and the human ego somehow be the same thing?

If both heaven and hell indeed do find their existences within the deepest levels of the human psyche (the Primordial Soul or collective unconscious), the collective nature of that largely alien mental dimension would probably produce some extraordinary and unanticipated consequences. Whereas in a single individual the ego might be only an insubstantial psychological element, in the collective after-death realm of the unconscious, where completely different rules would be in effect, the relative significance of this "psychological element" could be dramatically changed.

Those most likely to go to hell, according to tradition, would have egos which, having never been subordinated to anything beyond their own self-interest and self-aggrandizement, would be demanding, controlling, selfish, defensive, and generally malevolent to others. And once trapped within the unconscious (a dream-like realm in which like merges with like), such warped egos would find themselves becoming "collectivized":

> The deeper layers of the psyche lose their individual uniqueness as they retreat farther and farther into darkness. Lower down . . . they become increasingly collective until they are universalized . . .[1]

As the natural effects of the unconscious became evident, the normal distinctions between things would first become blurred, then indistinct, and then virtually nonexistent; all those multiple past-life egos would start to meld, intertwining and coalescing together, eventually forming a single undifferentiated mass of self-absorbed Ego. Growing larger with the death of every new insubordinate soul, it would grow in time into an impossibly huge megalomaniac of an Ego, a monstrous mistake of the unconscious, an artificially generated entity born and existing exclusively within the unconscious half of reality,[2] whose evil characteristics would be virtually indistinguishable from those of the traditional "devil."

The unconscious does not distinguish between "self" and "other"; this is its subjective nature,[3] and all its experience is perceived through this collective lens. The deeper into that unconscious one peers, the more absolute this collective nature becomes. In life, this is what allows one soul to bond with another, providing one person with the ability to sense and empathize with the feelings of another; as all social workers learn, conscious effort must be made to prevent such natural subjective, sympathetic reactions from overwhelming the rational intellect.

---

1 Jung, *The Archetypes and the Collective Unconscious*, para. 291, p. 173.
2 In psychological terms, this would be recognized as a huge "complex."
3 *"The right hemisphere [of the brain, governing the subconscious] appears to process information in a holistic manner."* — Springer and Deutsch, 55.

According to Division Theory, in death there would be no conscious mind to make that effort, and so those sympathetic reactions could be expected to reach their maximum effect. Since there is no reason to suppose this collective nature would otherwise be altered by death, this tendency of the unconscious to disregard differentiation and perceive all things as connected would seem likely, after death, to allow the multiple past-life egos within the unconscious to meld together, coalescing into a single unit,[1] which, again, is perhaps that psychic entity, the "devil."

A story in the Gospels provides an excellent illustration of such a "many-into-one" pattern. Jesus asked a certain "evil spirit" possessing a man to identify itself. This entity, repeatedly identified in the scripture as a single entity ("an evil spirit," "he," "him") obviously perceived itself as a single entity as well, since it used the phrase "My name." Yet it apparently also understood that, while single, it was at the same time also composed of many separate individuals, since it later also referred to itself as "we":

> When Jesus got out of the boat, a man with an evil spirit came from the tombs to meet him.... When he saw Jesus ... he shouted "What do you want from me, Jesus, Son of the Most High God?" ... Jesus asked him, "What is your name?" "My name is Legion," he replied, "for we are many."
> — Mark 5:2, 6-9

According to ancient legends and traditions, the dead become the possessions of the devil when they enter hell, becoming fully enslaved to his will. But might this not be because they already had, during their lives, pledged eternal devotion to him? Not knowingly, of course; but the devil may, in effect, disguise himself in life—as their own egos! And when these lost souls go through life placing the concerns of their own egos above all else, they would, unknowingly, be placing themselves in eternal servitude to the devil himself.

This collective unit would function as a single entity, indeed, as Lord, in that unconscious world, holding complete control over all its members. All those in hell would have gotten there by being fully, unquestioningly devoted to their own egos during life; and

---

1 In the subconscious, it is common for several related items to be blended together into a simple whole, by the process of "condensation," according to Freud in *The Interpretation of Dreams* (New York: Avon Books, 1965), 634-36.

once they had become residents in the unconscious realms and were no longer able to think clearly, they would be locked forever in the same belief and behavior patterns they supported when they first entered. As a result, whereas on earth the ego might merely be an insubstantial personality element, in hell it would attain the status of an evil, omnipotent despot who holds absolute control over all its members.

The Bible predicts that this devil will, at the Last Day, be placed in chains for a thousand years. Likewise, according to Division Theory, the human ego would also be restrained, forced into a subordinate position by the unavoidable presence of the Holy Ghost, once it became conscious and active in each person. So, in one version of the story, the human ego will be put in chains, forced into a subordinate position by the Holy Ghost; in another version the devil will be put in chains, forced into a subordinate position by God. Same story, different symbolism. Perhaps the ego *is* the devil.

Christianity has long maintained that this devil is the supreme adversary, the great and sole enemy of each and every person. Yet the Christian religion, as a whole, can also be defined as a creed which advocates *above all else* that the individual human ego be overcome, placed into a subordinate position in the psyche, subordinated to the higher power identified as God. Again, in one version the supreme adversary is the devil, in another version it is the ego. Again, same story, different symbolism.

The ego, when insubordinate, seems to be called the devil in the Western scriptures; he who has an insubordinate ego is said to be "one with" the devil. Likewise, when properly subordinate, this same human ego seems to be identified with Christ; he whose ego is properly subordinated to God is said to be "one with" Christ.

The Morning Star

This apparently potent human ego seems to have another name in the Bible also, a far more ancient title: the "morning star." And this morning star is a perfect symbol for the ego: just as the planet Venus, the real morning star, is like a smaller sun naturally subordinate to the real sun, disappearing in the dawn of the real sunrise, so also the human ego is like a smaller god,[1] which is, or at least

---

1 *"I said, 'You are Gods; you are all sons of the Most High.' But you will die like mere men; you will fall like every other ruler."* —Psalm 82:6-7.

should be, subordinate to the great God. This human ego likewise always disappears from view whenever God openly reveals Himself, just as Jesus' human ego disappeared, or at least became transparent, when the Spirit of God fell upon him.

In one passage, this morning star is identified with the devil himself (Isaiah 14:12), while in another it is identified with Jesus Christ (Revelation 22:16). Before the Fall of humanity, the Bible states that all the morning stars co-existed together happily and harmoniously (Job 38:7). And in the Last Day, those who "overcome" (their own egos?) will receive as their reward this same morning star as their permanent possession (Revelation 2:28; 2 Peter 1:19).[1]

The idea that the ego is of such paramount theological importance would clear up a passage that has confounded scholars for centuries. Isaiah 14:3-20 is a very curious passage which describes the descent into hell of Lucifer, the morning star, who surprises the denizens of hell when they see that he has joined them. But this morning star does not stay in hell; instead, after being "covered with the slain," he is "cast out of the tomb." He will not join his people in burial, the passage declares, for he has destroyed his land and killed his people. Part of this passage seems to refer to the devil (Lucifer, having wanted to raise his throne above God's, making himself like the "Most High"), but other parts sound like Jesus Christ (rising from the dead, being covered with the sins of the people, being a branch). This passage in Isaiah is puzzling because, while it clearly identifies its main character as Lucifer, this Lucifer carries the sins of the world on his shoulders and rises from the dead, logically pointing to identification of the character as Jesus Christ. Somehow, this character in Isaiah seems to be both Jesus and the devil at the same time! Such a paradox brings to mind a passage from the writings of Jung:

> The unconscious is not just evil by nature, it is also the source of the highest good; not only dark but also light; not only bestial, semihuman, and demonic but also superhuman, spiritual, and, in the classic sense of the word, divine.[2]

---

1 Of course, another way to say one was given permanent possession of his own ego would be to say he was given an "eternal name," or, simpler still, "eternal life."

2 Jung, *The Practice of Psychotherapy*, para. 389, p. 192.

This is most confusing. But if, in descending to the grave and accepting the guilt of all mankind, Jesus in effect became the personification of the collective human ego, then during this period he would have also become, if not the actual personification of the devil, then at least the substitute for him. Perhaps when he became Christ, Jesus *became* the collective human ego, or perhaps it is better to say that the collective human ego became him. They merged and became one. Perhaps, by merging and becoming one with God, Jesus also became one with humanity. If so, it would have been possible for him to be described in Isaiah both as devil and Christ at once, for when he descended into hell, he "reunited the opposites," and "made the two one."

Exiles From the Collective

If Division Theory is correct, it would reasonably be expected to provide explanations for most of the legends, beliefs, and phenomena that humanity has found reason to associate with death. Perhaps the most universal of these is the phenomenon of ghosts. Although belief in ghosts has almost always been at least somewhat controversial, virtually every culture and every people throughout history has had at least some traditional belief in ghosts and apparitions. Other than belief in an afterlife, no other facet of death seems to be as absolutely universal as belief in ghosts.

Today, according to a survey conducted by the University of Chicago's National Public Opinion Research Council, 42 percent of all Americans and a staggering 67 percent of widows believe they have had contact with the dead. Of those, 78 percent reported having seen a ghost, and the rest believed they'd heard or felt one.[1]

Such sightings seem at first glance to conflict with the expectations of Division Theory, since ghosts don't seem to have merged into the collective unconscious, but appear instead to have retained their separate identities, somehow hovering faintly on the threshold of the conscious realm of the living. Typical of ghost accounts is a legend in Ancient Assyria that told of Ekimmu, "an evil ghost of one who was denied entrance to the underworld and

---

1 Rosemary Ellen Guiley, *Harper's Encyclopedia of Mystical and Paranormal Experience* (New York: HarperCollins, 1991), 26-27.

was doomed to wander the earth."[1] Similar legends, suggesting that ghosts are the exception rather than the rule in the realm of the dead, can be found in virtually every culture throughout the world. Such souls, for whatever reason, seem either unable or unwilling to merge with the collective. In the Middle Ages, the Roman church taught that ghosts were souls trapped in purgatory until they paid for their sins,[2] and it is common to find stories in native folklore which maintain that the souls of the dead become ghosts only through sin or tragedy, i.e., when something goes wrong.

Although ghosts seem to somehow avoid being swallowed up in any unconscious collective, they do, however, exhibit many of the characteristics Division Theory predicts for a separated unconscious, and so provide further support for Division Theory's basic premise that the conscious and unconscious divide after death.

Haunting apparitions often seem to have emotional ties to the places they frequent.[3] Like "a hiccup in time," ghost appearances often either cyclically or endlessly replay events from the past. Ghosts are commonly reported to be re-enacting long-past emotional traumas, moving about in period clothing[4] and often following floorplans that no longer exist.[5] Such apparitions, researchers suggest, are merely unconscious recordings running on automatic,[6] possessing no more independent consciousness or self-awareness than is possessed by a video recording.

Ghosts, especially haunting ghosts, usually make no attempt to communicate with others; they act as if they are entirely unaware of the presence of the living. When the occasional communication occurs, it tends to be subjective in nature, often involving pictures or symbols. In short, ghostly communiques typically involve classic right-brain formatting of information. There are certain cases in which communicating to ghosts seems possible; exorcism rites occasionally appear to successfully convince a ghost to leave. The majority of ghosts, however—those which endlessly re-enact the

---

1 Rosemary Ellen Guiley, The Encyclopedia of Ghosts and Spirits (New York: Facts on File, 1992), 106.
2 Ibid., 15.
3 Guiley, Harper's Encyclopedia of Mystical and Paranormal Experience, 25.
4 J. Gordon Melton, ed., Encyclopedia of Occultism and Parapsychology, Vol. 1 (Detroit: Gale Research, 1996), 53.
5 Guiley, Encyclopedia of Ghosts and Spirits, 15.
6 Melton, 60.

same events—tend to respond to neither exorcism nor any other attempt at communication.[1] This characteristic lack of communication suggests that such ghosts possess no conscious awareness, that they are merely unconscious automatons, unaware psychic recordings. Although there is little consensus among researchers on the question of whether or not ghosts possess objective conscious intelligence, one of the most dominant schools of thought in the field holds that they do not, a holding that parallels Division Theory. Noticing that apparitions often appear to be sleepwalking, psychic research pioneer F.W.H. Myers suggested that ghosts are actually the unconscious dreams of the dead, somehow made visible.[2]

Other traits, too, offer evidence that perhaps ghosts are the separated and disembodied unconscious as defined in Division Theory. The cold spots often reported near ghosts[3] might betray the constant sensation of cold that would logically be experienced by a dead personal-soul. And, since the sense of smell is thought to be the most instinctual and therefore non-conscious sense man possesses, the frequency with which smells are reported in ghost sightings[4] reinforces the suggestion that ghosts function primarily in and from the unconscious hemisphere of reality.

Ghosts, then, offer an interesting perspective to Division Theory. The universality of ghost reports suggests that there may indeed be some personal-souls that do not enter any unconscious collective after death. These ghosts as reported do, however, exhibit many of the characteristic Division Theory traits of a separated and disembodied unconscious. The sensations attributed to their presence, their communication (or lack thereof), and the "behavior" they exhibit—mindlessly reenacting their unconscious-based, emotionally-charged memories ("treading the winepress") all fit into the scenario defined by Division Theory.

---

1   Guiley, *Encyclopedia of Ghosts and Spirits*, 14, 161.
2   Melton, 59, 581.
3   Ibid., 577.
4   Ibid.

APPENDIX B

RAPTURE BY DEATH

The WallBreaker

There appears to be a conscience in mankind which severely punishes the man who does not somehow and at some time, at whatever cost to his pride, cease to defend and assert himself, and instead confess himself fallible and human. Until he can do this, an impenetrable wall shuts him out from the living experience of feeling himself a man among men.

— C.G. Jung[1]

Division Theory's perspective into the Judeo-Christian prophecies not only offers fresh insights into Judgment Day's general resurrection, but also uncovers a mechanism capable of triggering such an event, showing how the dead might conceivably manage to break back into the conscious world some day.

All through the Biblical passages about the Last Day, there is much more than simply a spiritual upheaval being described; the prophecies also describe—repeatedly, vividly, horribly—a scene of great chaos on earth, great geological calamities and disasters which occur just prior to the "raising of the dead." Throughout all the Bible's prophecies of the Last Day, the same two separate themes are predominant: spiritual warfare and geological calamity. Perhaps these two themes are linked within the prophecies because they constitute a cause-and-effect sequence. From the perspective of Division Theory, the geological disaster could trigger the second, releasing the souls out of their unconscious confinement.

A planet-wide disaster of the sort described within these prophecies would be theoretically capable of knocking down the

---

1   Jung, *Modern Man in Search of a Soul*, 34-35.

wall which normally exists between the conscious and unconscious in the human psyche, if that disaster were traumatic enough to altogether overwhelm humanity's collective unconscious. Any number of causes could elicit an explosion of unbounded emotional distress, and this perhaps is what it would take to rip the wall between the conscious and unconscious in the human psyche.

It is common knowledge within the psychiatric field that excessive emotional stress can overcome the barrier between the conscious and unconscious in an individual's psyche, allowing the contents of the unconscious to temporarily flow freely into the individual's waking consciousness. Many short-term acute-care psychiatric facilities owe their very existences to this phenomenon. But if that emotional stress, instead of being limited to an individual, was experienced globally, and if that stress was so completely devastating that it did not just release the contents of the first level, the personal unconscious, but also the second level, the collective unconscious, the firm barrier which normally keeps humanity's lost souls from rising back up into consciousness might well be rendered ineffective.

The shock wave of intense, overwhelming trauma which would come flooding into humanity's collective unconscious from a planetary disaster such as that described within the biblical Judgment Day prophecies could conceivably "prime the pump" for an equal but opposite flooding outwards from the unconscious world, releasing everything within it, including those held captive there. And, from the perspective of Division Theory, the Biblical prophecies do in fact describe just such a scenario.

- The prophesied cataclysm is to be of planetary proportions:[1]

> The Lord is going to lay waste the earth and devastate it. . . .
> The floodgates of the heavens are opened, the foundations of the earth shake. The earth is broken up, the earth is split asunder, the earth is thoroughly shaken. The earth reels like a drunkard, it sways like a hut in the wind . . . it falls—never to rise again.
> — Isaiah 24:1,18-20

---

1 For other prophecies on a cataclysm of planetary proportions, see: Jeremiah 50:23; Zephaniah 3:8; Joel 2:30; Matthew 24:29.

> I watched as he opened the sixth seal. There was a great earthquake ... the stars in the sky fell to earth. ... The sky receded like a scroll, rolling up, and every mountain and island was removed from its place.
> — Revelation 6:12-14

The great emotional distress from such a catastrophe would have to be beyond all comprehension; the human grief and suffering which would inevitably follow devastation such as this would produce a universal cry of horror, far greater than anything that had ever been heard before.[1] The sheer, staggering force of all the survivors' combined emotional trauma flooding simultaneously into humanity's collective unconscious might well overwhelm it, effectively shutting it down. Just as there is a law in physics which demands that for every action there must be an equal but opposite reaction, so there may also be a similar law governing the dynamics of the psyche. If so, then after that flood of emotions was shotgunned into the unconscious world, that unconscious might in turn then shoot back out all its contents into the world of consciousness. The dividing wall separating the conscious from the unconscious would thus be completely ripped down:

> How broken and shattered is the hammer of the whole earth!
> — Jeremiah 50:23

> The sea [the unconscious] will rise over Babylon [the realm of the dead]; its roaring waves will cover her ...
> I will punish Bel in Babylon and make him spew out what he has swallowed. ...
> Waves will rage like great waters; the roar of their voices [of the dead] will resound. ...
> Babylon's thick wall will be leveled.
> — Jeremiah 51:42,44,55,58

Fury of the Trumpet

• The Judgment Day prophecies include repeated references to the sounding of a great trumpet. This theme reverberates throughout all the Last Day imagery:

---

1 For other passages on the Great Cry, see Isaiah 15:3, 33:7; Jeremiah 30:5, 46:12, 47:2, 49:21.

And in that day a great trumpet will sound.
— Isaiah 27:13

The sovereign Lord will sound the trumpet.
— Zechariah 9:14

• This trumpet is associated with the themes of the rapture and the resurrection:

Listen, I tell you a mystery: We will not all sleep, but we will all be changed—in a flash, in the twinkling of an eye, at the last trumpet. For the trumpet will sound, the dead will be raised imperishable, and we will be changed.
— I Corinthians 15:51-52

• It is also associated with wondrous and dreadful signs appearing in the sky:

At that time the sign of the Son of Man will appear in the sky, and all of the nations of the earth will mourn . . . and he will send his angels with a loud trumpet call, and they will gather his elect from the four winds . . .
— Matthew 24:30-31

The third angel sounded his trumpet, and a great star, blazing like a torch, fell from the sky on a third of the rivers and on the springs of water. . . . a third of the waters turned bitter, and many people died. . . . The fourth angel sounded his trumpet, and a third of the sun was struck, a third of the moon, and a third of the stars, so that a third of them turned dark.
— Revelation 8:10-12

• This trumpet also seems to be directly connected with the geological disaster within the Judgment Day scenario:

The first angel sounded his trumpet, and there came hail and fire mixed with blood, and it was hurled down upon the earth. A third of the earth was burned up . . . The second angel sounded his trumpet, and something like a huge mountain, all ablaze, was thrown into the sea.
— Revelation 8:7-8

• This trumpet seems to be directly connected with the "resurrection of the evil dead" theme:

> The fifth angel sounded his trumpet, and I saw a star that had fallen from the sky to the earth. The star was given the key to the shaft of the Abyss . . . and out of [the shaft] locusts came down upon the earth . . .
> — Revelation 9:1,3

• And, finally, a trumpet is connected with the end of the Judgment Day scenario, in which the kingdom of God becomes established on earth:

> The seventh angel sounded his trumpet, and there were loud voices in heaven, which said: "The kingdom of the world has become the kingdom of our Lord and of his Christ, and he will reign for ever and ever."
> — Revelation 11:15

So, from beginning to end of the entire scenario, trumpets remain a central theme of these Judgment Day prophecies. Assuming these are all related references, possibly even all to the same object, the prophecies describe it as having the following characteristics:

• It seems to be like a great trumpet for God to sound.
• It coincides with and/or causes very frightening sights in the sky.
• It coincides with and/or causes a third of the sky to be darkened.
• It coincides with and/or causes burning material to fall from the sky.
• It coincides with and/or causes a mountainous burning object to fall from the sky.
• It coincides with and/or causes a great star to fall from the sky.
• It makes a very loud noise that all can hear.
• It coincides with and/or causes a third of mankind to be killed.
• It coincides with and/or causes the rapture.
• It coincides with and/or causes the release of "locusts" from a burning Abyss.

- It coincides with and/or causes the resurrection.
- It coincides with and/or causes the establishment of the kingdom of God on earth.

This is not a trumpet! This is a comet! Comets often look like trumpets; their long tails can fan out widely, closely approximating the appearance of a great trumpet suspended in the sky. In fact, a comet's tail often assumes a pronounced curve to it, forming a perfect likeness of the ram's horns which were always used as trumpets in Biblical times. Of course, the world today is not as unfamiliar with comets as they were thousands of years ago; for a comet to come to be referred to as "God's Trumpet" today, it would have to be close enough to the planet to appear positively huge in the sky. Still, these prophecies do report that a full third of the sky is to be blocked out!

For a comet's tail to cover up that much sky, it would have to be dangerously close to the earth; and if it were, debris from that comet could easily become caught by the earth's gravitation and fall to the surface. Such debris would ignite while falling through the atmosphere, and although spectacular, would inevitably create worldwide panic. If that comet's composition included materials poisonous to human beings, that poison would be sure to eventually find its way into fresh water sources, causing widespread poisoning around the globe, again as these prophecies indicate.

And if a large enough portion of that comet's head also became caught in the earth's gravity, it would indeed seem like a great fiery mountain as it plummeted toward the earth. If something as large as this struck the earth, it would be sure to be heard around the world. And since two-thirds of the earth's surface is water, odds are it would fall in the sea.

If a flaming mountain plunged into the sea at supersonic speeds, any water in the vicinity that didn't instantly vaporize would surely start to boil. While seeming to belong in some modern science fiction novel, a vision of just such an event seems to have been foreseen long ago by Nostradamus:

By the heat ... upon the sea ... the fish shall be half broiled.
— II.03

Fish in the sea . . . shall be boiled . . . by heavenly fire.
— V.98

During the time when the hairy star is apparent . . . Struck from heaven . . . quaking earth.
— II.43

Of people and beasts shall be a horrible destruction . . . when the comet shall run.
— II.62

The dart of heaven shall make its great circuit, some die speaking, a great execution . . .
— II.70

• If the head of a comet the size of a mountain hit the earth, it would devastate the entire globe:

The Lord is going to lay waste the earth and devastate it. . . .
The floodgates of the heavens are opened, the foundations of the earth shake. The earth is broken up, the earth is split asunder, the earth is thoroughly shaken. The earth reels like a drunkard, it sways like a hut in the wind . . . it falls—never to rise again.
—Isaiah 24:1,18-20

I will make the heavens tremble; and the earth will shake from its place.
— Isaiah 13:13

• Even if the earth's position was not affected, the comet could cause an alteration in the earth's rotation; if so, the atmosphere would no longer move at the same speed as the earth's surface, causing the sky to appear to flash by at supernatural speeds:

I watched as he opened the sixth seal. There was a great earthquake . . . the stars in the sky fell to earth. . . . The sky receded like a scroll, rolling up, and every mountain and island was removed from its place.
— Revelation 6:12-14

Faith and Betrayal on Judgment Day

Death did not first strike Adam, the first sinful man, nor Cain, the first hypocrite, but Abel, the innocent and righteous. . . . He whom

God loves best dies first, and the murderer is punished with living.
— Joseph Hall[1]

Judgment Day, according to the new perspective provided by Division Theory, would bring a war within the minds and bodies of people; human consciousness would provide the battleground, human unconsciousness the armies. One army would take position before the battle starts; the devil's portion of the unconscious souls of humanity would have been released to wait on the battleground of the conscious living world.

God's influence would have to be totally withdrawn from the world before the evil dead could rush in, allowing mass possession and insanity to run rampant over the planet. For endless ages, the Bible indicates,[2] God held this evil back, but during Judgment Day He would withdraw His restraining forces to allow humanity to fall under the power of its ultimate adversary:

> That final day will not come until the rebellion occurs [souls of hell rebelling from their imposed captivity] and the man of lawlessness [the devil] is revealed [in direct human consciousness], the man doomed to destruction. . . .
> And now you know what is holding him back, so he may be revealed at the proper time. For the secret power of lawlessness is already at work [unconsciously], but the one who holds it back [the Holy Ghost] will continue to do so until he is taken out of the way. And then the lawless one will be revealed [will directly appear in human consciousness].
> — 2 Thessalonians 2:3,6-8

> [God says] I will turn my face from them, and they will desecrate my treasured place; robbers will enter it and desecrate it. . . .
> I will bring the most wicked of the nations to take possession of their houses; I will put an end to the pride of the mighty, and their sanctuaries will be desecrated.
> — Ezekiel 7:22,24

---

1 As quoted by John P. Bradley in *The International Dictionary of Thoughts* (Chicago: J.G. Ferguson Publishing Company, 1969), 193.
2 The nation of dead souls which God causes to attack us—when He steps aside and let them loose—have been waiting for all those endless years: "*O house of Israel,*" *declares the Lord,* "*I am bringing a distant nation against you - an ancient and enduring nation . . . their quivers are like an open grave . . . they will devour your sons and daughters . . . your vines and fig trees . . .*" — Jeremiah 5:15-17.

According to these scriptures, then, the unconscious contents of hell could not be released until the worldly presence of the Holy Ghost, which had been holding it back, was somehow removed out of the way. So long as the unconscious influence of this Holy Ghost even partially intruded into the world of conscious reality, the other side would apparently be forced to remain deeply hidden in the unconscious.

The "rapture" is perhaps the most controversial subject in Western religion. Only after this great event, it's thought, can the Last Day scenario begin, because it would be this rapture which would remove the Holy Ghost from the world. The rapture is expected to be a great, miraculous event in which Jesus himself briefly returns to whisk away all his faithful to safety,[1] far from the coming horrors of the Last Day.

The rapture has been widely discussed in the Christian West; many find it flattering to be told they might be involved in such a miraculous event. People may be disappointed in their expectations, however, because the perspective of Division Theory suggests that the true nature of the rapture has been misunderstood. This rapture is thought to have two purposes: to rescue God's devout, faithful followers from the horrors of Judgment Day, and to clear the way for the "wicked one" to assume control of the earth.

This rapture is generally pictured as being a miraculous event in which millions of people suddenly, mysteriously vanish into thin air, and yet, inexplicably, the rest of the world never even notices this unprecedented sociological event. But reason insists that if the world did suddenly lose a large number of people from every corner of the world for no apparent reason, the loss certainly would get noticed. Such a widespread recognition of the rapture by those who remain doesn't make sense, however; genuine proof of such a supernatural religious phenomenon would obviously warn them that Judgment Day was about to arrive. But the Bible suggests that the world would be taken totally by surprise,[2] falling easily into the Judgment Day trap.

It can be safely reasoned, then, that the rapture would not be obvious. And the only way for large numbers of people from every

---

1   Hal Lindsey, *The Rapture* (New York: Bantam Books, 1983), 41.
2   For passages suggesting that the rapture will not function as a warning to those who survive it, see I Thessalonians 5:2-4; 2 Peter 3:10; Revelation 3:3, 16:15.

walk of life to be removed from the planet without arousing suspicion is to do it the usual way, by having them all appear to leave this world through conventional means: death. The rapture, therefore, in order to remove large numbers of people from every corner of the planet, must appear to be a great worldwide catastrophe; might it not then be the very same catastrophe that starts the whole mess—the geological disaster? One event could do it all, it seems, very efficiently, very effectively; just the sort of quality workmanship that might be expected from a Supreme Being.

The same event needed to create the emotional flood that breaks down the mental wall and releases the dead unconscious souls could simultaneously "cleanse" the conscious world of the Holy Ghost, thus making it possible for the evil dead to actually venture out through the hole ripped in the wall.[1] Perhaps the only ones to die in Judgment Day's geological disaster, then, would be those who carried the awakened Holy Ghost within them; rather than being saved from the events of the Last Day, might the righteous of the earth in fact be the first to die in those events?

> The righteous perish, and no one ponders it in his heart; devout men are taken away, and no one understands that the righteous are taken away to be spared from evil.[2] Those who walk uprightly enter into peace; they find rest as they lie in death.
> — Isaiah 57:1-2

• Modern Christian theory maintains that those people who go through the rapture will be a generation who never know death. This would seem to be both true and not true, depending on one's definition of death. In one respect all would seem to be required to die;[3] all must die in the body:

> In Adam [the physical body] all die. . . .
> Flesh and blood cannot inherit the kingdom of God.
> — I Corinthians 15:22,50

---

1 Amos 4:3.
2 See also Job 14:13: *"If only you would hide me in the grave and conceal me until your anger has passed."*
3 On the inevitability of physical death for all the living, regardless of the rapture, see Ecclesiastes 7:2.

• But perhaps those taken in the rapture will only separate from their bodies, not separate their souls from their spirits. Instead of finding their souls entering the unconscious realm of death, they would maintain spiritual unity, becoming, in effect, an entirely new life form, a soul and a spirit without any human body:

> Listen, I tell you a mystery: We will not all sleep, but we will all be changed—in a flash, in the twinkling of an eye . . .
> — I Corinthians 15:51

• If so, then the only real miracle about the rapture would be that those who die in it would have been specifically hand-picked by God; only those who had awakened the Holy Ghost within them would be taken, and those who hadn't, wouldn't:

> I tell you on that night, two people will be in one bed; one will be taken and the other left. Two women will be grinding grain together; one will be taken and the other left.
> — Luke 17:34-35

• During such a worldwide catastrophe, where no place on the planet was safe, God would be able to efficiently and subtly remove His followers with no one the wiser. God could remove from danger the portion of mankind He claims as His own:

> A third of mankind was killed.
> — Revelation 9:18

• This rapture, according to these scriptures, would be but the first of two different "harvests" by God. The first such harvest would be of those who were consciously attuned with the Holy Ghost at the time of the catastrophe, while the second would come at the very end of Judgment Day:[1]

> In that day the Lord will reach out His hand a second time to reclaim the remnant that is left of His people. . .
> — Isaiah 11:11

---

1 On the spiritual Tribulation period occurring after the first harvest, the rapture, and before the second crop to be harvested is ready, see Amos 7:1. On the second harvest of souls, see also Jeremiah 6:9.

According to the Lord's own word, we tell you that we who are still alive [in the body], who are left till the coming of the Lord, will certainly not precede those who have fallen asleep . . . the dead . . . will rise first. After that, we who are still alive and are left will be caught up with them in the clouds to meet the Lord in the air. And so we will be with the Lord forever.

— I Thessalonians 4:15-17

Such a rapture would indeed be likely to be completely overlooked by the world. A great natural catastrophe would have killed a third of the world's population; in the middle of so much tragedy and confusion, no one would ever notice, or even consider the possibility that it had been the most moral, unassuming, longsuffering, selfless people who were struck down in the cataclysm.

Such a rapture would represent a final test of faith for the faithful. Seeing that the devout were falling on both right and left, believers would be sore tempted to conclude that their hopes for salvation were in vain, that their faith had been betrayed by the Almighty. Faith in the face of certain defeat and abandonment would seem to be the order of the day; how disappointing it would be to give up on God's promise mere moments before it was to be fulfilled! But how absolute the faith of those who did hold on despite all reason!

NOSTRADAMVS

Parallel Prophecies

The Sixteenth-Century Gnostic

Another seems to have been familiar with Division Theory, perhaps just as well as the Gnostics were: Michel de Nostredame. Better known as Nostradamus, this character has grown to legendary proportions in the 400 years since he lived, due to the legacy of 1,000 prophecies he left the world. While many dismiss him today, a number of his prophecies are widely believed to have come true over the last 400 years,[1] and they continue to be read just as they have been since their original publication.

It seems to be an almost universal condition of "prophets" that their prophecies be primarily religious-spiritual in nature, as those of the Hebrew prophets were. On the surface, Nostradamus is the exception to this rule; his prophecies seem almost exclusively political, and hardly religiously oriented at all. This seems doubly odd when one examines his personal letters, for in them he reveals himself to be a strongly religious person, whose paramount concerns were religious-spiritual in nature.[2] But if so, then why do his prophecies not reflect this nature?

The Inquisition may be the answer. Nostradamus lived during an era of extreme religious persecution; if he had openly authored any works of which the ruling powers didn't approve, they would have executed him without hesitation. If Nostradamus had seen

---

1 Jean-Charles de Fontebrune, *Nostradamus* (New York: Holt, Rinehart, and Wilson, 1980), viii, 436.
2 Henry Thomas, trans. and ed., *The Complete Prophecies of Nostradamus* (Oyster Bay, NY: Nostradamus Co., 1982), 3-8, in the letter of dedication to his son.

any hidden meaning in the Biblical prophecies or any suggestions about reincarnation, mass possession, or any of the rest, he would probably have been wise enough to realize that the church didn't want to hear about it.

With this in mind, a reexamination of Nostradamus's prophecies becomes very educational. It seems that he did recognize the secret message hidden within the books of the prophets and designed his own prophecies in the same manner. Perhaps, like the Jewish seers before him, Nostradamus (born a Jew himself) hid his own vision[1] of Judement Day in the midst of a collection of generic political predictions, thus securing his vision's place in history without risking execution.

A chief argument against any serious study of Nostradumus's ancient prophecies has been that their convulated, vague, nebulous style makes them subject to any number of interpretations. While I understand this genuine concern, it is nevertheless clear to me that many of his quatrains align themselves absolutely perfectly with Division Theory. In fact, many which seem confusing and nonsensical suddenly make perfect and obvious sense when viewed through the lens of Division Theory.[2]7x46

Nostradamus wrote just under 1,000 prophecies in all; of these, nearly 100 refer to Division Theory. I have included a number of them for examination here.[3]7x46

• On the fundamental division of human consciousness and the inevitable return of the dead souls during Judgment Day:

> The great tapestry [of life] is folded, and does not show except by halves for the greater part of its history. Those who had been chased far away out of the realm [the personal-souls of the dead] appear, harshly, so everyone will come to believe in their warlike act.
> — VI. 61

• On the souls' return being a part of God's plan to reunite Himself with all humanity, he wrote:

---

1 Thomas, 8.
2 Some of the most unmistakable are II.13, II.45, VI.61, and VII.24.
3 The translations are mine, from the French texts found in Henry C. Roberts' *The Complete Prophecies of Nostradamus* (Oyster Bay, NY: Nostradamus Company, 1982) and Erika Cheetham's *The Prophecies of Nostradamus* (New York: Putnam, 1980).

The King [God] will want to enter within the new city [Man]; his coming is by way of enemies storming in, captives [dead personal-souls] who are falsely liberated [temporarily raised from the dead] in order to speak and act.[1] The King will stay far away from the enemies through all of this.

— IX. 92

• On the reunion of the feminine souls and masculine spirits of all humanity:

The heavens weep excessively as Androgynous Man is born. Close to heaven, human blood responds [human souls cry out in pain as God draws near]. A great nation is re-created out of death too late. Late and early comes the expected help [for the Christians who find themselves pushed into the unconscious realms, Christ's return seems too late; for the hellish personal-souls who only briefly get to taste life again, Christ's return seems too early].

— II. 45

• On the opening of the mental wall between the unconscious soul and the conscious spirit:

In God's heaven, in the Kingdom of God, through force the great doors will be made to open, God and Man joined. The port [of the unconscious] destroyed, religion discarded [because it's no longer necessary once God and Man are directly joined], a serene day.

— X. 80

• On the troubles Christians would encounter with possession when God turns away:

When those of the cross [the Christians] find their senses troubled, in the place of that which is sacred [their own souls], they will instead see a horned bull [a devil]. Through the virgin [the unconscious], the pig's place [hell] will be packed full.[2] Order will no longer be maintained by the King [God].

— VIII. 90

• On the departure of the Holy Ghost and the onslaught of the souls from Hell:

---

1 Compare with Isaiah 10:5-7; Revelation 17:17.
2 Compare with Jeremiah 51:51.

The divine voice [the Holy Ghost] will be struck [silent] by heaven, and will not proceed further. From the unlocking [of the door], the secret [Holy Ghost] is shut up, so that people [armies of dead personal-souls] march over and above [you].[1]
— II. 27

• On Christians submitting under the pressure of mass possession:

Out of great discord the trumpet shakes. The broken covenant [between the soul and spirit] will raise [all] faces to heaven. Bloody voices [dead personal-souls] swimming within one's very blood, Those anointed with milk and honey [the Christians] lie with their faces on the floor [as the dead personal-souls overwhelm them].[2]
— I. 57

• A warning to voluntarily withdraw from consciousness to the safety of the unconscious realms during Judgment Day:

Leave, leave from [the land of] Genesis, everyone! The Age will change from one of Gold to one of Iron. Those against the betrayer of Babylon [Christ] will all be exterminated. Before the rush [of personal-souls], the sky will show signs.[3]
— IX. 44

• On Christians needing to take up Christ's cross rather than going into battle during the Day of the Lord:

The signal to go into battle [against the dead personal-souls] is not given, [Instead,] those of the garden [the conscious world] will be forced to leave there. The sign of the Great deliberate one [God] will be recognized, he who will make all his followers lie down and die.[4]
— X. 83

• On Christians resisting the urge to fight for their own lives during the siege, but instead placing all their faith in God and allowing themselves to be mentally submerged out of the conscious world of the living:

1   Compare with Psalm 66:11-12.
2   Compare with Isaiah 51:23.
3   Compare with Luke 21:25-26.
4   Compare with Mark 10:39.

By the abundance of tears shed, those from the top [are forced down] on the bottom, by the bottom coming all the way up to the very top. Having great faith, gambling to lose their lives, They die of famine by choosing to default [their own spirits].
— VIII. 100

• On the retiring of Christians into the unconscious realms, and the awakening of the personal-souls from hell:

Western citizens placed their treasure in the temple [the soul], And [then] retired within that secret place themselves [when] the temple is opened, the famished enslaved beasts delightedly regain consciousness, a horrible prey within.
— X. 81

• On the eventual end of spiritual death, when, instead of consciousness splitting apart at death, a guarantee of immediate reincarnation without memory loss is given:

The body without a soul is to be sacrificed no more. At the very day of death it is born again.[1] The divine spirit will make the soul rejoice, seeing the Word in its eternity.
— II. 13

Like the Hebrew prophets before him, Nostradamus made multiple references to each phase of Judgment Day. The references can be grouped under eight headings: an overview; the resurrection of the dead; incarnation fighting incarnation; two roads for Christians during Judgment Day; the rising of the devil; Jesus' Second Coming; the Wall being reformed; and the warning being sounded.

Part One: Quatrains Giving an Overview of the Judgment Day Scenario

The great theatre will bring itself back up straight.
The die is cast and the net is spread.
Those who put themselves first too much will tire of tolling
They were destroyed by arks that were split long ago.
— III.40

---

1 Compare with Isaiah 34:17, 56:5; John 3:16.

All the theatre of human history, with all the original players, will rise back up from the dead. Everything is already prearranged, and the trap is set. All the proud and selfish will tire of being dead; they were destroyed a long time ago when their own holy arks, the psyche, were split apart into soul and spirit.

> The free city of liberty was made a city of slaves
> And the shelter of the banished and dreamers.
> The King changes his fierce denial to them,
> From a hundred they will become more than a thousand.
> — IV.16

Conscious human life, which was originally designed for free spirits, eventually came to contain only those enslaved by sin. The human unconscious came to shelter the cast-off souls of the dead, deep inside itself. When God changes His denial of life and consciousness to these dead souls, they will multiply into more than a thousand conscious personal-souls all co-existing within the same living body.

> The bones of the hands and feet are tied up,
> Due to noise the house is deserted a long time.
> Through dreams, the buried will be exhumed,
> A healthy house, inhabited without noise.
> — VII.41

The remains of the dead, their personal-souls, are normally restrained in death by being imprisoned in the unconscious. Due to psychological disturbances (the soul's unconscious response to sin), those personal-souls were forced into death, thus deserting their spirits for a long time. But by material arising through the unconscious, those personal-souls who were dead and buried will be lifted from death, to occupy healthy bodies, without any more unconscious psychological disturbances.

> The royal scepter will be obligated to take on
> That which his predecessors had pawned.
> Afterwards the lamb will hurt them to understand,
> When they come to plunder the palace.
> — VII.23

The supreme ruler, Jesus, will be obligated to assume the debts which those rulers (living personal-souls) who came before him had accumulated. After he fulfills their debts, he will hurt them, to get them to understand the precarious nature of their position, when they come to plunder the physical world.

> There will be fire, flame, hunger, theft, wild smoke,
> Which will cause fainting, bruising hard to jar faith.
> Son of God! All creation swallowed up!
> Others are chased from the kingdom, enraged but not spitting.
> — XII.05

The hungry personal-souls from fiery hell will steal life from the living, causing the living to faint into the unconscious. This is intended by God to occur, giving people a "shove" in order to wake up their faith. At his Second Coming, Jesus absorbs all humanity within himself. Those who are chased into the darkness of the unconscious are furious, but powerless to object.

> The divine Word will give to creation that which comprises heaven and earth:
> Hidden gold into the mystic milk.
> Body, soul, spirit are all powerful,
> There is so much under the feet, on the throne of heaven.
> — III.02

Jesus, the "Word of God," will provide to humanity the most precious of all gifts, revealing a secret treasure hidden within life's most basic pattern: when body, soul, and spirit are all properly united, they become all powerful, and so much power and resources become available that it's like sitting on the throne of heaven itself.

> Those who are second or third yet make first class music
> Will be sublimely honored by the King,
> Even though they are fat, thin, even half emaciated.
> The only yield of the false source of pleasure will be to make one debased.
> — X.28

Those who do their very best even without recognition will be greatly honored by God, even though they may not seem outwardly deserving. But the only thing that comes from seeking benefits for oneself is to compromise the integrity of one's own soul.

The faint voice of a soul is heard under holy ground,
Human flame shines for the divine voice.
The earth will be stained by the blood of the solitary ones.
And the sacred temples of the impure are destroyed.
— IV.24

The Holy Ghost can be faintly heard within one's own soul; the human spirit shines brightly under the influence of this Holy Ghost. The earth will be stained by the evil of those who wish to remain independent of this Holy Ghost. And the personal-souls of the impure will be destroyed.

Part Two: Quatrains on the Resurrection of the Dead

Bones from the three-leveled vessel will be found
By those searching for a profound, enigmatic treasure.
Those thereabout this stone hollow and lead seal
Will not be in repose.
— V.07

Dead personal-souls, the remains of the living (which are composed of three parts—body, soul, and spirit—when alive) will be found in the unconscious by those searching for the secrets of life and death. But those found to still reside in this ancient tomb will not be at rest.

Whoever opens the discovered tomb,
And does not close it again promptly,
Evil will befall him, and he won't be able to say
Which is better, a British or Norman king.
— IX.07

Whoever purposely tries to awaken the dead personal-souls hidden deep within his own psyche, and does not immediately cease such efforts when he does make contact, will suffer great evil, and will end up in such a state that he won't be able to tell the difference between the thoughts of one life and the next.

What a pity it will be—before much longer
Those who gave will be forced to take.
Naked, famished, cold, they will mutiny,
To get across mountains, making great disorder.
— VI.69

Before much more relative time elapses since Christ's resurrection (Nostradamus wrote in the 1500s), those dead personal-souls who treated people unjustly when alive will finally find themselves on the receiving end. Bodiless, hungry for life, such dead personal-souls from hell will eventually revolt from their captivity, crossing the barrier between the conscious and unconscious, causing great trouble in the world.

> The deformed ones are born out of suffocating horror
> Into the inhabitable city of the great King.
> The severe edict of the captives revoked,
> Hail and thunder beyond all estimation.
> — V.97

The warped personal-souls of the evil dead are reborn out of the suffocating horror of hell itself, reappearing in the place where people live, in the "Temple of God," the human body. When the severe ruling which originally condemned these personal-souls to experience death's division of soul and spirit is revoked, there will be unimaginable distress on the earth.

> To the enemy, the enemy promised its faith.
> Not kept, the captives are returned.
> The principal ones are taken near death,
> And the rest, clothed, the rest are damned for being supporters.
> — X.01

To Christ, the true enemy is a person who is faithful only to himself and his own ego. Instead of being kept eternally imprisoned in the realm of death as they had expected, the unconscious personal-souls of the dead are released from their captivity and returned to conscious life. The most important and precious of the living, the Christians, are taken very near death, swimming in the unconscious, while all the rest, those who refuse to give up their physical bodies again, are condemned for supporting the insubordinate human ego and all its works.

> Three-leveled vessels full of captives of all ages.
> The time is good for evil, sweet for the bitter ones.
> Others are prey to the barbarians, who, in their haste, will be too soon.
> They were anxious to see the feather shake in the wind.
> — X.97

The living, naturally composed of three parts, secretly contain captive dead personal-souls from all the ages of history. At first, Judgment Day is pleasant for the evil dead, sweet for hell's bitter and resentful residents. Others become the prey of these barbarians, who, in their haste to return to life, rise from the dead before it is safe to do so. Those of the living who woke them were also hasty, anxious to see proof that their past personal-souls truly existed within, and could really speak through subtle voices, such as "channeling."

Part Three: Quatrains on Incarnation Fighting Incarnation

After the truce is made,
From new clothes comes malice, plotting, and machination.
The first to die will be one who produces evidence
The "pleasure policy" is a trap.
— IV.06

After the evil personal-souls are reunited with their original conscious spirits, as soon as they put on physical bodies again, conflict and evil intention will follow, as each newly risen personal-soul struggles to become the dominant identity within the psyche. After these personal-souls begin to emerge from the unconscious, the first to reenter that realm of death will be those who recognize that using this regained physical life only to again pursue pleasure is a mistake, a trap that will end up destroying them entirely.

The populated places will be uninhabitable:
A great division to obtain fields:
Realms given to those incapable of prudence:
Death and dissention among brothers.
— II.95

During Judgment Day, the living will be unable to stay where they had been living, their own bodies. There will be great division and conflict among all those awakened dead who wish to occupy the body, but they are all frenzied, none cautious. While technically they are all related incarnations of one another, each of these personal-souls try to press the others back into the realm of the dead.

The child in front of the father will be killed,
The father, afterwards, will enter the chaff.

The people of the land of Genesis will be striving,
Their leader lying in their midst like a log.
— X.92

The personal-souls of one's later incarnations will be pressed into the unconscious realm of death by the souls of those incarnations which preceded them. The earlier personal-souls will later be fully extinguished, judged to be only good as food for the fire. All the souls of Creation will be struggling together, while Christ lies perfectly still right in their midst.

By hunger, the prey will make the wolf a prisoner,
And the attacker will then be in extreme distress,
The born one finds the last one in front of him.
The great do not escape from the middle of the pressing crowd.
— II.82

The denizens of hell, so hungry for life, will become the distressed prisoners of the very ones they sought to attack. The living will find their previous incarnations appearing directly before them in their conscious awareness. Those who are more proud than humble won't be able to escape, becoming trapped in a crowd of their peers.

Part Four: Quatrains On the Two Roads for Christians During Judgment Day

Whom neither plague nor sword could destroy
Dead on the mount's summit, struck from heaven.
The abbot will die when he sees ruined
Those of the shipwreck trying to catch the rock.
— II.56

There will be some, of whom neither sin's plagues nor death's dividing sword can separate soul from spirit; it will be these, the wholest of the whole, who die in the rapture. Having climbed to the highest level of true Christianity, truly "living" in Christ, they are the ones struck down by heaven. After this rapture has removed the Holy Ghost from the world, effectively wrecking the "ship" of the church, the remaining leaders of that now purely earthly church will mourn when they see many who only then begin to seek faith, the "rock" of Peter.

The army of the sea will stand before the city,
Then go away for a little while.
A citizen army will then hold the land.
The fleet returns to take back the great stolen thing.
— X.68

Christ's unconscious army from heaven will momentarily stand before the city of human consciousness during the rapture, then will briefly depart, allowing the army of the evil dead to occupy human consciousness. Then Christ's legions will return, repossessing the conscious spirit which the evil dead had stolen from the living.

Before the battle, the great wall will fall,
The great are to die, a death too sudden and bewailed.
The church being imperfect, most will swim,
Near the river of blood, the earth is tainted.
— II.57

Before Judgment Day's final battle, the barrier separating the conscious and unconscious will fall, and those who are truly great in God's eyes will die sudden deaths, causing mourning around the world. The Christian church is imperfect—although many people do believe in Christ, few truly "live" in him, so most of the world's professing Christians will end up swimming in the unconscious during Judgment Day. The entire earth is approached by the unconscious' river of personal-souls from hell, and takes on hell's dishonor.

Instead of the bride, the maids slaughtered,
Murder a great mistake, none will survive;
Within the well, clothed ones drowned,
The spouse extinguished by high poison.
— IV.71

The most faithful and pure Christians will become Christ's "spouse" during Judgment Day, being consciously united to him in the rapture, when they die quickly from poisonous death that comes from the sky. Many professing Christians, however, instead of becoming Christ's "bride," will remain unmarried "maids" who are later slaughtered by the evil dead during Judgment Day, sent off alone into the unconscious. These believers will consider their own murders a horrible mistake; they thought they had understood that God was not going to allow such a thing to happen to them! All who stay clothed in their physical bodies during the rapture will later be drowned in the unconscious by the risen evil dead.

> The great army that will be driven out
> In a moment will be needed by the king.
> Because the faithful word which had been promised from afar will
> be false and distorted,
> They will be left naked, in pitiful disarray.
> — IV.22

Those who voluntarily enter the unconscious prior to Christ's Second Coming and those who were removed in the rapture will be simultaneously asked to return en masse, at the very moment of the Second Coming. But because the message of the Christian faith came from so long ago, time severely deteriorated its original message; for this reason, many of the world's believing Christians, misguided about what their faith truly required, will not be taken in the rapture, but will instead suffer being tossed out of their bodies by the evil dead, to be left in pitiful condition for a time.

> Many will be confounded in their expectation,
> The inhabitants will not be pardoned,
> Who thought to persevere in their resolution.
> But they will not be given a great deal of spare time off.
> — VIIIB.01

Many professing Christians, those who believed in but did not fully "live" in Christ, will be confounded in their expectation that they would be spared the tribulations of Judgment Day: they will not be pardoned, even though they thought that their belief alone would be enough to keep them alive and safe. But they will not have to wait long in the unconscious realms.

> The undersigned to a worthless deliverance
> Will receive contrary advice from a multitude.
> Changing their monarch puts their thoughts in peril.
> They will see themselves shut up in a cage.
> — IX.47

Those who, during the tribulation of Judgment Day, worry that their trust in Christ's promise of deliverance was mistaken, will be encouraged by many to turn away from him. But changing their loyalties from Christ to their own egos, their own self-interests, will open them up to thoughts which can place them in mortal danger. Those who do desert Christ during Judgment Day will be betrayed by such poor judgment; they will end up permanently imprisoned in the unconscious when Judgment Day is over.

> In the conflict, those who are great yet are valued as little
> At their ends will do an astonishing deed.
> While the king sees that which he required,
> During a feast he stabs the proud.
> — II.55

During Judgment Day, those who are great yet who receive no great recognition, the true Christians, will do something amazing by trusting in Christ enough to enter the unconscious realm of death voluntarily. When God sees this, the act of pure faith He will be waiting for, He will destroy all the evil dead while they are still feasting on the conscious life, thus destroying all those too proud to submit to Him.

> The great army led by a young man
> Will give itself up into the hands of the enemies:
> But the old man born to the half-pig
> Will make neighbors sue their friends.
> — III.69

A great number of Christians in the world, following Jesus' injunctions to "give to those who ask" and "turn the other cheek," will voluntarily give up and allow the clamoring souls around them to force them into the unconscious. But the ancient devil, the unconscious offspring of the insubordinate human ego (which is so selfish and cruel it does not deserve to even be called "human"), will cause great conflict between those personal-souls who, popping up to consciousness in the same body, choose to remain and fight for rights of possession.

> By deceitful trickery, the commander of the group
> Will make the meek ones leave their vessels.

They come out, murdered by the chief renouncer of baptism.
After that, by an ambush, they give him his just deserts.
— IX.79

The devil, who commands the evil dead, will trick the meek (the Christians) into leaving their conscious bodies. They come out, murdered by the devil/ego, who rejects all submission to God. After that, by an ambush, the Christians return, and pay that devil the justice he deserves.

There will be a king who will give the opposite,
The exiles raised over the kingdom:
The poor chaste nation will swim in blood.
And will even flourish a long time under such a design.
— V.52

God will exchange death for life and life for death;[1] the souls exiled in death will be raised up to take over the kingdom of the living. The Christians, poor yet pure, will swim in the unconscious realm of death, and will even be comfortable and safe in that place.

From where it had been thought famine would come,
From there will come fullness.
The eye of the sea is reached by way of bestial miserliness:
One man will be given to another food stuffs.
— IV.15

The realm of the dead, into which the Christians are pushed during Judgment Day, is expected to deprive them of what they need, but instead they will find total satisfaction when they enter there. They enter that place, the center of the unconscious, because the beastly personal-souls who enter their conscious world are selfish and will not share life with them. Instead, the evil dead consume the life force of the living as if it were food.

Wisdom and understanding[2] being in the world,
Public blood is shed for new truths.

---

1   As in Amos 9:13: " 'The days are coming,' declares the Lord, 'when the reaper will be overtaken by the plowman, and the planter by the one treading grapes . . .'"
2   Instead of "wisdom and understanding," Nostradamus actually wrote " 'the rose' in the world," but elsewhere, in quatrain V.31, Nostradamus stated that "the rose of the world" is "wisdom and understanding," which does fit in well with quatrain V.96, concerning, as it does, "truth" and "speaking truth."

Every one who speaks the truth will have their mouths closed,
Then, the awaited one will come late to their distressful need.
— V.96

Once Jesus, the personification of wisdom and understanding, has been reborn in the world, the personal-souls of the living start to be pushed down into the unconscious realms by the awakened dead, once the truth of the unconscious existence of the dead is recognized. Once the reawakening of the evil dead has begun, all who mention the truth of Christ will be banished into the unconscious by those evil dead. Then, their awaited Savior will not save them right away, but will make them wait awhile in the unconscious realms.

In a short time sacrifices will return,
Opposers will be put to martyrdom.
No more will there be monks, abbots, novices;
Honey will be more cherished than wax.
— I.44

During Judgment Day, the evil dead will deceitfully encourage all the living to make "small sacrifices," to temporarily step aside so that the dead can have a chance to briefly regain consciousness. But many of the living, especially all those who oppose this plan, will be made into human sacrifices, becoming trapped in that unconscious. All those connected with the Christian church will thus be deported into the unconscious, and the teachings of Christ will be granted no respect. All associated with the church will be considered worthless; only physical delights will be recognized as valuable.

The buried will come out of the tombs.
The strong of the church
Will be tied with chains,
Poisoned by the offspring of a pimp.
— VII.24

The personal-souls of the dead will rise back to life. Those Christians who find more glory in strength and pride than in Christ's meekness and humility will be imprisoned and restrained within themselves, poisoned from within by the devil, the inevitable unconscious companion of those who sell their inner virtue for mere self-aggrandizement.

The just will be wrongfully put to death,
Publicly extinguished from their midst.
[Then] so great a plague will come to rise in that place,
That the judges will be forced to flee.
— IX.11

The Christians will be wrongfully put to death during Judgment Day, executed by evil personal-souls who have appeared right in the midst of their own psyches. Following this, so great a plague will rise up within that same psyche that those same personal-souls will then be forced to flee back into the unconscious themselves.

The nocturnal race from the land of Genesis is dried up with hunger.
Immediate hope will come to those who faint.
The hellish order will be at a breaking point.
Their group won't be accepted at the great port.
— II.64

Dead personal-souls from the land of Creation are now trapped in the dark side of human consciousness, dried up by a lack of the living spirit. But during Judgment Day, this will change, and immediate hope will come to those who faint away into that unconscious. The order which normally controls the unconscious realms is about to break and fail, but those personal-souls from hell will never be allowed in conscious living bodies after Christ returns.

After the conflict comes the eloquence of the injured one
For a little while in his web of holy rest.
The anointed one does not admit the great to deliverance
But instead the enemies are fittingly repaid.
— II.80

After entering the unconscious during Judgment Day, good personal-souls get to enjoy the eloquence of Christ, the "crucified one," resting with him for a while in his unconscious heaven. Christ, also called the "anointed one," does not allow the egotistic and proud to be saved, counting them instead as enemies who should be repaid with justice.

Part Five: Quatrains on the Devil Rising

A false image will come to expose the true landscape.
The urns of the tombs will be opened.
Sects and holy philosophy will swarm,
Black for white and new for old.
— VII.14

The devil, the false unconscious mirror image of the human ego, will expose the true nature of human existence; the unconscious vaults containing the personal-souls of the dead will be opened. Numerous sects and religious philosophies will spring up in the world as a consequence of the rising of these personal-souls, teaching many falsehoods, and all the while exchanging new personal-souls for old ones.

When the Sun is eclipsed in broad daylight,
The monster will be seen.
It will be interpreted in quite other ways.
They will not care about expense, but no one will have provided for it.
— III.34

When the light of human consciousness starts to be eclipsed during life instead of at death, that secret hidden monster, the devil, the unconscious offspring of the human ego, will be able to be clearly perceived by the living for the first time in history. No one, however, will comprehend what it is they are truly encountering. Those who foolishly rush to awaken their own past-life personal-souls will not care about the consequences of this act, consequences for which they will be totally unprepared.

When the beast so familiar to humanity
Comes to speak after great labor and leaping,
The lightning shall be so hurtful to a virgin,
That she'll be taken from the earth and suspended in the air.
— III.44

Shortly after the evil dead start to reawake, the human ego's unconscious "alter-ego," the devil, will begin to communicate and act in waking human consciousness. The Second Coming of Jesus Christ (which will be "like lightning") will be so injurious to those "pure of soul," the virgin-like truest Christians, that they will be removed from the earth altogether, in the rapture.

Part Six: Quatrains on the Second Coming

Royal Priest drawn down too low,
A great flow of blood will come out his mouth.
The angelic reign breathing by royal authority,
A long time dead, alive in the city of the dead, like a stump.
— X.56

Jesus Christ, both king and priest, was drawn down too low into the human unconscious by his death. But at the Second Coming, an explosive instant of infinite pain will burst out of him like a flash of lightning, when all humanity's soul-pain, which he experienced unconsciously at his crucifixion and resurrection, will finally be granted full conscious release, utterly melting all those personal-souls occupying the highest levels of consciousness at that exact moment. Then the personal-souls of heaven will enter the vacated conscious living bodies and start breathing again, having been returned to life by the will of God. They had been dead a long time, yet not truly dead, but only unconscious and dormant.

By lightning entering into the ark,
Gold and silver are melted.
Of two captives, one will devour the other.
The greatest in the city lie down, they all swim submerged.
— III.13

By the "lightning" of the Second Coming entering into the human psyche, the holy ark containing the living spirit, the spirit and soul are permanently melded together. But prior to Christ's Second Coming, whenever there are more than one of the raised captive evil dead occupying the same psyche, each will try to devour the other. True Christians all submit, and are forced to swim far beneath the surface of consciousness.

In closed temples the lightning will fall.
The natives there will be distressed by their own strength.
Beasts and men together, the wave will touch the wall.
The more weakly armed ones will go under by hunger and thirst.
— III.06

The "lightning" of the Second Coming will fall within the psyches of those who have closed themselves off to Christ. Those therein will suddenly find that the very strength they sought is a curse instead of an advantage. Personal-souls and devils together, the wave of the unconscious will touch the wall of soul-pain within the psyche. The weak will then be the lucky ones, for they will be already submerged within the unconscious when the "lightning" falls.

> The false shadow of the holy kingdom
> Will make the life of the strong illegal.
> The promised vow, the uncertainty of the ark.
> The King of the golden connection will give a legitimate wall.
> — X.45

The devil, the false unconscious mirror image of the conscious ego, will insure that only those forceful enough to keep themselves alive and conscious during Judgment Day will be condemned. The time will have come for God's promise, that "all who call on the name of the Lord will be saved," to be tested, when the "ark" of the self becomes uncertain and insecure. God, the master of the connection between the soul and spirit, will establish a proper wall to keep the evil dead apart from living consciousness.

> The fugitives and the banished are recalled,
> Fathers and sons filling up the upper chambers.
> The cruel father and his followers will be suffocated.
> His son, the worst of all, will be submerged in the pit.
> — IV.53

When the good personal-souls who had been banished into the realm of death are finally recalled, many generations of the same self will join together, filling up the upper levels of consciousness. The insubordinate human ego, and all those devoted to it, will be suffocated by a lack of life and consciousness. The offspring of that ego, the devil, will be totally submerged in Christ's soul-pain.

> The natural ones are high, high not low.
> The late return will make the sad contented.
> The reconciled one will not be without disputes,
> In applying and losing all his time.
> — X.84

During Judgment Day, those who have fully regained the natural unity between their souls and spirits will be raised up in the rapture, instead of being lowered into the unconscious realms. But those who are lowered into the unconscious will think their Savior is late in rescuing them; however, when he finally does come they will be completely satisfied. Those evil personal-souls who only become reconciled to Christ at the last moment, while being rewarded with eternal life for their faith, will still suffer, by being forced to obey him all the time.

> By unbridled love, the crossed brother
> Will cause one who rises up too high to die by divine power.
> Fleet into a thousand years, the frantic, crazed female,
> Both will die after the drink is drunk.
> — VIII.13

Because of his unlimited brotherly love for all humanity, Christ suffered the agony of the cross. This sacrifice gave him the divine power and right to cause all dead personal-souls who rise back up to consciousness before he does to die. The personal-souls from heaven are granted continuous life, while the insane evil souls return to the unconscious. Both those who remain alive during the Second Coming and those evil souls who return to hide in the unconscious at that moment will die when Christ's full cup of soul pain is poured out upon them.

> Closed eyes shall be opened by an ancient fantasy.
> The clothing of the solitary ones shall be brought to nothing.
> The great monarch will punish their frenzy,
> Snatching the treasure from in front of their temples.
> — II.12

The closed eyes of the dead will be reopened by the devil, the artificially evolved unconscious mirror image of the insubordinate human ego. The physical bodies of those who choose to remain independent and alone, who refuse to join with Christ, will be taken from them by force. God will punish the "feeding frenzy" of the reawakened evil dead, snatching their newly regained treasure, life itself, from their grasp.

> The bright splendor of the joyous maid
> Will shine no longer, long will she be without salt

With merchants, ruffians, abhorrent wolves
All a universal monstrous jumble.
      — X.98

Maiden-like because they refused to "marry" Christ, the evil dead will be overjoyed to regain the splendor of living consciousness at the beginning of Judgment Day, but the taste of life will be taken away from them again during Christ's Second Coming. These lost personal-souls will return together into the deepest reaches of humanity's collective unconscious. There, all of them, deceitful and wicked in every way humanity has devised, will coalesce into a single jumbled unconscious mass.

The false images puffed up with gold and silver
Will be thrown into the lake of fire after the kidnapping.
At the discovery, all quenched and disturbed.
Precepts inserted, written in stone.
      — VIII.28

Their egos were revived by reuniting their personal-souls and spirits. After kidnapping the bodies of the living, the evil dead will be condemned into the fire of Christ's soul-pain. All evil will be quenched, and the whole universe changed around, when the subconscious existence of Christ is discovered inside each personal-soul. New laws will then be written directly into humanity's souls by Christ's conscious presence.

The deceiver will be put into the dungeon,
and bound fast for a while.
The clergy is united, and the chief, with his cross upright,
Pointed upward, will draw in contented ones.
      — VIII.95

At the end of Judgment Day, the devil will be imprisoned in the deepest unconscious, the churches and religions of the world will be united, and Christ, once again alive and strong, and finally reigning, will draw all the personal-souls of humanity toward heaven.

The great old enemy dies of poison,
Conquering an infinite number of sovereigns.

It will rain stones, they will hide under rocks,
In vain will death present arguments.
— II.47

Humanity's greatest and oldest enemy, the devil, the unconscious mirror image of the insubordinate human ego, will finally die from all the poisonous soul-pain it swallowed but never digested over the long course of history. When it does die, this will in turn overcome all the insubordinate human egos of which it was composed. This will all happen when rocks rain from the sky, and humanity finally discovers that withdrawing to the unconscious realm of death can no longer save them from the pain of God's correction.

The inhuman tyrant will die a hundred times.
In his place will be put a wise, kind man.
All the court will be under his hand.
He will be made angry by the reckless evil one.
— X.90

The devil, formed out of insubordinate human egos, will die over and over when all those insubordinate egos die themselves during Judgment Day. In the place of that devil-ego will be put the ego consciousness of Christ himself. He will be a stern judge, who reacts angrily to those who are rash and malicious.

Born under the shadows into a nocturnal life,
He will, in reign and bounty, be sovereign
And will make his blood reborn from the ancient urn,
Renewing a golden age instead of a brass one.
— V.41

The Holy Ghost was born into an unconscious existence 2,000 years ago at Christ's Resurrection. When Christ returns to conscious physical life, his reign will be sovereign and unlimited. He will reincarnate, forming a new personal-soul from his ancient Primordial Soul, living again in order to usher in a far superior age.

The great King, abandoned by the physical ones,
Is alive by strength, not the tricks of a Jew.
He and his people placed high in the kingdom,
Grace given to a people who envy Christ.
— VI.18

Christ, abandoned by those who wish to remain physical, returns to conscious physical life through his own integrity, not by some dishonorable trick. He and those he calls his own will be placed high in the scheme of things to come, when preference will be given to those who truly appreciate Christ.

> The great Christian will be chief of the world,
> The furthest behind, loved, feared, dreaded,
> His fame and praise will surpass the heavens,
> And he will be satisfied with the sole title of Victor.
> — VI.70

At the end of Judgment Day, Christ will find himself in total control of all humanity. His conscious psyche, sitting inside the furthest reaches of every human mind, makes him simultaneously loved and feared. Although he will receive great praise, his only concern was to achieve victory over the insubordinate human ego.

Part Seven: Quatrains on the Wall Being Reformed

> From the angelic kingdom the unworthy are chased away,
> The counselor, through anger, will be put in the fire.
> His adherents will drop so low
> That the illegitimate will be half accepted.
> — III.80 (III.82 in some editions)

At the Second Coming, the evil dead are chased away by the personal-souls of heaven, while the devil is put in the fire of Christ's pain. The devil's followers, those with insubordinate egos, will drop to such a low level of unconsciousness that even they will be accepted as partially useful in the kingdom of God.

> The human reign of the offspring of an angel
> Will make his reign stay in peace and union.
> War captives form half of his wall,
> They will keep the peace maintained a long time.
> — X.42

The peaceful reign of Christ's new incarnation will continue without end, thanks to the perpetual union of soul and spirit. Those evil personal-souls who are captured during Judgment Day will prove useful, forming half of Christ's "plumb line" wall needed to control humanity's behavior; the fixed, ominous yet inert presence of these evil ones will act as a reminder, keeping humanity at peace for a long time.

Part Eight: Quatrains on the Warning Being Sounded

> He who shall have been charged to destroy
> Temples and sects changed by fantasy
> Will bring more harm to the rocks than to the living
> By ornate language recaptured with the ears.
> — I.96

One will be commissioned to clean away all the erroneous changes which have divided human religion into all the bickering denominations in existence today. Clearing away all these doctrinal mistakes will shake some people's faith (the "rock" of Peter), but not those who already live in Christ. Such changes will be possible because the true meaning of the specific wording of the prophecies will have finally been recaptured for all to hear.

> O vast Rome, your ruin draws near,
> Not of your walls, but of your blood and substance.
> One sharp in letters make so horrible a mark,
> His sharp point goes all the way to the quick.
> — X.65

The ruin of the Roman Church draws near, by the destruction, not of its political being, but of its doctrine and canon. The impact made by scholarship reaches to the very core of the Church's teachings.

BIBLIOGRAPHY

Aristotle. *On the Soul.* New York: Penguin Books, 1986.

Armstrong, Karen. *A History of God.* New York: Alfred A. Knopf, 1994.

Atharvaveda: Sanskrit Text with English Translations. Trans. by Devi Chand. Colombia, MO: South Asia Books, 1982.

Atwater, P.M.H. *Beyond the Light.* New York: Birch Lane Press, 1994.

Bhagavad-Gita (Song of God). Trans. by Swami Prabhavananda. New York: New American Library, 1972.

Bhattacharyya, Sibajiban. "Indian Philosophies." In *The Encyclopedia of Religion.* Vol. 7. New York: MacMillan, 1987.

Bible. New International Version.

Bible, Thompson Chain Reference. Indianapolis: B.B. Kirkbride Company, 1983.

Bijlefeld, Willem A. "Gnosticism as a Christian Heresy." In *The Encyclopedia of Religion.* Vol. 8. New York: MacMillan, 1987.

Bijlefeld, Willem A. "Reincarnation." In *The Encyclopedia of Religion.* Vol. 8. New York: MacMillan, 1987.

Bloom, Harold, ed. *Modern Critical Views: Sigmund Freud.* New York: Chelsea House Publishers, 1985.

Bradley, John P. *The International Dictionary of Thoughts.* Chicago: J.G. Ferguson Company, 1969.

Brandon, S.G.F. *The Judgment of the Dead.* New York: Charles Schribner's Sons, 1967.

Bremman, Jan. "Soul: Greek and Hellenistic Concepts." In *The Encyclopedia of Religion*. Vol. 13. New York: MacMillan, 1987.

Budge, E.A. Wallis. *The Egyptian Book of the Dead*. New York: Dover, 1967.

Budge, E.A. Wallis. *Osiris and the Egyptian Resurrection*. Vol II. New York: Dover, 1973.

Campbell, Joseph. *The Hero With a Thousand Faces*. Princeton, N.J.: Princeton University Press, 1949.

Cheetham, Erika. *The Prophecies of Nostradamus*. New York: Putnam, 1980.

Cohn, Norman. *Cosmos, Chaos, and the World to Come*. New Haven: Yale University Press, 1993.

Coogan, Michael David. "Canaanite Religion: The Literature." In *The Encyclopedia of Religion*. Vol. 3. New York: MacMillan, 1987.

Cooper, Alan. "Canaanite Religion: An Overview." In *The Encyclopedia of Religion*. Vol. 3. New York: MacMillan, 1987.

Davies, Steven. "Soul." In *The Encyclopedia of Religion*. Vol. 13. New York: MacMillan, 1987.

De Fontebrune, Jean-Charles. *Nostradamus*. New York: Holt, Rinehart, and Wilson, 1980.

Elliot, William. *Tying Rocks to Clouds*. Wheaton, IL: Quest Books, 1995.

El Mahdy, Christine. *Mummies, Myth, and Magic*. New York: Thames and Hudson, 1989.

Evans-Wentz, W.Y., trans. *The Tibetan Book of the Dead*. London: Oxford University Press, 1981.

Freud, Sigmund. *The Interpretation of Dreams*. New York: Avon Books, 1965.

Giles, Mary E. "Saint John of the Cross." In *Great Thinkers of the Western World*. New York: HarperCollins, 1992.

Gnoli, Gherardo. "Iranian Religions." In *The Encyclopedia of Religion*. Vol. 7. New York: MacMillan, 1987.

Grey, Margot. *Return From Death: An Exploration of the Near-Death Experience.* London: Arkana, 1985.

Grottanelli, Cristiano. "Dragons." In *The Encyclopedia of Religion.* Vol. 4. New York: MacMillan, 1987.

Gruen, Arno. *The Betrayal of the Self.* New York: Grove Press, 1986.

Guiley, Rosemary Ellen. *The Encyclopedia of Ghosts and Spirits.* New York: Facts on File, 1992.

Guiley, Rosemary Ellen. *Harper's Encyclopedia of Mystical and Paranormal Experience.* New York: HarperCollins, 1991.

Head, Joseph, and L. Cranston. *Reincarnation: The Phoenix Fire Mystery.* New York: Crown, 1977.

Hinson, E. Glenn. "Origen." In *Great Thinkers of the Western World,* ed. by Ian P. McCreal. New York: HarperCollins, 1992.

Howe, Quincy. *Reincarnation for the Christian.* Philadelphia: Westminster Press, 1974.

Hundersmarck, Lawrence F. "Paul Tillich." In *Great Thinkers of the Western World.* New York: HarperCollins, 1992.

Jacobsen, Thorkild. *The Treasures of Darkness.* New Haven: Yale University Press, 1976.

Jung, C.G. *Two Essays on Analytical Psychology* (Vol. 7); *The Structure and Dynamics of the Psyche* (Vol. 8); *The Archetypes and the Collective Unconscious* (Vol. 9i); *Aion: Researches into the Phenomenology of the Self* (Vol. 9ii); *Psychology and Religion: East and West* (Vol. 11); *The Practice of Psychotherapy* (Vol. 16); *The Development of Personality* (Vol. 17). In *The Collected Works of C.G. Jung,* trans. by R.F.C. Hull. Princeton: Princeton University Press, 1969.

Jung, C.G. *Modern Man in Search of a Soul,* trans. by W.S. Dell and Carey F. Barnes. New York: Harcourt, Brace, 1933.

Kramer, S.N. *Sumerian Mythology.* Philadelphia: American Philosophical Society, 1944.

Lao Tzu. *Tao Te Ching (The Way of Life).* Trans. by R.B. Blakney. New York: New American Library, 1983.

Leff, Gorden. "Cathari." In *The Encyclopedia of Religion*. Vol. 2. New York: MacMillan, 1987.

Lindsey, Hal. *The Late Great Planet Earth.* New York: Zondervan Publishing House, 1979.

Lindsey, Hal. *The Rapture.* New York: Bantam Books, 1983.

Long, J. Bruce. "Reincarnation." In *The Encyclopedia of Religion*. Vol. 8. New York: MacMillan, 1987.

Long, J. Bruce. "Underworld." In *The Encyclopedia of Religion*. Vol. 15. New York: MacMillan, 1987.

Magill, Frank N., ed. *Masterpieces of World Philosophy.* New York: HarperCollins, 1990.

Melton, J. Gordon, ed. *Encyclopedia of Occultism and Parapsychology*, Vol. I. Detroit: Gale Research, 1996.

Moody, R.A. Jr. *Coming Back: A Psychiatrist Explores Past-Life Journeys.* New York: Bantam, 1992.

Moody, R.A. Jr. *Life After Life.* Boston: G.L. Hall, 1975.

New Catholic Encyclopedia. New York: McGraw-Hill, 1967.

Oesterreich, T.K. *Possession: Demonical and Other*. New York: University Books, 1966.

Pagels, Elaine. *The Gnostic Gospels.* New York: Random House, 1979.

Pennington, M. Basil. "Saint Bernard of Clairvaux." In *Great Thinkers of the Western World.* New York: HarperCollins, 1992.

Pritchard, James B., ed. *Ancient Near Eastern Texts Relating to the Old Testament*, 3rd Ed. Princeton: Princeton University Press, 1969.

Progoff, Ira. *Jung's Psychology and Its Social Meaning.* New York: Grove Press, 1953.

Purington, Marjean D. "William Blake." In *Great Thinkers of the Western World.* New York: HarperCollins, 1992.

Ries, Julian. "Immortality." In *The Encyclopedia of Religion*. Vol. 7. New York: MacMillan Publishing Company, 1987.

Rig Veda. Ed. by Barend A. Van Nooten and Gary B. Hilland. Cambridge, MA: Harvard University Press, 1994.

Riviere, Claude. "Soul: Concepts in Primitive Religions." In *Encyclopedia of Religion*. Vol. 13. New York: MacMillan, 1987.

Roberts, Henry C., trans. and ed. *The Complete Prophecies of Nostradamus* (Oyster Bay, NY: Nostradamus Company, 1982.

Robinson, James M., translator's director. *The Nag Hammadi Library in English*. San Francisco: Harper & Row, 1977.

Sabom, Michael. *Recollections of Death: A Medical Investigation*. New York: Harper & Row, 1982.

Satapatha Brahmana in the Kanviya Recension. W. Caland, ed. Delhi: Motilai Banarsidass, 1983.

Seidel, Anna. "Afterlife: Chinese Concepts." In *Encyclopedia of Religion*. Vol. 1. New York: MacMillan, 1987.

Seldes, George. *The Great Thoughts*. New York: Ballantine Books, 1985.

Springer, Sally P., and Georg Deutsch. *Left Brain, Right Brain*. New York: W.H. Freeman and Company, 1985.

Strong, James. "Dictionary of the Hebrew Bible." In *The New Strong's Exhaustive Concordance of the Bible*. New York: Nelson Publishers, 1984.

Swedenborg, Emmanuel. *Heaven and Hell*. New York: Swedenborg Foundation, Inc., 1979.

Thomas, Henry, trans. and ed. *The Complete Prophecies of Nostradamus*. Oyster Bay, NY: Nostradamus Company, 1982.

Tillich, Paul. *The Dynamics of Faith*. New York: Harper, 1957.

Tober, Linda M., and F. Stanley Lusby. "Jewish Afterlife." In *The Encyclopedia of Religion*. Vol. 6. New York: MacMillan, 1987.

Toynbee, Arnold, and Arthur Koestler, et al. *Life After Death*. New York: McGraw-Hill, 1976.

The Upanishads: Breath of the Eternal. Trans. by Swami Prabhavananda and Frederick Manchester. Hollywood: Vedanta Society of Southern California, 1948.

Van Baaren, T.P. "Afterlife: Geography of Death." In *The Encyclopedia of Religion*. Vol. 1. New York: MacMillan, 1987.

Wickes, Frances G. *The Inner World of Choice*. Englewood Cliffs: Prentice-Hall, 1963.

Zandee, Jan. *Death as an Enemy According to Ancient Egyptian Conceptions*. New York: Arno Press, 1977.

Zaechner, R.C. *The Dawn and Twilight of Zoroastrianism*. London: Oxford, 1961.

Zerries, Otto. "South American Religions: An Overview." In *The Encyclopedia of Religion*. Vol. 13. New York: MacMillan, 1987.

Hampton Roads Publishing Company

. . . for the evolving human spirit

Hampton Roads Publishing Company
publishes books on a variety of subjects
including metaphysics, health, integrative medicine,
visionary fiction, and other related topics.
For a copy of our latest catalog, call toll-free,
(800) 766-8009, or send your name and address to:

Hampton Roads Publishing Company, Inc.
134 Burgess Lane
Charlottesville, VA 22902